On Absolute War

On Absolute War

*Terrorism and the
Logic of Armed Conflict*

Eric Fleury

LEXINGTON BOOKS
Lanham • Boulder • New York • London

Published by Lexington Books
An imprint of The Rowman & Littlefield Publishing Group, Inc.
4501 Forbes Boulevard, Suite 200, Lanham, Maryland 20706
www.rowman.com

6 Tinworth Street, London SE11 5AL

British Library Cataloguing in Publication Information Available

Library of Congress Cataloging-in-Publication Data

Library of Congress Cataloging-in-Publication Data Available

ISBN 978-1-4985-6541-7 (cloth)
ISBN 978-1-4985-6543-1(pbk)
ISBN 978-1-4985-6542-4 (electronic)

Contents

Preface and Acknowledgments

This book draws on the work of Carl von Clausewitz, principally his treatise *Vom Kriege* (*On War*) to improve the theoretical analysis of terrorism. At first glance, there is an obvious incongruity in the notion of a Clausewitzian approach to terrorism. Clausewitz (1780–1831) was a Prussian veteran of the Napoleonic Wars and renowned scholar of military affairs whose writings presupposed a direct clash of opposing forces, whether of regular armies or popular militias. The notion of a clandestine cell deliberately targeting non-combatants and striking fear in a mass audience for the sake of extracting political concessions was entirely beyond his frame of reference. Accordingly, my intention is not to treat Clausewitz's works as the source for a strategy of counterterrorism. *On War* is a peerless source of wisdom, and its scores of pithy aphorisms make it eminently quotable, but one cannot isolate its tidbits of advice from the particular social and political context that prompted their formulation.

For an American audience in particular, reading Clausewitz as a tactical manual would compound a preexisting tendency of devising military solutions to political problems. A reader consulting Clausewitz in search of a blueprint for victory is likely to focus on key concepts such as "the decisive engagement" and "the center of gravity," and in doing so transform from theoretical concepts into ever-present possibilities that swing the advantage to whomever most ably exploits them. In fairness to this instrumental interpretation, Clausewitz frequently emphasizes the utility of conceptual signposts for condensing the infinite complexity of real-life phenomena down to manageable dimensions. His purpose in writing *On War* was to identify and preserve the essential truths of warfare that would remain relevant relevance across the inevitable changes in technological means and political ends. War paradoxically derives its nature from the infinite mutability of its core com-

Preface and Acknowledgments

ponents, particularly the "trinity" of fighting spirit, military expertise, and political calculation. Translating this to the page requires a dialectical comparison between pure concepts and relevant practical applications, which approaches a resolution between theory and practice but never quite achieves it since there will always be new circumstances and information to disrupt any settled conclusions.

The drawback of this dialectical format is that it invites the incautious reader to cherry-pick the concept that fits their preconceptions and then pursue it headlong without proper regard for circumstantial variations or second-order effects. For example, fixation on the decisive battle tends to equate quantity with efficacy, so that victory becomes a matter of right-sizing a force structure and drawing the enemy into combat through the gravitational pull of its presence. This approach has proven especially counterproductive against insurgents who seize upon the propaganda value of a foreign occupation to replenish their losses indefinitely and thereby postpone the decisive battle while taxing the enemy beyond its strength and patience. The "center of gravity" exists in much of the modern military literature as a critical vulnerability that one's forces must seek out and destroy. With respect to terrorists, this promotes a focus on one particular aspect of the network as decisive, the elimination of which gives an illusion of victory as the group mutates and converts its tactical loss into propaganda gains.

Many of the scholars who have noticed the disjuncture between Clausewitz and modern warfare suggest that understanding the latter requires jettisoning the former. This interpretation reduces his writing to its most superficial exegesis. The datedness of Clausewitz's historical examples and the weakening of concepts such as the decisive battle in no way invalidate Clausewitz's methodology. Among the countless books and monographs filled with strategic principles and tactical formulae, *On War* remains unmatched in its ability to link the time-bound aspects of military art and science to the permanent interplay of human nature and historical evolution. Anticipating vast changes in warfare and reluctant to predict the specific course they would take, Clausewitz provided an intellectual structure for keeping theory abreast with changes in the character of war, one that will remain intact so long as human beings employ organized violence to advance political interests.

Extraordinary changes in technology, ideology, and governing structures have invalidated many if not most of Clausewitz's specific prescriptions, but these very changes should prompt the modern scholar to return to the same theoretical foundation that Clausewitz consulted in order to reckon with the seismic impact of the Napoleonic Wars. His spirited critique of the doctrinaire approach to military theory is all the more important now that contemporary readers might be tempted to regard Clausewitz as doctrinaire himself as many of his observations become more remote from recent experience.

Rather than treat *On War* as an instruction manual for military professionals, readers both military and civilian should engage with the text to challenge their most deeply-held assumptions regarding the efficacy and purpose of military force.

My research on this topic began with the intention of using Clausewitz to evaluate the concept of the "war on terror." I am hardly the first to do so, but the existing scholarship typically focuses on critiquing Western military doctrine for failing to advance political objectives, often with pointed references to Clausewitz's writings on guerrilla warfare and popular mobilization against occupying forces. I will use Clausewitz's methodology to engage in a much more comprehensive, dialectical comparison of war and terrorism. My main purpose is to show how I terrorism, which sprung from the same historical forces that motivated the writing of *On War*, affirms the underlying theory of war while intentionally subverting its normative basis. Elaborating the systemic origins of terrorism, its strategic and tactical dimensions, as well as the reasons for its increasing role within the international system will enable scholars and policymakers to understand its subsequent forms in light of its basic nature.

Studying Clausewitz trains the mind to view everything as a paradox, and so I have come to recognize that every one of the countless solitary hours that I spent researching and writing depended on the assistance, counsel, and sacrifice of others. At Lexington Books, Joseph Parry, Madhumintha Koduvalli, and Bryndee Ryan were tremendously helpful in lifting this project off of the ground and then providing the finishing touches, always ready to provide advice when asked while granting me enough independence to forge ahead with confidence. I would like to thank each of the students at the College of the Holy Cross who enrolled in my Terrorism course from 2016 to 2018 and were patient enough to let me test the ideas that would come to form this book. Two students deserving special mention are Maggie Connolly and Julia Doyle, who were exceptionally helpful with the index and overall formatting process. I am indebted to those who took time to look over drafts and provide invaluable suggestions, namely my dear friend and graduate school mentor David Clinton, as well as my friends and Holy Cross colleagues Alex Hindman and Erin Brooks. David Steenburg provided the invaluable perspective of the intelligent non-academic reader. This book is immeasurably better than it was prior to their input, and all remaining shortcomings are entirely my own.

Most importantly, this book is only possible due to the support and sacrifice of my family. My parents encouraged my interest in war and terrorism from an age when I was probably too young to read about such things, but I owe much of my academic career to their efforts to cultivate my intellectual curiosity and work ethic. My wife, Christina, is effectively the co-author of this book, not only for bringing the discerning eye of a high school English teacher to the editing process but even more importantly by accommodating the demands of the writing process with with inexhaustible patience. Finally, I owe this book to my children, Charles and Jane. My daily responsibilities as a father maximized the value of writing time when it was available, and they reminded me every day that there are things more important than work. The joy they brought to my life made it much easier to spend two years of work on a sobering topic. With that said, I should also mention that having two toddlers gave me a valuable opportunity to research the effectiveness of terrorism firsthand.

Chapter One

Terrorism and War

INTRODUCTION

Prior to the September 11th attacks, the idea of waging war against terrorism would have struck most American politicians as a useful rhetorical device for marshaling public anger in the wake of an attack, not an actual condition of belligerency. The U.S. had periodically used military force to retaliate against states for their roles in sponsoring specific acts of terrorism, but such acts fell squarely within the domain of coercive diplomacy rather than war. U.S. warplanes struck Libya in 1986 for its role in a bomb that killed two American servicemen at a German nightclub and then Iraq in 1993 after uncovering a plot to assassinate former President George H.W. Bush during a visit to Kuwait. Despite the use of warlike measures, the obvious intent in both instances was to dissuade the regime in question from any further provocative acts, not to bring them to heel through force of arms.

During this same period, the use of American military power against non-state organizations were similarly inclined toward chastisement more than combat. During the Lebanese Civil War, the U.S.-led Multi-National Force had attempted to subdue various anti-government militias as part of its peacekeeping mission, but President Reagan opted for withdrawal over retaliation following the October 1983 bombing of the Marine barracks in Beirut. Following Al Qaeda's bombing of the U.S. embassies in Nairobi, Kenya and Dar es Salaam, Tanzania in August 1998, the subsequent missile strikes in Sudan and Afghanistan were patently insufficient for dealing a major blow to the organization. While the Clinton administration certainly hoped to kill Osama bin Laden and eliminate his alleged access to chemical weapons, the strikes were designed to pressure the National Islamic Front and Taliban regimes into abandoning their support for the elusive Saudi and his band of self-proclaimed *mujahideen.*[1] Apart from these isolated measures, terrorism in both its foreign and domestic variants was understood to be a predominantly criminal matter, albeit one periodically requiring military means, and not an enemy to be defeated.[2]

Since the 9/11 attacks, the concept of war against terrorist organizations has become a bedrock assumption of American foreign policy and political culture. While the specific term "Global War on Terror" fell out of fashion after the George W. Bush administration left office, a rare bipartisan consensus has held firm regarding the primacy of military force in the struggle against terrorism. Long after the public has grown frustrated with the high costs and dissatisfying results of prolonged combat in Afghanistan an Iraq, the U.S. has reduced the costs of waging war only to expand the scope of the campaign to Pakistan, Syria, Libya, Yemen, Somalia, and elsewhere. Years of sustained engagement with a diffuse and clandestine enemy have led to substantial revisions in military doctrine and vast improvements in the methods of disrupting terrorist networks. These innovations, however, have precluded a more fundamental examination of how to understand the nature of war between such dissimilar combatants. Unless policymakers better understand how each side defines victory, the respective roles of force and negotiation in achieving it, and how these two models interact with one another, they will find themselves trapped in a battle that they can neither win nor bring to a stop.

There has long been considerable overlap between terrorism and war. Non-state militants throughout the twentieth century adopted the structures, nomenclature, and capabilities of conventional armies to try and compete with nation-states on an equal footing and thereby gain a moral and political status commensurate with their capabilities.[3] In response, states such as the United Kingdom and France pioneered counterinsurgency tactics that integrated military force and police power, adjusting to the harsh necessities of asymmetric warfare while winning the hearts and minds of the populace.[4] Furthermore, terroristic methods are hardly the exclusive province of non-state actors. A state's use of indiscriminate bombing or targeted assassination in the course of conventional warfare, counterinsurgency, or police action is not less terroristic because its perpetrator wears a uniform and operates within a clearly recognizable chain of command. The state almost always "kills noncombatants more efficiently, more routinely and in far greater numbers"[5] than non-state organizations.

The September 11th attacks have effectively negated any notion of equivalence between the practitioners of conventional war and terrorists in public discourse. The prevailing assumption behind the campaign against terrorism is that the enemy is a pitiless and relentless force of pure malevolence. As Bush's chief speechwriter David Frum and Undersecretary for Defense Richard Perle argued, terrorists "cannot be deterred. They cannot be appeased.

The terrorists kill and will accept death for a cause with which no accommodation is possible."[6] The only logical response to such an implacable and pervasive threat was a proactive and open-ended struggle that would go on as long as it took to completely discredit the ideology of militant Islam. It was both necessary and right to "take the battle to the enemy, disrupt his plans, and confront the worst threats before they emerge" in order to defend the "single surviving model of human progress"[7] that the advanced Western democracies represented. The patent superiority of democracy and the rule of law, combined with preponderant American military power, produced a "marriage of democratic idealism with the exercise of pre-emptive power."[8] Eliminating terrorist organizations, and overthrowing the regimes that give them aid and comfort, would clear the space in which the natural popular desire for freedom would blossom. This in turn would win over initial skeptics and "produce a benign form of the domino dynamic"[9] in which each success beget further success. Its victories gave proof that the defeat of terror would secure and expand the blessings of freedom.

Yet the pursuit of victory against terrorism quickly encountered the operational limits of employing methods of conventional warfare against an enemy that refused to submit to the test of a major battle. Occupying territory and inflicting casualties often had little long-term effect against organizations capable of falling back on a global network of "virtual sanctuary"[10] to reconstitute their sources of funds, fighters, and sympathy. Al Qaeda's status as America's primary antagonist required contesting it at every point of contact. Given the unlimited scope of its potential influence, this led to a vast expenditure of American resources well out of proportion to Al Qaeda's actual capacity to inflict harm.[11] Meanwhile, states such as Pakistan confounded the attempted bifurcation of states into the opponents and enablers of terrorism, cooperating in efforts to apprehend terrorist leaders while simultaneously curtailing American objectives in order to safeguard its domestic legitimacy and pursue its longstanding rivalry with India in Afghanistan.[12] In Afghanistan and Iraq, the promised transition from despotism to democracy foundered on ethnic and sectarian rivalry, rampant corruption, and militant organizations with sufficient determination, military skill, and popular support to refuse their designation to the dustbin of history.

Coming to power largely in response to public frustration with the war on terror, the Obama administration attempted a more pragmatic course correction with a multifaceted approach of "countering violent extremism (CVE)." CVE divides counterterrorism into three categories. The first is combating militant organizations, through law enforcement measures when possible and with military force when necessary. The second category is "building specific alternatives, narratives, capabilities, and resiliencies" that reduce the susceptibility of "target communities" to radicalization and recruitment. The third category consists of diplomatic efforts "to promote good governance and the rule of law" with the aim of resolving the political and societal conditions in which terrorist movements take root. [13]

Despite significant modifications in tactics and rhetoric, CVE did not entail a fundamental reconsideration of the Global War on Terror's strategic premises. As U.S. forces severely formally terminated combat operations in Iraq and Afghanistan, and placed greater reliance on "soft power"[14] to curb the appeal of radicalism, the basic assumption of an indefinite commitment with the end of destroying terrorism went unchallenged. The Defense Department cites the legal condition of armed conflict to justify the use of drone strikes for the targeted killing of suspected terrorists, often at the cost of stoking anti-Americanism and delegitimizing local governments. [15] While U.S. forces have struggled to preserve a stalemate against the Taliban, diplomats refuse to grant it a negotiating status commensurate with its bargaining power or standing within Afghan society. Following Obama's departure, U.S. officials promised another course correction that combines the confrontational swagger of the Bush years with the skepticism regarding large-scale interventions that characterized the Obama approach, while still regarding terrorism as an existential threat and promising to deliver a total victory.

In the attempt to fine-tune the struggle against terrorism, the U.S. has become involved in a set of wars that it can fight indefinitely at a relatively low cost, but cannot afford to win, lose, or halt with a formal acknowledgement of a status quo. In the process, war and terrorism have become ever more integrated, as both sides have adapted to a protracted struggle by learning to mirror one another's advantages. [16] Western militaries have adapted themselves to the dimensions of counterterrorism while militant organizations such as Islamic State and the Taliban take on the features of states, occupying territory with large military forces and operating a sophisticated bureaucracy. [17] As Iran and the U.S. arm their respective Shi'a and Kurdish proxies, Iraq formally deputizes sectarian militias into its army, and Syria wages unlimited warfare against it own citizenry, the fine line dividing an army from a terrorist organization has turned into a wide and blurry spectrum. [18]

U.S. counterterrorism policy has remained behind the curve of political developments in part due to the absence of an objective standard of evaluation, relying instead on an amalgamation of long-established principles and resonant lessons of recent experience. The elusiveness of a decisive outcome against Salafi-Jihadism has increased sensitivity to the costs of direct American involvement abroad, without shaking the basic commitment to destroy the ideology through military force and political reform across the Islamic world. No matter how much the U.S. refines the art of counterinsurgency or reallocates the burdens of combat and reconstruction between the Great Powers, international institutions, and local allies, the wider campaign perpetuates an unstable political environment in which militants continually persist and evolve.[19] To avoid falling between the stools of security at home and stability in areas of vital interest, the U.S. and its allies must reevaluate the nature of the conflict itself, and not just revise its tactics. A more complete theoretical understanding of terrorism and war will provide decision-makers with a framework for fitting longstanding objectives and public preferences within the possibilities and limits of political and military action.

This book will provide a theoretical overview of the relationship between terrorism and war. To establish a basis of comparison, I will draw on the work of Carl von Clausewitz, chiefly his classic treatise *Vom Kriege* (*On War*), which was published posthumously in 1832 and is widely regarded as the most important theoretical contribution to the study of warfare in the Western tradition.[20] Most famous for his declaration that "war is merely the continuation of policy by other means,"[21] Clausewitz constructs a theory of war through a dialectic between the abstract notion of absolute war (*absolute kriege*) and war as it is in reality (*der eigentliche krieg*). Absolute war is a "pure concept of war"[22] featuring two antagonists engaged in a continuous and all-consuming struggle, locked in a cycle of escalation and reciprocity with "no logical limit to the application of that force,"[23] and tending toward a climactic moment when one side decisively imposes its will upon the other. Clausewitz uses the notion of absolute war to provide an idealized standard pure combat, and he insists that it is neither possible nor desirable to replicate it in the real world.

The main argument of this book is that terrorism is an attempt to approximate a condition of absolute war in reality as much as possible. Terrorism is not a specific form of warfare, such as a direct engagement or asymmetric insurgency, which is characterized by a typical arrangement of actors, methods, and intentions.[24] Nor does it serve as a description of a combatant's overall purpose, despite common parlance positing the existence of "terrorists" and "terrorist organizations" who presumably exist for no other purpose than to wreak havoc. Rather, terrorism is a method for bypassing the traditional limits of warfare, especially friction and reciprocity, in order to achieve a complete and irreversible political result. Terrorist tactics deliberately break down logistical and normative restraints on the organized use of deadly force, replacing the subtleties of political calculation with relentless progression toward a decisive result, which forces allies and enemies alike to follow suit or fall behind. Terrorism is decisive to the extent that it compels a target audience to reorient their loyalties around the architects of the campaign and contribute to a process of continuous and theoretically unlimited escalation. Even if the enemy refuses to capitulate, the campaign itself leads to the formation of a thoroughly militarized community that harmonizes its political objectives with the internal logic of war, and is therefore immune from effective retaliation.

Terrorism may be the work of a small and clandestine cadre, an organized contingent of guerrilla fighters, or agents of the state. In any case, the decision to utilize terrorism emerges from a preexisting network of actors and objectives, and its adoption does not preclude subsequent or even simultaneous reliance on more conventional methods of combat and negotiation. Even acts most closely associated with terrorism, such as the deliberate targeting of noncombatants or acts of violence with more symbolic than material effect, are better understood as violations of the laws of war that are likely to feature on both sides of a conflict rather than inherent features of terrorism. Terrorism does not describe a type of actor or action, but rather a conviction that the worthiness of an objective places it above all other moral and political considerations. Although few, if any, terrorist campaigns will actually achieve the ends that justify the means, they may prove able to perpetuate themselves indefinitely, or pose a serious enough threat as to force significant concessions. At the very least, an unsuccessful campaign can still lay the groundwork for a community that is then capable of defending its interests by more conventional means.

Clausewitz provides the ideal model around which to frame a theoretical examination of terrorism because it presents a direct challenge to his account of how war should operate in reality while seeking to recover the ideal that he regarded as a hypothetical condition. Just as the Napoleonic Wars prompted Clausewitz to establish a theory of war that made sense of the profound changes in its conduct,[25] the increasing overlap of war and terrorism requires an evaluation of their common theoretical heritage and patterns of historical interaction. Significant modifications in the "grammar" of warfare make it all the more important to reevaluate the corresponding shifts in its underlying "logic,"[26] and thereby maintain a reasonable connection between military means and political objectives. A theory of war was meant to equip the monarchs of the post-Napoleonic Restoration with a basic template for fighting a nineteenth-century war while keeping those new technologies and tactics within diplomatic channels. Likewise, modern states cannot prepare for twenty-first century warfare without proper regard for the political structures that enshrine principles of restraint, mutuality, and prudence.

TERRORISM, WAR, AND THE CONTEMPORARY RELEVANCE OF CLAUSEWITZ

Theories of Terror

Before proceeding to the analysis, it is necessary to address likely objections to the contention that Clausewitz's methodology can improve the study of terrorism. The first objection is that terrorism is not amenable to any kind of comprehensive theoretical analysis. Walter Laqueur comments that "given the specific difficulties involved in the study of terrorism . . . it is not surprising that there has been no stampede to search for a general theory explaining the phenomenon."[27] The same characteristics that keep terrorism at the forefront of the public consciousness and policy agendas also make it difficult to conduct a theoretical analysis of the phenomenon as a whole. The vast range of methods and purposes within and between campaigns resists encapsulation within a singular framework, and draw comparison to a variety of lenses such as war, crime, and religion.[28] The term gains traction from the psychological impact of an action rather than the action itself, and so the meaning attached to it will vary depending upon the assumptions and reactions of various audiences.[29] Its pejorative connotations lend the term equal weight as a term denoting a discrete sphere of activity and a label that rival governments and non-state actors use to delegitimize one another.[30]

The obstacles to conceptualizing terrorism in general terms have favored an inductive method of studying cases to generate conclusions on specific aspects of terrorism. The findings drawn from this approach have tended to correspond with the "images of analysis" (also known as levels of analysis), which explain political behavior through three lenses: human behavior, organizational structures, and the systemic pressures common to a set of actors.[31] Although studies based on the images of analysis can generate valuable insights on specific cases, the images of analysis framework betrays its origins in the context of interstate relations and foreign policy analysis, making it insufficient for accommodating the far less steady ground of terrorism.[32]

First-image analysis of terrorism has the appeal of providing a rational explanation for the confounding question of why an individual would engage in terrorist activity, risking so much with little prospect of reward. After decades of psychological research failed to conclusively demonstrate the presence of a "terrorist personality,"[33] first-image analysis now focuses on aspects of human nature that motivate certain types of terrorist activity and the social conditions most likely to activate them. Marc Sageman attributes the decision to join militant organizations to "cliques" that "facilitate the development of a shared collective social identity and strong emotional feelings for the in-group." The process of socialization, especially for individuals "temporarily alienated from society," shifts their perception of themselves and the world around them in a way that reinterprets the willingness to kill and die into a heroic and selfless act.[34] Drawing on evolutionary biology, Bradley Thayer and Valerie Hudson describe suicide terror (in their case, focusing on Islamic societies) as a strategy designed to "help alpha males secure their dominant position in the social hierarchy, ensure that threatening out-groups face violence, and dampen the inevitable social instability of a polygynous society." Providing material rewards for the families of *shuhadaa* ("martyrs") and promising ample sexual rewards in the afterlife discou-

rages non-alpha males from challenging their inferior status and directs them
toward increasing the reproductive prospects of themselves and their families.[35]

No matter how well first-image theories explain their chosen cases, they
necessarily cover a subset of a subset, requiring a unique linkage of psychological or biological predilections with an amenable social environment in
order to gain plausibility. No theory will cover every example within the
case, or apply to other cases of terrorism. For example, Thayer and Hudson's
model fails to account for the many suicide bombers who have been married
and had children, were from well-connected families, or born and educated in
a non-polygynous society like Western Europe. Its most conspicuous omis-
sion is the role of women in such campaigns, even though female suicide
operatives in Lebanon, Turkey, Sri Lanka, Chechnya, and Palestine have all
proven more deadly on average than their male counterparts and more resistant to detection.[36] First-image theory necessarily turns every example outside
of its scope into an outlier, no matter its importance. An explanation of
terrorism based on psychological or biological impulses cannot provide an
explanation beyond the decision to undertake the act itself, which leaves out
crucial considerations such as target selection, timing, and the public justification provided for the act.

Early efforts at second-image analysis classified forms of terrorism by
ideology, structure, characteristic tactics and many other considerations,
which led to there being "almost as many typologies of terrorism as there are
analysts."[37] As an alternative, scholars have examined the influence of different regime types and religious traditions on the motivations of individual
motivation and organizational strategy. For example, William L. Eubank and
Leonard Weinberg launched an ongoing discussion over the question of
whether democracies are particularly susceptible to terrorist attacks, and if
so, the proper means of redressing that vulnerability.[38] A number of scholars,
notably Mark Juergensmeyer and Jessica Stern, have analyzed the role of
religious traditions motivating terrorist attacks. Juergensmeyer comments
that terrorism "comes naturally to activists from a religious background"
since the actions constitute a form of "public ritual" infused with the symbol-
ism and spectacle befitting a religious rite.[39] Stern views religious terrorism
as a convergence that takes shape "only when there is a large supply of
young men who feel humiliated and deprived; when leaders emerge who
know how to capitalize on those feelings; and when a segment of society—
for whatever reason—is willing to fund them."[40]

As with the first image, a second-image explanation gains its greatest
plausibility when it can isolate its designated variable across a variety of
cases. In international politics, a theory of second-image causation such as
the democratic peace proposition (which posits that war between two democracies is practically unthinkable) can identify the independent variables that

distinguish a democracy from other states and then measure the correlation of those variables across multiple cases with designated outcomes, in this case the absence of war.[41] Quan Li has applied this method toward terrorism, arguing that "institutional constraints" within a democracy increase the number of transnational terrorist attacks that it is likely to endure,[42] but those constraints may just as easily be a response to terrorism rather than its cause. The designation of "Islamic" or "Christian" terrorism suffers from the opposite problem, too readily attributing a single cause to the hodgepodge of political and religious factors that motivate and mobilize members and invite sympathy from a broader audience.[43] Second-image comparisons either underdetermine the degree of correlation by focusing on outcomes and obscuring the question of motive, or overdetermine it by affixing a label reflecting whichever characteristics happen to be the most salient to the observer.

In contrast to "reductionist"[44] approaches that study the whole of a subject through the parts, third-image analysis locates the structural forces that lay the permissive structural conditions for terrorism, instead of the characteristics of the actors in question. Rhonda Callaway and Julie Harrelson-Stephens locate the roots of terrorism in states that violate "security rights" and "create an incentive for people to seek extra-systemic means of political expression,"[45] but are not so repressive as to smother all opposition. Michael Mousseau finds that terrorism is most likely among the "patrons and lieutenants" of "clientalist hierarchies" that fear losing their privileged position to the forces of globalization and "market civilization."[46] In both cases, terrorism is the eminently rational response of a threatened group against an intolerable status quo. Just as a state will put aside ideology or international law to advance a pressing interest, the questionable morality of terrorism pales before its practical utility for a combatant with no other alternative at its disposal.

Third-image analysis of international politics assumes a universal motivation of state behavior, whether that be the achievement of enough security to deter external threats or the elimination of those threats through the establishment of hegemony.[47] Because states mutually recognize one another and utilize a common currency of military, economic, and diplomatic power, theorists have a consistent baseline for linking structural conditions with expected behaviors.[48] In the absence of a constant such as international anarchy, there is no way to conceptually link terrorist movements that derive from different structural causes, or predict the specific means by which the affected population will redress their grievances. Third-image analysis amends the flaws of unit-level analysis by supplying a universal motive for terrorism, but in doing so loses its power to explain the interaction among tactical assets, target audiences, and political objectives that animates a specific campaign.

Another consequence of the inductive study of terrorism has been its near-total cleavage into state and non-state forms, with very little direct comparison of their underlying logic beyond their shared penchant for targeting civilians and inspiring fear.[49] State terror appears to be a more appropriate subject for the images of analysis since it retains the essential variables of the individual decision-maker, a formal institutional framework, and a clearly defined role within the international system. The problem with this approach is that it buries the unique dynamics of terrorism within the bounds of state-centric assumptions. Terrorism becomes the exclusive brainchild of a "personalist dictator" given the assumption that the leader's preferences have practically unrestrained influence on state policy.[50] A second-image emphasis on structure or ideology can no more explain the timing of a single-party or military dictatorship's terror campaign than its decision to go to war. Third-image explanation positing state terror as a rational means of shoring up internal strength against external threats says nothing about why some states engage in terror and others do not when all are subject to similar systemic pressures.

The insufficiency of any single image has encouraged terrorism scholars to adopt the "neo-classical" method of integrating multiple images into a single model, positing systemic pressures which are then "translated through intervening variables at the unit level."[51] A standout example of this approach is Robert Pape's *Dying to Win: The Strategic Logic of Suicide Terrorism.* Pape attributes suicide terrorism to a summation of three factors, each of which correspond to an image of analysis: the structural condition of a foreign military occupation, the institutional variable of a democratic occupier, and the individual motive of repelling a foreigner (almost always of a different religion) from one's homeland.[52] Accordingly, Pape suggests that the key to defeating suicide terrorism is for the United States to increase homeland security to defend against attacks by the current generation, and to implement an "offshore balancing"[53] strategy by to discourage the emergence of a new generation.

Pape's reduction of suicide terrorism to a predictable sequence of cause and effect imposes fixed characteristics onto a contingent arrangement of social factors. Suicide terror, as with other forms of terrorism, constantly changes based on the mutual influence of cultural expectations, organizational interests and individual willpower within a given context.[54] For example, the Islamic State (commonly referred to as ISIS) invalidates every one of Pape's criteria, as it has used suicide terror to expand and defend its own territorial occupation, drawing its volunteers mainly from foreign fighters instead of the local population, and overwhelmingly targeting coreligionists, including fellow Sunnis.[55] Terrorism achieves its distinct psychological effect by consistently defying expectations. Inductive theorizing at its best takes a snapshot of terrorism, contextualizing in a particular form at a particular moment. Without the ability to define terrorism beyond the behavior of specific actors and circumstances, the relentless innovation of terrorist activity will ensure that theory perpetually remains one step behind practice.

Clausewitz's theory of war provides a model for an alternative mode of theorizing about terrorism. Clausewitz set his own understanding of war against theorists who defined it as either an art or a science. For theorists who regard war as an art, each example is a unique and creative interplay of individual will, physical material, and environmental circumstance, the result of which chiefly depends on the skill of the practitioner.[56] Clausewitz's theory attributes great importance to individual talent, but that concept alone cannot "serve as a scaffolding on which the commander can rely for support," since it is impossible to reconstruct the precise interplay of talent and external forces after the fact. As soon as the commander employs his own talents on the battlefield, "he will find himself outside the model and in conflict with it,"[57] providing a unique example that will prove to be of little utility to future practitioners.

Alternately, a science of war posits a set of principles and laws, such as the maintenance of interior lines or achievement of numerical superiority at the critical moment, which promise "some sort of resolution" to the "maelstrom of opinions"[58] surrounding military affairs. Clausewitz shares the scientific concern for an objective knowledge of war, while insisting that "no prescriptive formulation universal enough to deserve the name of law can be applied to the constant change and diversity of the phenomenon of war." Generalizations and even doctrines can develop around widely practiced routines, methods, and tactics, but the application of principles and rules will never be automatic, and so should be expressed as "simple truths" that leave ample room for individual judgment.[59]

Clausewitz distinguishes his own theory from either approach by interpreting war as "part of man's social existence," specifically "the clash between major interests, which is resolved by bloodshed."[60] As a product of human interaction, its only permanent feature is that it always derives its particular shape from the intellectual and emotional qualities of its specific combatants. As Peter Paret points out, the "urge to understand the use of violence, turn it into a science, and make it predictable" must not confuse the aspects of war that are amenable to precise measurement or pithy summation with the thing itself. The confluence of moral and material factors will generate discernible patterns of action within a given era, but if a theory of war is to "pass the test of reality,"[61] it must isolate the intangible elements that ultimately define the essence of the concept. A theory of terrorism must proceed along similar lines. Echoing Alan Beyerchen's description of war, terrorism comprises "not a single reaction, but dynamic interactions and anticipations" which "can be theorized only in qualitative and general terms, not in the specific detail needed for prediction."[62]

As Clausewitz describes it, a theory of this kind undertakes three tasks. First, it must "clarify concepts and ideas that have become . . . confused and entangled,"[63] clearly defining the essential features of the subject at hand. Next, that definition should "show how one thing is related to another," pointing out how the operation of concepts in reality result in patterns, rules and wherever possible, "that nucleus of truth we call a principle."[64] Finally, a theory should establish an "intellectual apparatus" that connects the "natural talent"[65] of the practitioner with the accumulated wisdom of experience, reflection, and common sense. Theory cannot "equip the mind with formulas for solving problems, nor can it mark the narrow path on which the sole solution is supposed to lie," but it can "give the mind insight into the great mass of phenomena and of their relationships," which allows the practitioner to "rise into the higher realms of action."[66] No theory of terrorism can obviate the necessity of practical judgment, but it can clarify the boundaries in which prudential judgments are made.

Clausewitz and Modern War

A project that applies Clausewitz to contemporary warfare must also engage the body of criticism that has challenged the place of Clausewitz atop the rank of military theorists. Such arguments typically fall under one of three headings: perniciousness, irrelevance, and incoherence. Generations of critics have accused Clausewitz of being a proponent of militarism. This view gained traction during and after the World Wars, when Clausewitz's popularity in his native Germany prompted a view of him as a "typical Prussian" whose teachings "indoctrinated"[67] his countrymen with a pseudo-philosophy of aggression and brutality. British general and author Basil Liddell Hart helped to popularize the view of Clausewitz as the "evil genius of military thought" and the "apostle of total war"[68] obsessed with massive formations and relentless offensives.

The accusation of Clausewitz being a bloody-minded warmonger represents a classic case of selective quotation, which given his dialectical method leads to criticisms on contradictory grounds.[69] On one hand, Philip Meilinger blames Clausewitz for an American tendency "to view war as a climactic, and usually bloody, clash of arms"[70] without proper regard for the broader social and political environment. On the other hand, John Keegan begins his *History of Warfare* by proclaiming that "war is not the extension of policy with other means,"[71] challenging Clausewitz's most famous statement and its implication that the horrors and complexities of warfare are subject to rational summary and some degree of control. Different parts of the text do appear to contradict one another, especially when cited out of context, but Clausewitz cannot be both a prophet of battle for its own sake and a cynical proponent of war as a morally neutral political instrument. His theory of war includes the possibility of war as both unrestrained and limited, which in neither case amounts to outright advocacy.

In the post-Cold War era, the most frequently leveled charge against Clausewitz is that of irrelevance. In this understanding, *On War* reflects the experience and assumptions of warfare characterized by decisive battlefield engagements between functionally identical states capable of mobilizing their resources with the express purpose of achieving a distinct political objective.[72] The "new wars" scholars question Clausewitz's ability to explain diffuse and prolonged contests between states and amorphous, asymmetrical entities.[73] Martin van Creveld argues that developments in technology, international law, and concern for the perspectives of individual soldiers and civilians leaves Clausewitz unable to explain the most important aspects of modern warfare.[74] Mary Kaldor argues that Clausewitz's notion of war as a "contest of wills" has given way to a "mutual enterprise" of indefinite and inconclusive conflict.[75] As globalization breaks down traditional state identities, war becomes a means of securing ethnic and religious identities or an opportunity for personal profit rather than a means of achieving political aims.[76]

The advocates of a "post-Clausewitzian"[77] approach accurately point out major changes in the art of war, the new actors capable of waging it, and the necessity for a reexamination of long-held tenets regarding the use and purpose of military force. However, "an account of the actors is not tantamount to an account of the conduct of war,"[78] and innovations of method do not necessarily result in changes to the underlying theoretical properties. Van Creveld argues that Clausewitz's model is dependent upon a clear distinction of people, army, and government,[79] but Clausewitz used these examples "as an illustrative device" to describe violence, probability, and rational purpose "through examples that would have made sense to his contemporaries."[80] Kaldor argues that the absence of decisive battle in modern warfare exhausts the usefulness of absolute war as a theoretical standard, since conflicts are more likely to drag on at at relatively low levels rather than hurtle toward a climactic moment. This critique misrepresents absolute war as an inherent tendency of all wars rather than ultimate potentiality. Absolute war is also a question of scope rather than scale. Contemporary "wars without end" that spread like wildfire across state borders and obliterate the distinction between soldier and civilian are just as prone toward the absolute as the "wars without limits"[81] of the nineteenth and twentieth century. War approaches the absolute not as it becomes more destructive, but to the extent that it conflates the logic of war with political calculation.

The third criticism of Clausewitz is that because he died before completing *On War*, the text is more a collection of insightful quotations than a coherent theory of war.[82] This line of argument finds support in two notes that Clausewitz wrote regarding his progress on the text. In the first, written in July 1827, Clausewitz announced his intention to rework the "rather form-less mass" of the first six books so that it better clarifies the difference between war intended to "overthrow the enemy"[83] versus a war of limited objectives. In a second, undated note, possibly written as late as 1830, he declares that "the first chapter of Book One alone I regard as finished," and that the manuscript as a whole was "nothing but a collection of materials from which a theory of war was to have been distilled."[84] Azar Gat attributes these notes to a "drastic change of direction"[85] in the last years of his life from a single-minded focus on battle to a broader exploration of war and politics. According to Gat, Clausewitz's failure to properly update the text in accordance with the changes in his thought explains how so many commen-tators could draw such drastically opposing conclusions.

Critics are correct to point out that Clausewitz is not an infallible guide to the warfare of his own time, much less any other period. In addition to the imperfections of the text, which was published posthumously under his wid-ow's direction, Clausewitz himself warns the reader of the limitations of theoretical and historical inquiry. He repeatedly insists that the most impor-tant lessons will elude those "who know war only from books."[86] Clause-witz's reluctance to draw on more remote historical examples, which are "bound with the passage of time to lose a mass of minor elements and details that were once clear,"[87] now renders much of his text obsolete for all except military historians. It is impossible to determine with certainty whether his maxims regarding the inherent superiority of defensive warfare and the con-centration of forces at a decisive point were meant as literal advice for the commander or as hypotheses that he intended to reevaluate and critique.

The limitations of Clausewitz's text serve as reminders that he should not be a source of unquestioning reverence, but his notes indicate that the pur-pose of the revisions was to align the text with his "main ideas which will be seen to govern this material," which he regarded as "the right ones."[88] Chief among these main ideas was the "fascinating trinity"[89] (*wunderliche Dreifal-tigkeit*) which concludes the first chapter of Book One. The trinity, as Chris-topher Bassford notes, "ties all of Clausewitz's many ideas and binds them into a meaningful whole."[90] The trinity consists first of primordial violence, the "blind natural force" of hostility and passion that motivates a combatant, and a people as a whole, to endure the hardships of warfare and to inflict harm on the enemy. Second is "chance and probability," the element of uncertainty in which "the creative spirit is free to roam" in the form of military experts who devise and execute tactics, strategy, and logistics more skillfully than the enemy. Third, and most important, is the "element of subordination," the awareness that war is an "instrument of policy . . . subject to reason." Although each component of the trinity takes on an infinite num-ber of shapes in reality, the concept represents the essential truth of war as "more than a true chameleon" and yet featuring "dominant tendencies" that recur one way or another in every example. Comparing the ideal nature of the trinity with its real-life application sets forth a "theory that maintains a balance between these three tendencies, like an object suspended between three magnets."[91]

By completing the first chapter to his satisfaction, Clausewitz successfully laid the groundwork for what he hoped "might bring about a revolution in the theory of war."[92] Once Clausewitz had defined the principal elements of the theory and supplied a means of comparing them, all that remained was to test them against the evidence at his disposal. The remainder of the text proceeds as an elaboration on the qualities of mind, material, and circumstance that shift the balance among the components of the trinity and the types of warfare that result from these innumerable arrangements. Even though Clausewitz did not always interpret the evidence convincingly, and new evidence calls for a modified analysis, the theory does not stand or fall on the applicability of the text in its entirety. *On War* retains its usefulness by providing a model for scholars to assess changes to the warfare of their own time in light of its history and fundamental nature, laying the foundation for a process of studying war that, like the text itself, is destined to remain unfinished.

Several generations of Clausewitzian scholarship indicate that changes in the conduct of war do not simply make *On War* more or less relevant, but rather downplay certain aspects while restoring others to renewed significance. During the Cold War, politicians such as Senator J. William Fulbright claimed that "nuclear weapons have deprived force of its utility as an instrument of national policy."[93] In response, Samuel Huntington argued that the atomic age prompted a reassertion of the military as the instrument of the nation state and the attendant policy that "precedes war, determines the resort of war, dictates the nature of the war, concludes the war, and continues on after the war."[94] Traditional Clausewitzian strategy retained the virtue of common sense, especially compared to either fanciful scenarios of a winnable nuclear war or an equally dangerous faith in the automaticity of Mutually Assured Destruction.[95] The excruciating failure of U.S. efforts in Vietnam prompted a renewed interest in Clausewitz as a vital corrective to a misplaced faith in technological superiority as a military panacea.[96]

The end of the Cold War uncovered new avenues for Clausewitzian theory. Retired British general Rupert Smith argues that the need "to win the will of the people"[97] has replaced the destruction of enemy forces as the supreme objective of war, and that this indicates not the obsolescence of Clausewitzian warfare bur rather its proliferation to a host of non-state actors. Low-intensity conflict and peacekeeping operations are no less in need of alignment between the calculations of the political leadership and the morale of soldiers on the ground.[98] M.L.R. Smith argues that the notion of guerrilla warfare as separate from Clausewitz's paradigm reflects a tendency to classify warfare by distinctive tactics in the hope of devising "general operational solutions,"[99] which replaces strategic thinking with technocratic doctrines.

The post 9/11 era has similarly continued the tradition of applying Clausewitz's theory to the dominant security concerns of the age. Antulio Echevarria argues that the struggle against terrorism "has shown that each of the tendencies in Clausewitz's wondrous trinity remains alive and well."[100] The globalization of technology and information has only amplified ideological hostility, the role of chance and uncertainty, and the political ramifications of individual actions such as a suicide bombing or desecration of a Quran. Sergei Boeke and Bart Schuurman explain the 2013–2014 French intervention in Mali as an incomplete Clausewitzian operation, as France successfully integrated its own military and political objectives but failed to reconcile those with the long-term political needs of Mali itself.[101] As David Lonsdale argues, the war on terror was a perfect opportunity to demonstrate the Revolution in Military Affairs (RMA) brought about by information technology, that would eliminate uncertainty, permit a surgical focus on high-value targets, and thereby delegitimize the concept of the Clausewitzian engagement. This initial optimism has foundered on the persistent need for ground forces to ascertain accurate intelligence, as well as the recognition that forces can exploit an informational advantage to inflict crippling damage on an entire society, or compensate for an informational disadvantage with indiscriminate violence.[102]

The common thread running through each of these works is that the failures of modern strategy stem not from a dogged adherence to Clausewitzian thinking, rather from the failure to apply it properly. This book continues the tradition of employing a Clausewitzian lens to understand contemporary warfare more clearly, albeit with much a closer examination of the ways in which terrorism both imitates and challenges the classic Clausewitzian view of war. Terrorism is an isomeric variation of war, circumventing its logistical and normative limitations in order to arrive at a purer expression of its fundamental dynamics and thereby produce results beyond the capabilities of a conventional combatant. War presumes two (or more) trinitarian arrangements that inflict harm upon one another in pursuit of relative gains. A terrorist campaign also combines primordial violence with a calculation of probabilities in service of a political objective, but the objective is directed principally toward the destruction and reconstitution of its own trinity rather than an external goal. Terrorism is a process of escalation though which a combatant achieves a perfect synthesis of political direction, military skill, and popular enthusiasm. To the extent that it accomplishes this feat, it can revert to more conventional forms of war, such as direct combat or insurgency, and pursue external objectives with a qualitative advantage over enemies against whom it could have never prevailed in a symmetrical contest.

The vast majority of Clausewitz's text addresses the problems that result from failure of theory to endure the complexities of practice. The concept of strategy, tactics, attack, defense, and morale gain their significance from the grim realities of the battle countermanding the best-laid plans of generals. This book will similarly focus on the ways in which terrorist campaigns adjust after they fall short of absolute war, as they are bound to do in one way or another. Every successful terrorist campaign has had to adjust, postpone, or temporarily put aside its timetable for total victory on behalf of more immediate political considerations, and those who have refused to do so rarely lasted long enough to mount an effective campaign.[103] This presents an even more serious problem for a terrorist campaign than for a conventional combatant, which can adapt its objectives in light of changing circumstances. A terrorist campaign cannot compromise or significantly alter its primary objective without undermining its own *raison d'être*, and it must pursue that objective "like a shark in the water: it must keep moving forward—no matter how slowly or incrementally—or die."[104] The crux of a terrorist campaign is the ability to perpetuate a narrative of inexorable momentum while navigating the same difficulties of logistics, morale, and shifting political winds that bedevil all combatants. A credible threat of imposing absolute war hinges on the appearance of having bent physical and political reality to one's will.

PLAN OF THE BOOK

Clausewitz begins his text with a dialectical comparison of absolute war and real war to establish the baseline of his theory. The middle books go into painstaking detail on aspects of strategy and tactics with illustrative examples from recent history, especially the campaigns of Napoleon and Frederick II of Prussia. He concludes it by dividing real war into subcategories of wars either fought toward a decisive conclusion or with limited objectives in order to trace out the possibilities of war in his own day and the foreseeable future. This book follows a similar progression with respect to terrorism, allowing for a side-by-side comparison with war. I will begin with a dialectical comparison of terrorism and conventional warfare to flesh out their essential similarities and differences as well as their influence upon one another. I will divide terrorism into its state-directed and non-state variants as a basis for evaluating historical and contemporary cases. Both types of terrorism share the basic goal of forming a new and thoroughly militarized community through a process of rampant escalation, and employ a strategy that seeks to minimize the effect of reciprocity with respect to its prospective enemies. Given their fundamental similarity of political and strategic objectives, the main difference between the two basic types of terrorism is the dialectic of terrorist and target, either the state attacking its people or a people attacking a state. Consequently, a theory of terrorism will develop in accordance with evolving notions of the relationship between the state and peoples.

A dialectical method is necessary for imposing intellectual discipline on a phenomenon that is characterized more by its dynamism than fixed characteristics that can be comprehensively enumerated. In the opening sentences of *On War*, Clausewitz announces that he will forego a comprehensive definition of war. Instead, he will "proceed from the simple to the complex"[105] and develop a conceptual map that traces the path by which abstract concepts manifest themselves in reality, so that the practitioner can then understand reality in light of those concepts. Accordingly, his text begins with the essential features of war itself and the task of theorizing on it, followed by the elements of strategy, the nature of battle, tactical questions of organization, offense, and defense, and then a review of the theory's implications for contemporary warfare. In the following chapters, I will follow this progression, moving from the present chapter's defense of theory to the theory itself, followed by its practical implications and role within broader dynamics of historical change.

In chapter 2, I will elaborate upon absolute war and explain its significance for Clausewitz's theory. I will then compare it with the development of warfare after Clausewitz's time, particularly by contrasting it with "total war," and describe how terrorism emerged from the same social and political conditions that he identified as likely to push warfare closer toward the absolute than had previously been possible. Chapter 3 will analyze the strategy of terrorism, especially concerning the moral qualities that constitute an effective campaign and the principles of strategic success and failure. I will compare terrorism with warfare on critical elements of strategy including genius and morale, unity of command, and suspension of hostilities. I will then elaborate upon the strategy of state-directed terrorism, and compare the theoretical ideal with the example of the Soviet Union under Stalin. Chapter 4 will turn to the strategy of non-state terrorism, again developing a theoretical construct and then comparing it with a host of examples ranging from the Fenian and *Narodnik* campaigns of the late nineteenth century to contemporary examples such as Hamas.

Chapter 5 will compare the nature of battle in conventional war and terrorism. It will compare each form of battle in terms of the nature of the offense and defense, the culminating point of victory, and the center of gravity. I will then turn to the specific dynamics of combat with state-directed and non-state terror, and review the examples of Saddam Hussein's Iraq and Al Qaeda. In chapter 6, I will review the theory in the light of contemporary cases that integrate the traditional features of war and terrorism, most notably the Taliban and Islamic State. I will explain how the theoretical conception of terrorism as an approximation of absolute war is particularly useful for understanding the convergence of warfare and terrorism, as well as formulating a rational response to it.

Although the book is primarily a theoretical investigation, no theory can stand apart from the circumstances that prompted its formation. In this case, this work is the product of reflection on the experience of the U.S. and its allies engaged in an indefinite war against terrorism without a clear sense of how to win or even how to fight effectively. In light of that experience, my intention is to help the public to refine their expectations regarding terrorism and the use of military force to combat it. The public's relative insularity from the vicissitudes of the war against terror combined with sustained fear of the terrorist threat has reinforced a series of faulty perceptions regarding the nature of the conflict, especially a magnified sense of danger and an unrealistic expectation of outright victory. A more sophisticated understanding begins with thinking through the concept of terrorists as combatants operating within a three-dimensional political space, and not as psychopathic criminals or automatons driven solely by ideology.

Clausewitz's emphasis on war as an extension of policy means that war is a phase of political interaction. Thinking of terrorism in terms of war means that terrorism is a transient, if reoccurring, phase of action, one that does not permanently fix the identity of the participant. Terms such as "state sponsor of terrorism" and "terrorist organization" would be analogous to designating any state that has fought a war as a "belligerent" after the war concludes. Like war, terrorism ends, and typically on terms far short of the total victory that it heralds in its propaganda. Once that phase concludes, utilizing similar tactics against the erstwhile terrorists is no more appropriate than using warlike measures in a time of peace. The temptation to deal with terrorism through principally military means has degraded a proper understanding of the fulness of war and what it necessarily entails. Analyzing terrorism as a variant of war locates its tactical and strategic aspects within a broader political context, and reasserts the supremacy of political judgment in formulating the appropriate response.

NOTES

1. Martha Crenshaw, "Coercive Diplomacy and the Response to Terrorism," in *The United States and Coercive Diplomacy*, eds. Robert J. Art and Patrick M. Cronin (Washington, D.C.: United States Institute of Peace Press, 2003), 326–327.

2. Lindsay Clutterbuck, "Law Enforcement," in *Attacking Terrorism: Elements of a Grand Strategy*, eds. Audrey Kurth Cronin and James M. Ludes (Washington, D.C.: Georgetown University Press, 2004), 140–141.

3. Bruce Hoffman, *Inside Terrorism* (New York: Columbia University Press, 2006), 21–2.

4. See Frank Kitson, *Low Intensity Operations: Subversion, Insurgency, Peacekeeping* (Harrisburg: Stackpole Books, 1971), 13–28; David Galula, *Counter Insurgency Warfare: Theory and Practice* (New York: Frederick A. Praeger, 1971), 32–46.

5. A.J. Coates, *The Ethics of War* (New York: Oxford University Press, 2016), 323.

6. David Frum and Richard Perle, *An End to Evil: How to Win the War on Terror.* New York: Random House, 2004), 34

7. George W. Bush, "Commencement Address at the United States Military Academy," (speech, West Point, NY, June 1, 2002) White House Archives, https://georgewbush-whitehouse.archives.gov/news/releases/2002/06/20020601-3.html

8. Melvyn Leffler, "9/11 and the Past and Future of American Foreign Policy," *International Affairs* 79 (2003): 1047.

9. Jonathan Monten, "The Roots of the Bush Doctrine: Power, Nationalism, and Democracy Promotion in U.S. Strategy," *International Security* 29 (2005): 149–150.

10. Magnus Ranstorp, "The Virtual Sanctuary of Al-Qaeda and Terrorism in an Age of Globalisation," in *International Relations and Security in the Digital Age*, eds. Johan Ericsson and Giampiero Giacolmello (New York: Routledge, 2007), 37–38.

11. John Mueller, *Overblown: How Politicians and the Terrorism Industry Inflate National Security Threats, and Why We Believe Them* (New York: Simon & Schuster, 2006), 13–14.

12. Seth G. Jones, *In the Graveyard of Empires: America's War in Afghanistan* (New York: W.W. Norton, 2010), 259–263.

13. " Department of State & USAID Joint Statement on Countering Violent Extremism." U.S. Agency for International Development. http://pdf.usaid.gov/pdf_docs/PBAAE503.pdf .

14. Colin Dueck, *The Obama Doctrine: American Grand Strategy Today* (New York: Oxford University Press, 2015), 84.

15. Michael J. Boyle, "The Costs and Consequences of Drone Warfare," *International Affairs* 89 (2013): 19–22.

16. James A. Russell, "Into the Great Wadi: the United States and the War in Afghanistan," in *Military Adaptation in Afghanistan*, eds. Theo Farrell et al. (Stanford: Stanford University Press, 2013), 53.

17. Audrey Kurth Cronin, "ISIS Is Not a Terrorist Group: Why Counterterrorism Won't Stop the Latest Jihadist Threat," *Foreign Affairs* 94 (2015): 87–88.

18. Leonard Weinberg and Susanne Martin, *The Role of Terrorism in Twenty-First Century Warfare* (New York: Oxford University Press, 2017), 2–5.

19. Andreas Krieg, "Externalizing the Burden of War: The Obama Doctrine and US Foreign Policy in the Middle East," *International Affairs* 92 (2016): 97–113.

20. Michael Howard, *Clausewitz: A Very Short Introduction* (New York: Oxford University Press, 2002), 1, 62–78.

21. Carl von Clausewitz, *On War*, trans. Peter Paret and Michael Howard (Princeton: Princeton University Press, 1984), 69.

22. Ibid., 90.

23. Ibid., 77.

24. Bard E. O'Neill, *Insurgency and Terrorism: From Revolution to Apocalypse* (Dulles: Potomac Books, 2005), 33–36.

25. Daniel Pick, *War Machine: The Rationalization of Slaughter in the Modern Age* (New Haven: Yale University Press, 1996), 29.

26. Clausewitz, *On War*, 605.

27. Walter Laqueur, *A History of Terrorism* (New Brunswick: Transaction Publishers, 2012), 144.

28. Alex P. Schmid, "Frameworks for Conceptualising Terrorism," *Terrorism and Political Violence* 16 (2004): 212–214.

29. Peter R. Neumann and M.L.R. Smith, *The Strategy of Terrorism: How it Works, and Why it Fails* (New York: Routledge, 2008), 2.

30. Anthony Richards, *Conceptualizing Terrorism* (New York: Oxford University Press, 2015) 26.

31. Kenneth N. Waltz, *Man, the State, and War: A Theoretical Analysis* (New York: Columbia University Press, 2001), 12.

32. Jason Franks, *Rethinking the Roots of Terrorism* (New York: Palgrave Macmillan, 2006), 26.

33. Andrew Silke, "Cheshire-Cat Logic: The Recurring Theme of Terrorist Abnormality in Psychological Research," *Psychology, Crime & Law* 4 (1998): 53.

34. Marc Sageman, *Understanding Terror Networks* (Philadelphia: University of Pennsylvania Press, 2004), 154–155.

35. Bradley A. Thayer and Valerie Hudson, "Sex and the Shaheed: Insights From the Life Sciences on Islamic Suicide Terrorism," *International Security* 34 (2010): 52–53.

36. Lindsey O'Rourke, "What's Special About Female Suicide Terrorism?" *Security Studies* 18 (2009): 687.

37. Quoted in Alex P. Schmid and Albert J. Jongman, *Political Terrorism: A New Guide to Actors, Authors, Concepts, Data Bases & Literature* (New Brunswick: Transaction, 1988), 40.

38. Quoted in Alex P. Schmid and Albert J. Jongman, *Political Terrorism: A New Guide to Actors, Authors, Concepts, Data Bases & Literature* (New Brunswick: Transaction, 1988), 40.

39. Mark Juergensmeyer, *Terror in the Mind of God: The Global Rise of Religious Violence* (Berkley: University of California Press, 2017), 157.

40. Jessica Stern, *Terror in the Name of God: Why Religious Militants Kill* (New York: HarperCollins, 2003), 236.

41. Zeev Moaz and Bruce Russett, "Normative and Structural Causes of Democratic Peace, 1946–1986," *The American Political Science Review* 87 (1993): 632–636.

42. Quan Li, "Does Democracy Promote or Reduce Transnational Terrorism?" *Journal of Conflict Resolution* 49 (2005): 278–297.

43. Jeroen Gunning and Richard Jackson, "What's So Religious About 'Religious Terrorism?'" *Critical Studies on Terrorism* 4 (2011): 378.

44. Kenneth N. Waltz, *Theory of International Politics* (Boston: McGraw Hill, 1979), 18.

45. Rhonda Callaway and Julie Harrelson-Stephens, "Toward a Theory of Terrorism: Human Security as a Determinant of Terrorism, *Studies in Conflict & Terrorism* 29, no. 7 (2005): 684.

46. Michael Mousseau, "Market Civilization and Its Clash With Terror," *International Security* 27, no. 3 (2002): 5–29.

47. John Mearsheimer, *The Tragedy of Great Power Politics* (New York: W. W. Norton, 2001), 22.

48. Alexander Wendt, *Social Theory of International Politics* (New York: Cambridge University Press, 1999), 233–238.

49. Ruth Blakeley, "State Terrorism in the Social Sciences: Theories, Methods, and Concepts," in *Contemporary State Terrorism: Theory and Practice*, eds. Richard Jackson et al. (New York: Routledge, 2010), 12–27.

50. Jessica L.P. Weeks, *Dictators at War and Peace* (Ithaca: Cornell University Press, 2014), 29–32.

51. Gideon Rose, "Neoclassical Realism and Theories of Foreign Policy," *World Politics* 51 (1998): 146.

52. Robert Pape, *Dying to Win: The Strategic Logic of Suicide Terror* (New York: Columbia University Press, 2005), 21–22.

53. Ibid, 246–250.

54. Jeffrey William Lewis, *The Business of Martyrdom: A History of Suicide Bombing* (Annapolis: Naval Institute Press, 2012), 14–17.

55. Michael Weiss and Hassan Hassan, *ISIS: Inside the Army of Terror* (New York: Simon & Schuster, 2015), 168.

56. Clausewitz, *On War*, 148.

57. Ibid., 140.

58. Ibid., 134.

59. Ibid., 151–152.

60. Ibid., 149.

61. Peter Paret, "Clausewitz," *Makers of Modern Strategy: From Machiavelli to the Nuclear Age*, ed. Peter Paret (Princeton: Princeton University Press, 1986), 190.

62. Alan Beyerchen, "Clausewitz, Nonlinearity, and the Unpredictability of War," *International Security* 17, no. 3 (1992–1993): 73.

63. Clausewitz, *On War*, 132.

64. Ibid., 578.

65. Ibid., 147.

66. Ibid., 578.

67. Quoted in Christopher Bassford, *Clausewitz in English: The Reception of Clausewitz in Britain and America* (New York: Oxford University Press 1994), 123.

68. Quoted in Ibid., 129.

69. Hew Strachan, *Clausewitz's On War: A Biography* (New York: Grove Press, 2007), 193–194.

70. Philip Meilinger, "Busting the Icon: Restoring Balance to the Influence of Clausewitz," *Strategic Studies Quarterly* 1, no. 1 (2009): 116.

71. John Keegan, *A History of Warfare* (New York: Vintage Books, 1994), 1.

72. T.V. Paul, "The National Security State and Global Terrorism: Why the State Is Not Prepared for the New Kind of War," in *Globalization, Security, and the Nation State: Paradigms in Transition*, eds. Edsel Aydinli and James N. Rosenau (Albany: State University of New York Press, 2005), 51.

73. Bart Schuurman, "Clausewitz and the 'New Wars' Scholars," *Parameters* 40 (2010): 90.

74. Martin van Creveld, *More On War* (New York: Oxford University Press, 2017), 4–8.

75. Mary Kaldor, "In Defense of New Wars," *Stability: International Journal of Security and Development* 2 (2013): 1–16.

76. Mary Kaldor, *New & Old Wars: Organized Violence in a Global Era* (Malden: Polity, 2012), 72–74.

77. Edward Luttwak, "Toward Post-Heroic Warfare," *Foreign Affairs* 74, no. 3 (1995): 122

78. Isabelle Duyvesteyn, "Rethinking the Nature of War: Some Conclusions," in *Rethinking the Nature of War*, eds. Jan Angstrom and Isabelle Duyvesteyn (New York: Routledge, 2005), 231.

79. Martin van Creveld, *The Transformation of War* (New York: Free Press,1991), 49.

80. Thomas Waldman, *War, Clausewitz, and the Trinity* (New York: Routledge, 2016), 165.

81. Mary Kaldor, "Inconclusive Wars: Is Clausewitz Still Relevant in These Global Times?" *Global Policy* 1, no. 3 (2010): 275.

82. John E. Shephard, Jr. "*On War*: Is Clausewitz Still Relevant?" *Parameters* 20, no. 3 (1990): 8

83. Clausewitz, *On War*, 69.

84. Ibid., 70.

85. Azar Gat, *A History of Military Thought: From the Enlightenment to the Cold War* (New York: Oxford University Press, 2001), 201.

86. Clausewitz, *On War*, 180.

87. Ibid., 173.

88. Ibid., 70.

89. Ibid., 89.

90. Christopher Bassford, "The Primacy of Policy and the 'Trinity' in Clausewitz's Mature Thought," in *Clausewitz in the Twenty First Century*, eds. Hew Strachan and Andreas Herberg-Rothe (New York: Oxford University Press, 2007), 75–77.

91. Clausewitz, *On War*, 89.

92. Ibid., 70.

93. Quoted in Peter R. Moody, "Clausewitz and the Fading Dialectic of War," *World Politics* 31 (1979), 418.

94. Samuel P. Huntington, *The Soldier and the State: The Theory and Politics of Civil-Military Relations* (Cambridge: Harvard University Press, 1985), 65.

95. Bradley S. Klein, *Strategic Studies and World Order: The Global Politics of Deterrence* (New York: Cambridge University Press, 1994), 52–74.

96. Harry G. Summers, *On Strategy: A Critical Analysis of the Vietnam War* (New York: Random House, 2009), 196.

97. Rupert Smith, *The Utility of Force: The Art of War in the Modern World* (New York: Alfred A. Knopf, 2007), 305.

98. Ibid., 241–242.

99. M.L.R. Smith, "Guerrillas in the Mist: Reassessing Strategy and Low-Intensity Warfare," *Review of International Studies* 29 (2003), 24.

100. Antulio J. Echevarria II, "Clausewitz and the Nature of the War on Terror," in *Clausewitz in the Twenty First Century*, 217.

101. Sergei Boeke and Bart Schuurman, "Operation 'Serval:' A Strategy Assessment of the French Intervention in Mali, 2013–2014," *The Journal of Strategic Studies* 38 (2015): 801–825.

102. David J. Lonsdale, *The Nature of War in the Information Age: Clausewitzian Future* (New York: Frank Cass, 2004), 109–112.

103. Adam Dolnik, "The Dynamics of Terrorist Innovation," in *Understanding Terrorism Innovation and Learning: Al Qaeda and Beyond*, eds. Magnus Rainstorm and Magnus Normark (New York: Routledge, 2015), 76–95.

104. Hoffman, *Inside Terrorism*, 234.

105. Clausewitz, *On War*, 75.

Chapter Two

Absolute War in Theory and History

The term "absolute war" receives mention only a handful of times in *On War*, and its different invocations do not always suggest the same meaning. Clausewitz's use of the term at times suggests a purely abstract condition and at other times an increasingly relevant standard for evaluating the warfare of Clausewitz's own day and age.[1] This apparent contradiction has led some scholars to argue that "Clausewitz did not have an intelligible theory of absolute war," and that the idea itself is "meaningless."[2] This is the most severe example of misinterpreting Clausewitz's dialectics for self-contradiction, since the distinction between absolute war and real war constitute the fundamental dialectic of the text. Absolute war entails the continuously escalating use of emotional and intellectual resources to break the will of an enemy. It defines the theoretical essence of war and frames its historical evolution within a consistent, rational framework. Although no combatant ever has or ever will achieve this condition due to physical, emotional, and political limits on the pure logic of armed combat, nor can they afford to give up on the possibility of its realization, given the perpetual risk that their opponent is better able or more willing to bypass those restraints.

Warfare in Clausewitz's lifetime had provided a visceral demonstration of how some combatants could come much closer to the absolute than others, forcing their opponents to escalate in kind or suffer a calamitous defeat. The raised states of warfare, even a single battle, relative to earlier eras prompted Clausewitz to divide real war into two variants, one featuring decisive clashes for major stakes and the other limited to lower levels of violence and limited objectives. Many commentators have regarded terrorism as a modern variant of limited war, comparable to guerrilla warfare or insurgency.[3] However, the same social and political forces that prompted Clausewitz to subdivide real war also introduced terrorism as a means of transcending the limits of real war and restoring the pure concept of the absolute to the practice of warfare. Notions of popular sovereignty, combined with the productive capacity to outfit massive armies, introduced the potential for creating a state capable of leveraging its military potential and public support toward an unprecedented degree of supremacy over its rivals. But before taking the field against its enemies, a terrorist campaign was necessary for purging an existing trinity of its traditional limits and infusing it with the will and capacity for unlimited escalation toward a truly decisive result which it could impose unilaterally.

Clausewitz identifies the French Revolution as the moment that signified the decisive turn in modern warfare, and the 1793–1794 Reign of Terror represents the introduction of the term "terrorism" into the lexicon.[4] Whereas war entails the direction of force by one community against one another, the ultimate purpose of terrorism is to direct the full energy of a community against itself, forcing it to escalate or perish. *La Terreur* represents the first systematic attempt to use warfare as an agent of social transformation, pushing a people to the brink of annihilation so that they overcome the limits of historical possibility and emerge as a perfectly unified and thoroughly mobilized community. Despite failing in that purpose, the soaring rhetoric and shocking brutality of the Terror left behind a legacy of revolutionary urgency and popular mobilization that persists, in both its state and non-state forms, as the basic ideational template of a terrorist campaign. By serving as a historical point of origin on which to anchor the concept of terrorism, the Reign of Terror illustrates the approximation of absolute war in reality and provides a permanently valuable standard for comparison with subsequent examples.

THE PURE CONCEPT OF WAR:
ABSOLUTE WAR IN CLAUSEWITZ'S TEXT

The Nature of Absolute War

As a "typical educated representative of his generation,"[5] Clausewitz's theory of war reflects the traditions of the Enlightenment and Romanticism which were common to a Prussian of his profession and social station. In accordance with the prevailing methods and assumptions of the time, Clausewitz's quest for objective knowledge unfolds through a dialectical comparison of its rational and irrational elements, with the fullness of reality reflecting an ever-shifting mixture of each. Commencing the theory with an ideal type is a means of isolating the permanent features of war from broader social reality with which it interacts. The contrast between the ideal and the real then clarifies the "intervening variables" of psychology and historical contingency that divert from the logical concept of war without diluting its overall explanatory power.[6] In this respect, absolute war serves the same function that the "state of nature" did for theorists such as Hobbes, Locke, Rousseau, and Hume.[7] Just as the state of nature reaches back into a hypothetical antiquity to uncover the irreducible features of society and government, absolute war draws the most direct possible connection between war and human nature in order to define the possibilities and limits of warfare in all times and places.

Clausewitz's summation of war as "nothing but a duel on a larger scale . . . an act of force to compel our enemy to do our will" is only a partial description of any actual war, but it captures the essence of the thing itself. Absolute war is the logical extrapolation of the abstract duel, with no input whatsoever from the specific actors, actions, and circumstances that constitute its real-life operation. Such a condition is no more attainable in reality than the contented solitude of Rousseau's natural man, nor does it represent the supreme truth of war any more than Hobbes's grim account of the state of nature means that life itself is solitary, poor, nasty, brutish, and short. Nonetheless, both absolute war and the state of nature have a practical utility beyond that of a mere thought experiment. Hobbes admits that no society has ever lived up to his grim description of nature, but he also warns that a society will resemble it if it lacks the protections of the social contract and the sovereign power. Likewise, every war retains the potential to exhibit aspects of absolute war to the extent that social and political forces operate in accordance with the internal logic of armed conflict.

Absolute war consists of a set of dialectics in which both components have free rein to achieve their full expression. First is the dialectic of the duel, which in turn sets up a means-end dialectic of using force for the purpose of imposing one's will upon the enemy.[8] Regardless of whether their intention are offensive or defensive, the end result is the same so long as the wills of the two sides are incompatible, each refuses to accede to the other, and both are willing and able to assert their will through force. The entirety of the relationship between the two entities consists of their opposed wills, making it impossible for any conclusion other than the victory of one and the defeat of the other. At the precise moment that they each commit to the use of force on behalf of their respective wills, the contest becomes an end unto itself irrespective of the original dispute, the achievement of which now requires the complete disarmament of the enemy. Lacking any means other than warfare to interact with one another, any slackening of resolve is tantamount to outright capitulation.

This dialectic of ends and means sets up another dialectic within the means themselves, with passion and reason serving as the two principal elements of force. Upon the initial outbreak of war, each side expends only as much energy as it deems necessary to accomplish its objective. As the effort expands into a mutual attempt at disarmament, both sides will tax their emotional and intellectual resources accordingly. Even if the combatants have no particular feelings of hostility toward one another, "the emotions cannot fail to be involved" as individuals inflict and endure greater levels of violence. The inherent stress of combat at least requires that both sides cultivate "hostile intentions" commensurate with the task, or else their citizens will lack the willpower to kill the enemy, risk their own lives, and suffer the privations of the campaign. Absolute war also draws on the ingenuity of its participants as much as their raw passion. Breaking the enemy's will requires "more effective ways of using force than the crude expression of instinct." Contrary to the belief that the progress of civilization diminishes the role of the passions, Clausewitz upholds modern technology and organization as a concrete manifestation of the "the impulse to destroy the enemy,"[9] and the intensification of that impulse will drive a more advanced society to produce deadlier instruments and utilize them with greater precision. While no amount of civilization can reduce war to a chess match, the rational direction of force prevents the infliction of pain and destruction for its own sake. The mutual dependency of passion and reason gives even absolute war some semblance of limits.

The unrestricted play of passion and reason then sets up the dialectic between the combatants themselves, which carries them both to the logical extremes of war as the conflict persists. In the absence of any external limitation or standard of conduct, "the sole criterion for preparations . . . would be the measures taken by the adversary,"[10] triggering a continuous sequence in which every action instantly prompts an equal and opposite reaction. Implacably committed to imposing their will, either side can only achieve victory by rendering their opponent "utterly defenseless"[11] in the face of an intolerable and unavoidable threat of further pain. As each side calculates its own efforts against the capabilities and determination of the enemy, the cycle of innovation and adaptation will continue unabated until both have deployed their material and psychological resources to the limits of human potentiality.

Absolute war is a depiction of human nature applied entirely and exclusively to war. With the whole of their emotional and intellectual faculties engaged in the overthrow of the enemy, each side derives its motivations, methods, and objectives exclusively from the struggle itself. As theoretical entities with no specific culture or personality, one can assume them to be equal in their rationality, enthusiasm, and overall capacity. This means that the two sides will interpret and respond to threats in similar ways, ascend the ladder of escalation at the same speed, and make up for any material deficiency with a comparable advantage in morale, or vice versa.[12] Only combatants that mirror one another in the "combined effects of [their] aim and strength"[13] are capable, much less willing, of engaging one another without pause and reciprocating each and every one of the other's moves. Likewise, only armed forces built on parallel models can hope to achieve a qualitative advantage in every avenue of competition, thereby nullifying the possibility of further resistance.

Clausewitz describes the commencement of absolute war as the point "in which two mutually destructive elements collide"[14] and traces its logic of inexorable escalation, but he does not describe how it ends. The entire war constitutes a single, winner-take-all engagement since there is no break in contact between the two sides, both of whom fight steadily increase their share of resources and commitment to overthrowing the other. However, this does not mean that it must eventually conclude with a decisive outcome, or conclude at all. No matter the results of specific engagements between forces, absolute war "is indivisible, and its component parts (the individual victories) are of value only in their relation to the whole." Under conditions where "everything results from necessary causes and one action rapidly affects another,"[15] combatants always react as the situation demands and never succumb to the doubts and fears that would allow an opponent to exploit the psychological effect of a tactical advantage toward a strategic breakthrough. The iron law of reciprocity ordains that every action will be answered in kind, and that one side's expectation of victory will remain strictly proportional to the other side's dread of defeat, ensuring that neither will ever achieve the distinct superiority necessary for victory.

If there is one flaw in the otherwise perfect logical constructs that are the combatants in an absolute war, it is their failure to recognize that their enemy is as tenacious a combatant as they are, which given the assumption of rationality should have discouraged them from fighting in the first place. As ahistorical entities free of any internal or external restrictions on their conduct of war, there is no reason to believe that either combatant would actually reach the point at which submission would be preferable to continuing the struggle. The longer the battle persists, the ongoing and reciprocal commitment of resources and resolve raises the stakes even further and completes the overlap of the internal logic of warfare and the character of the combatants. The equality of the sides implies that only two outcomes are possible. The first is that the steadily increasing scale of the means will push the contest to the point of mutual annihilation once they suitably destructive weapons and summon the will to use them despite the risk of retaliation in kind. The second possibility is that the joint evolution of passion and reason will make war a "ceaseless activity" that perpetually "arouse[s] men's feelings and inject[s] them with more passion and elemental strength." As escalating levels of enthusiasm and operational sophistication tie together more and more individuals within a "stricter causal chain," each individual "would be more important, and consequently more dangerous,"[16] as the battlefield extends to every point of contact between one people and another. Absolute war is decisive insofar as it leads a community to destruction or turns it into a perfect fighting machine invulnerable to defeat no matter the cost or the caliber of the opponent.

Absolute War: Abstraction or Perfection?

Every time that Clausewitz discusses absolute war in the text of *On War*, he immediately follows up the description with an insistence on its remoteness from reality. After introducing the concept in the first chapter of Book One, Clausewitz announces a "move from the abstract to the real world" and proceeds with a detailed account of how actual wars differ from "the almost invisible sequence of logical subtleties"[17] that make up absolute war. In Book Eight, the last of the text, Clausewitz emphasizes that absolute war is a "general point of reference"[18] with chiefly pedagogical rather than practical value. He makes this point to set up his further classification of real war into its decisive and limited variants, taking care that the reader does not confuse this classification with the still more fundamental classification of absolute war and real war with which he began the treatise.

Its utter separateness from reality does not mean that absolute war is a pure abstraction. Absolute war represents one extreme in a vast range between what Youri Cormier describes as "unlimited and limited political aims serving as the moderators and accelerators of the dynamics between the more and less extreme forms of war."[19] Some wars are more absolute than others, and those that approach it have come closer to capturing an authentic essence. This seems to contradict Clausewitz's dismissal of absolute war as merely a theoretical device, and in some passages, he appears to regard it a source of admiration and even imitation. He repeatedly points to the still-fresh experience of Napoleon as having "rather closely approached its true character, its absolute perfection."[20] In his chapter on "The People in Arms," he describes guerrilla warfare as the "elemental violence of war"[21] overcoming the artificial and hollow restraints of social and political convention. Throughout the text, his oft-repeated claim that in battle, "direct annihilation of the enemy's forces must always be the dominant consideration"[22] appears to cross the line from theoretical postulate to practical imperative.

These ambiguities within the text have generated competing interpretations over the relationship between absolute and real war, especially once the total war and the prospect of nuclear annihilation removed all practical restrictions on the destructive effect of warfare.[23] Scholars such as Jon Tetsuro Sumida understand absolute war as both a theoretical concept of maximal violence and a distinct type of real war, characterized by one side seeking the other's destruction "as a matter of policy."[24] R. Harrison Wagner reframes the progression from real to absolute war as an initial attempt to shape prospective negotiations in one's favor through limited force, the failure of which prompts one side to undertake an increasingly "absolute" effort to completely disarm the other and impose terms unilaterally.[25] Others push this idea further by arguing that for Clausewitz, "the true nature of war had to be sought in absolute war" and its inexorable tendency toward "untrammeled violence."[26] In this understanding, Clausewitz may have been sensitive to the infinite variety of political aims that define and limit war aims, but the superior strategy is always "the one that aims at making the enemy defenseless through destroying his armed forces in decisive battle."[27]

While portions of Clausewitz's text lend credence to these interpretations, blurring the qualitative distinction between absolute war and real war invalidates the concept as Clausewitz describes it. For absolute war to represent the optimal standard of conduct for real life combatants, then "every war in history would have shown the same general pattern of escalation,"[28] or else the concept would lose its validity as soon as it failed to manifest itself. Clausewitz insists that absolute war is a "pure definition," separate not only from war as it is fought but also how "it ought to be fought."[29] To the extent that historical practice mirrors theoretical precision, this is as much a cause for trepidation as admiration. As Raymond Aron states, absolute war prompts Clausewitz to feel "a kind of sacred horror, a fascination comparable to that wakened by cosmic catastrophes." Clausewitz feels "neither delighted nor indignant,"[30] at the prospect, as it is a philosophic ideal entirely distinct from the practical ideal of war as an extension of policy by other means.

The nature of absolute war remains fixed throughout the text of *On War*, although its significance for the argument shifts as Clausewitz employs it for different purposes. As Clausewitz moves from the simple to the complex, the original dialectic of absolute and real war generates additional dialectics that maintain the basic distinction while refining its applicability to reality. The description of absolute war in Book One is a "Platonic ideal"[31] that exhibits its own incompleteness by virtue of all the real-life factors that it lacks, and thereby proves the need for a theory attuned to the immediate facts of experience. In the middle books (Three through Seven) on strategy and tactics, the destruction of enemy forces is the battlefield equivalent of absolute war, the original truth of the engagement that exists prior to the modifications of reality but is nonetheless subordinate to their influence. In Book Eight's chapters on decisive and limited warfare, a reminder on the absolute potential of war serves as a warning that the ideal of warfare as a rational instrument of policy is no more achievable than the pure logic of escalation. For Clausewitz, absolute war is the distant light by which all political entities cast a shadow of war in their own distinct image, and like the sun, it would reduce them to ashes if they were to approach it too closely.

From Absolute War to Real War

Absolute war is unachievable in practice for two sets of reasons. The first is "friction," the innumerable physical and intellectual limitations of human nature that make a continuous process of escalation toward a climactic decision physically and emotionally impossible to achieve for even the most motivated and capable antagonists. All of warfare is "an uncharted sea, full of reefs"[32] that subjects rational thought to the play of uncertainty and probability. All thought and action takes place under ever-changing constraints of space, time, and resources, which instantly compromises the integrity of the plan at the moment of execution. After one side acts, the other must balance the impulse to respond quickly and decisively against the time and thought required to discern and carry out an appropriate response, prompting an interval of deliberation based on information that is often contradictory, incomplete, or inaccurate.[33] Once a course of action is decided upon, its success depends on countless variables such as weather, terrain, logistics, and proper coordination among the agencies of implementation. The annals of military history are filled with stories of misplaced or miscommunicated orders, extreme weather conditions turning armies into an inert mass, and errors of judgment so monumental as to defy rational explanation.

Friction also results from the sheer variability of human will and ability. Even if the two sides agreed to commit their full resources in a pitched battle at a mutually agreed upon time and place, and did not commence the battle until both commanders declared their troops to be at full readiness, there is no guarantee that either army would operate at optimum effectiveness. As soldiers suffer from fatigue, fear, hunger, illness, or discontentment, they will be unable or unwilling to follow orders and exploit opportunities on the battlefield.[34] Energy that would ideally be directed against enemy forced is instead consumed in the provision of food, shelter, medical care, training, and enforcement of discipline.[35] For commanders fortunate enough to have courageous and motivated soldiers at their disposal, "the natural tendency for unbridled action and outbursts of violence must be subordinated to demands of a higher kind: obedience, order, rule, and method."[36] Perfecting the fighting spirit of an army requires its subjection to "frequent exertions . . . to the utmost limits of its strength,"[37] so that the process of refinement carries with it the risk of attrition and exhaustion.

Friction is a universal and inescapable condition, although it will never impact both sides equally. En route to the battlefield, one army may lose contact with its supply train, succumb to an epidemic, or stumble into a better-prepared enemy detachment. The performance of the troops will result from the sum total of their training, morale, experience, and sheer luck.[38] The most perspicacious commanders can only be effective by giving orders that bear a meaningful resemblance to the willingness and capacity of their forces. Since war is only a temporary and partial aspect of human activity, its particular demands must regularly give way before the broader aspects of human nature. The conditions of war, from the physical danger facing the soldier to the burden of responsibility placed upon the commander, will trigger the very psychological qualities that impede its efficient operation.[39] An army's collective desire to win a battle can never triumph completely over the desires of its individual members for survival, comfort, or freedom from responsibility.[40] As commanders gauge the extent of their vulnerabilities, the most sensible decision could be to postpone the engagement, commit only a portion of their forces, or withdraw. Courage is the supreme virtue of war, but the "interplay of possibilities, probabilities, good luck and bad that weaves its way throughout the length and breadth of the tapestry" means that courage is just as likely to be the frank acceptance of an unpleasant necessity rather than an unfailing counsel of boldness.[41]

The physical and psychological aspects of friction break down the theoretical conception of war as a continuous, self-contained engagement tending toward a total decision. The impossibility of bringing all of one's forces to bear makes it equally impossible for one side to destroy the enemy's forces in a single roll of the iron dice, and so "the tendency is always to plead that a decision may be possible later on."[42] The incompleteness of the single engagement "gives rise to the completely different activity of planning and executing these engagements themselves, and of coordinating each of them with the others in order to further the object of the war." This introduces the hierarchy of tactics and strategy, the former being the "use of armed forces in the engagement" and the latter "the use of engagements for the sake of the war."[43]

Depending upon the dimensions of the theater, the pace of events, and the correlation of forces, the task of the strategist is to manage the sequence between engagements in a manner that either preserves material and psychological advantages or amends its disadvantages. The patient allocation of resources and marshaling of resolve will either tip the scales of the next battle in one's favor or convince an enemy to terminate the war given the perceived likelihood of defeat or unacceptable losses. Of course, an eminently reasonable decision to await favorable developments cannot escape the risk that fortunes will not improve but instead sink further.

The possibility of ending a war through negotiation introduces politics as the second major restraint on absolute war. Wars do not begin *sui generis*, as "neither opponent is an abstract person to the other," and conflict between them "never breaks out wholly unexpectedly."[44] Since the two combatants are complex political identities with relations that precede their hostility, coexist alongside it, and will persist after the war's conclusion, hostility represents only a fraction of their total interaction, albeit potentially a very high one. Their objective is invariably the imposition of their will on the other, but the actual substance of that will and the amount of force that its imposition requires will depend upon the specific dispute between them and the degree of hostility that it produces.[45] Assuming that war remains preferable to negotiation or inaction, a combination of "weak motives for action"[46] and awareness of relative inferiority may limit the scope of an offensive campaign or counsel a defensive posture until opportunities for decisive action emerge.

Politics adds another level of decision-making on top of strategy and tactics that relates the commencement, conduct, and termination of the war to a "supreme consideration"[47] of ends. As the strategist plans the engagement with an eye toward subsequent engagements, the political leadership plans and executes the war in light of the desired postwar settlement and projections regarding the next war. Disarming an enemy may be necessary in strictly military terms, but is still imprudent if the effort leaves forces too exhausted to maintain the conditions of the peace or leaves other areas of strategic significance vulnerable to attack in the interim.[48] A force defending its own territory can only enjoy the attendant tactical advantages if the people within that territory are willing to accept the sacrifices necessary for diminishing the strength of the attacker.[49] Requisitioning supplies from enemy civilians is an ideal method for sustaining an offensive campaign beyond its supply lines, but the victims of a conquering army will quickly turn into the scourge of one in retreat.[50]

With these and countless other considerations in mind, leaders charged with determining "the degree of force that must be used against the enemy" must "adopt a middle course" between "too small an effort" and a "maximum exertion" which would "cease to be commensurate with ends."[51] Warfare is "not merely an act of policy but a true political instrument, a continuation of political intercourse, carried on with other means."[52] The test of success in warfare is the utilization of strategic and tactical logic to the exigencies of politics. The art and science of combat are rational on their own terms, since the dialectic of force and the imposition of one's will permits the formulation of principles and rules connecting available means with a fixed end. As Bernard Brodie points out, the battlefield considered in isolation generates principles of action, such as the rapid pursuit of a defeated enemy, but the idiosyncrasies of political calculation "show the limitations of even the worthiest rule" and its utter subordination to the "tyranny of circumstance."[53]

The Trinity

The first chapter of *On War* is the only part of the text in which the dialectical comparison of opposites actually leads to a resolution, which likely explains why Clausewitz regarded it in his accompanying notes as the only finished chapter.[54] In the classic fashion of nineteenth-century German idealism, the thesis of absolute war followed by the antithesis of real war concludes with the synthesis of the trinity. The trinity is the refraction of absolute war through the prisms of friction and politics, turning the dialectics of means-ends and passion-reason into hostility, calculation, and policy, components that are theoretically intact while subject to infinite variation. War is a "fluid, unstable, and non-linear activity,"[55] and so the trinity links theory with practice by identifying the principal agents of change and outlining how variations within and among its components push war toward the extremes of a "war of extermination" or "simple armed observation."[56]

The first component of the trinity, the "blind natural force"[57] of primordial violence, filters the universal tendencies of the passions through the dynamics of conflict between specific peoples. Hostility between peoples is necessary for war to occur, and numerous factors can exacerbate, mitigate, or redirect it, which will shape the objectives of war and often diverge from them as the act of combat generates its own emotional effects.[58] The resumption of a long-simmering feud may lend the air of existential struggle to what would otherwise be a contest of limited aims. Alternately, war-weariness or fear of escalation may prompt reconciliation or restraint between arch-rivals. The intensity and duration of hostility is so erratic because war is almost never between peoples as such. Conflicts typically result from threats to specific interests, incompatible notions of honor, or prospects of short-term gain. It is possible that "where there is no national hatred and no animosity to start with, the fighting itself will stir up hostile feelings."[59] Typically, such feelings are more the product of a dispute than its cause, and may cool down just as suddenly as they flare up.

Turning to the other half of the passion-reason dialectic, the calculation of probabilities translates the purely competitive logic of absolute war through the medium of friction. In general, commanders seek to reduce the burden of friction for themselves and increase it for their enemies. Yet commanders will invariably encounter friction that they are either unable or unwilling to overcome. Aside from the inherent limits of geography or technology, politics introduces its own constraints, even if these amount to reckless interference when considered strictly on the grounds of military utility.[60] A *modus vivendi* with the enemy may prohibit certain target sets or weapon systems. The political leadership may place loyalists rather than experts in senior military positions, or refuse to pursue a decisive victory if the public will not tolerate high casualties. These measures deserve criticism if they are at the service of a faulty policy, but the military is not equipped to judge the wisdom of a policy any more than a tool judges its user. The freedom of the military "creative spirit"[61] ironically hinges on the security of the political unit, which in turn assures that security by shaping and directing the military instrument in accordance with its own discrete purposes.

Although the political objective enjoys nominal supremacy within the trinity since it defines the original purpose of the war, the actual experience of war is as likely to weaken its authority as affirm it. Alienation of public opinion may redirect primordial violence against the leadership in the form of a popular revolution, and the military may cite its operational expertise as cause to mute, ignore, or supersede political oversight. Warfare is only sensible as a political exercise, and yet the government will not sustain its legitimacy if it is militarily incompetent. Clausewitz himself betrays conflicting attitudes regarding the desirability of political control over warfare and the reality of combat as the acid test of strategy and policy.[62] Ideally, one side can "make the war more costly" for the other through a combination of threats and "general damage"[63] to the point where the mere prospect of a decisive engagement is sufficient to sap the enemy of the will to fight. The task of the statesman is to convert the "terrible-battle-sword" that exhausts its user into a "light, handy rapier," achieving the political object of war through precise use of "thrusts, feints, and parries"[64] and husbanding as much energy as possible for the next campaign. At the same time, the statesman armed only with an "ornamental rapier"[65] is like a bank with no cash reserves, left with the fragile hope that the enemy never calls to collect on the account.

The progression from absolute war to real war to the trinity mirrors the experience of the practitioner who first studies war in its theoretical properties, encounters its grim realities, and then learns to interpret individual phenomena as parts of its overall character. Through reflection and experience, human beings can achieve objective knowledge of warfare through the observation of subjective forces.[66] The trinity is the two-way bridge connecting the innumerable, unique facets of individual experience to the intractable conditions of human existence. On one hand, this model assures practitioners that their descent into the murky details of reality remains answerable to rational evaluation and that prudent management of chance and uncertainty is always possible. On the other hand, it cautions the practitioner that a war which is perfectly logical on its own terms can nonetheless overwhelm the rational capacities of its participants.

CLAUSEWITZIAN THEORY AND
THE EVOLUTION OF "REAL WAR"

Clausewitz, Machiavelli, and the Nature of International Politics

Despite the central importance of politics in Clausewitz's theory of war, the text of *On War* lacks any direct references to the nature of the state or international politics. For some commentators, this is proof that the validity of the theory stands and falls on the political assumption of Clausewitz's time and place, or that he mistook those assumptions for the immutable nature of things.[67] This critique fails to evaluate *On War* in the context of Clausewitz's political opinions, about which he wrote extensively in letters and other writings. As Hugh Smith describes it, Clausewitz's additional work outlines his view of the state, in which the "internal arrangements must allow for maximum development of its potential in order to meet the demands of its international circumstances while at the same time providing opportunities for its citizens to make the greatest use of their talents."[68]

Clausewitz's view of the state as a complex organism that is rational in its pursuit of the national interest and spirited in its defense of national honor was hardly the time-bound view of a standard nineteenth-century Prussian. Clausewitz challenged both the Hohenzollern monarchy for its stubborn refusal to acknowledge the "irreversible tendency toward greater participation in government by the people" and the German liberals for their Kantian belief that liberalism would inevitably spell the end of war.[69] Aspects of Clausewitz's theory, especially the conception of war as an extension of policy by other means, are as much a statement of his preferences for how politics ought to be conducted as declarations of how it really operates. The theory does not depend upon any particular political arrangement or preference, since it presumes the impending likelihood of tremendous political change. Whether the post-Napoleonic international system moved to recapture the stolidity of absolutism and the balance of power or hurtled toward democratic revolution and continental wars, the theory captures those aspects of international politics that will remain in place so long as war itself is a feature of political life.

As a scholar, German patriot, and outspoken advocate of reform within the Prussian military, Clausewitz was profoundly influenced by Machiavelli. Among his early manuscripts is a note that lists the "chief rules of politics" in unequivocally Machiavellian terms: "never be helpless; expect nothing from the generosity of another; do not give up an objective before it becomes impossible; hold sacred the honor of the state."[70] He later wrote that "no book on earth is more necessary to the politician than Machiavelli's," that he "gives some remarkable rules, which will remain valid forever." The only flaw of *The Prince* was that it described political reality "with a certain lack of decency" and thus lent credence to hypocrites who "heap proud disdain and sentimental revulsion"[71] on Machiavelli's arguments while putting them to use when it suits their purposes.

For a state such as Prussia, meager in resources and surrounded by more powerful rivals, Machiavelli's advice to be "either a true friend and a true enemy"[72] was for Clausewitz "the basic code for all diplomacy."[73] In an 1809 letter to philosopher Johann Fichte, he critiqued Machiavelli for fixating on the military methods of the past, but found in his writings "the true spirit of war" as "mobilizing the energies of every soldier to the greatest possible extent and in infusing him with warlike feelings."[74] Seeking the renewal of the Prussian state after its devastating loss to Napoleon at the Battles of Jena and Auerstedt in 1806, at which Clausewitz was present, he found a kindred spirit in Machiavelli's reflections from amid the wreckage of Florence during the Italian Wars. Machiavelli's recommendation of cold-blooded *ragione di stato* and impassioned citizen militias eager to fight on behalf of the virtuous prince stuck a chord with Clausewitz's call for an army of permanently mobilized *Landwehr* conscripts motivated by patriotic sentiment and thus capable of fighting beyond the range of their officer's whips.[75]

Machiavelli's name does not appear in *On War* "but his ideas are frequently in evidence." Clausewitz assumes an international arena "permanently in flux, lacking finality" in which "conscience and other ethical concerns were extraneous to fundamental political realities."[76] Under these anarchic conditions, the one certainty is the perennial possibility of war between independent and egoistic polities. In addition to borrowing many of Machiavelli's historical examples as well as his penchant for quotable axions, Clausewitz draws on his understanding of violence as an elemental force that explicitly and implicitly gives shape to political life. Machiavelli's and Clausewitz's respective contempt for the wars of the *condottieri* and the *ancien regime* as a "degeneration of the art of war" was a reaction against the "half-measures, indecisiveness, and inactivity"[77] which could not hope to compete against the more absolute forms of warfare introduced by French king Charles VIII in his 1494 invasion of Italy and then Napoleon three centuries later.

Having each witnessed the destruction of their states at the hands of foreign invaders, the purpose of both authors is to remind their reader of the stark consequences of failure to heed the "effectual truth" of violence in politics and the necessity of using it "virtuously."[78] However brutal and treacherous a Machiavellian system may be, each prince's chief interest in survival incentivizes them to concentrate political and military authority within their own hands, and thereby retain the flexibility to escalate and de-escalate conflict as circumstances dictate. Unlike the two functionally identical states in a condition of absolute war, an entire network of identically motivated states have too many potential threats to ever bend their entire focus onto any one of them. Consequently, the pursuit of war should remain strictly proportional to its prospective rewards and the likelihood of acquiring them compared to the risks, especially when the loyalty of the public and the faithfulness of allies is never given without an expectation of mutual benefit.[79]

Clausewitz converts Machiavelli's observations and recommendations into a systematic theory of war and the state. The baseline assumption is that domestic and international politics alike are an unending zero-sum struggle for power, the awareness of which should promote a general interest in relative gains over high-risk, high-reward ventures. But while it is certainly in the long-term interest of rivals to affix constraints on the scope and scale of competition, there is no guarantee that the arrangement of technological forces and political interests will ensure compliance. Periods of relative stability will favor symmetrical competition over limited stakes, and in times of major convulsions, various players will either seek to rewrite the rules in their favor or take shelter under those most likely to succeed in that task. The sheer variety of interests and exogenous factors renders it impossible to make predictions, except that the system as a whole and its individual units are trapped in an endless cycle of crisis and resolution. Politics is the art of identifying the character of one's own environment relative to this cycle, and securing the most advantageous possible position within it. Warfare is the *ultima ratio* for determining both the balance of power among states and the overall character of the system after successive rounds of unit-level conflict. The conclusion of every military and political struggle lays the foundation for a new one, either to affirm or displace the most recent iteration of the status quo.

The Nature of Trinitarian War

The trinity summarizes the theoretical forces underlying the nature of war and captures the full panoply of influences on unit-level decision-making within a Machiavellian environment.[80] The decision to go to war, and the "degree of force that must be used against the enemy" once war is decided upon, results from the two states weighing the scales between their respective "political demands" as well as their comparative "strength of will, their character, and abilities."[81] After determining one's own motivations and capabilities relative to the enemy, the political leadership must also evaluate the relative standing of allies and enemies as well as "the political sympathies of other states"[82] that may flip from one category to the other in the course of the conflict. The political objective takes shape and evolves through the constant recalculation of material and psychological elements within and beyond the state, and one side will at some point calculate that war is no longer worth the political cost, a question which faces the prospective victor as much as the loser. Since every state within a trinitarian system finds security within patterns of interaction that are both reciprocal and predictable, and so they should be as hesitant to inflict a condition of absolute war as they would be to endure it.

The system as a whole aggregates the trinitarian sets of its constituent states, and from their iterated interactions develops its own "general character" of popular attitudes, military doctrines, and political demands that Clausewitz refers to as "the spirit of the age" (*zeitgest*).[83] In extremely rare cases such as Imperial Rome, one state's trinitarian synthesis gives it undisputed mastery over its rivals, allowing it to imprint its own character onto the system itself.[84] In other cases such as Alexander the Great or the Mongol conquerors, weak political organization prevented them from leveraging their tactical advantages into lasting superiority.[85] Neither set of cases achieve the true dimensions of absolute war for the simple reason that they were only absolute for the losing side.

As the instruments of war became increasingly lethal, and bureaucratic centralization increased the resources available to governments, the internal logic of war would suggest that the reduction of friction inexorably propelled war closer to the absolute. In fact, the development of technology and social organization had uneven political effects, with the character of states determining the use of military methods more often than the reverse. In modern Europe, sustained contact and rough parity among the great powers fostered a system-wide identity and promoted conventional agreements on the legitimate use of force, adherence to which indicated conformity to governing principles and norms of coexistence.[86] The balance of power in eighteenth-century Europe was both a consequence of the "narrow base" of available technology, manpower, and finance, as well as an affirmation of the logical, Newtonian universe at the heart of Enlightenment theory. Commanders such as Sweden's Charles XII and Frederick the Great with the talent of an Alexander or Caesar fought at a time when "even the most ambitious ruler had no greater aims than to gain a number of advantages that could be exploited at the peace conference."[87] One who had only experienced war of this kind could be forgiven for thinking that war was a progressive science that continually diminished the role of bloodshed and popular fury in the achievement of the political objective.[88]

"The God of War Himself"

Clausewitz's two decades of experience fighting in the Revolutionary and Napoleonic Wars convinced him that war was finally capable of approximating its absolute condition in reality. As both "sovereign of the country and as well as the military chief of the army," Napoleon used battle as his principal form of diplomacy and ultimately erased the distinctions between the interests of the state, the fortunes of the army, and the passions of the French people. His troops were armed no differently than those of Frederick the Great a generation before, but their eagerness to fight for the prospect of *la Gloire*, the prospect of social mobility, or desire for plunder introduced tactical possibilities far beyond the armies of *l'ancien regime.*[89] This combination of fighting spirit and grand ambition enabled Napoleon to overwhelm an enemy army, conquer its territory, and undermine the vast coalition arrayed against him by dangling offers of territorial compensation in exchange for peace before repeating the cycle again.[90]

Napoleon was the apotheosis of military genius, "the God of War himself,"[91] but warfare approached the absolute only when his enemies were capable of utilizing his own methods against him and turn a singular example of genius into an exchange of escalating blows.[92] Prussia's reconstitution with a massive army of *Landwehr* conscripts, Tsar Alexander's refusal to surrender after the fall of Moscow, and the *guerrilla* resistance of the Spanish represent the three critical aspects of what would later be called total war: armies of trained and patriotic professionals, the government's willingness to fight to the finish rather than bargain in the traditional manner, and most importantly, the direct and enthusiastic participation of the masses.[93] For Clausewitz, "the peoples' new share in these great affairs of state" was the most revolutionary for the nature of war, tearing down social barriers to escalation that "are not so easily set up again." Whenever "major interests are at stake," the union of political and popular objectives will replace the subtle maneuvers of war between governments with the "elemental fury"[94] of masses committed to defeating an enemy with whom compromise was unthinkable.

Naturally, the conduct of the war fell short of the absolute in many respects, most notably the impossibility of achieving a decisive outcome through battle that could not be reversed within at most a few years.[95] Even the most critical battles were never of equal importance to both sides, as Napoleon moved from waging wars of conquest to a desperate struggle to survival, while the Coalition moved in the opposite direction.[96] Yet by the time Napoleon finally embarked for his final exile on St. Helena, every major state in Europe had drawn on an unprecedented portion of its resources and rallied its people to stake their national destiny on the field of battle. From that point forward, any people with the right combination of resources, ideology, and national character could either make their government a force to be reckoned with, or if sufficiently disillusioned with that government, undertake their own form of war by other means.[97]

Napoleon is central to Clausewitz's text not only because of his impact on the author's life, but also because he is the great exception that ultimately proves the rule of absolute war being unachievable in reality. While he personified the theory of war unlike anyone in history, his illustrious career ended in catastrophe because not even he could confine the totality of war to its ideal dimensions. As skillfully as he kept together an effective and loyal fighting force to the bitter end, he could not fully imprint his mastery of war onto the politics of the French state, which ultimately refused to follow its leader into oblivion after Waterloo. In spite of this failure, Napoleon's legacy of a motivated, professional, and centrally directed "Nation in Arms" was that all wars would henceforth retain the possibility of approximating the absolute. In previous eras, logistical and normative limits on political structures made escalation all but impossible. After Napoleon, any state could rally a people to its banner with the right combination of propaganda and organizational skill, either by maximizing its own resources or drawing on universal ideologies to redraw the lines of political loyalty. [98]

For the monarchs and statesmen of the Vienna System, their experience of popular warfare could have been a cautionary tale or an opportunity to substitute French hegemony with their own. While Metternich and Castlereigh secured treaties "charged with protecting Europe against both aggression and domestic upheaval," Tsar Alexander invoked grandiose principles of religion and liberty that could hypothetically "let [him] march his armies across Europe to combat [his] conception of revolutionary danger." [99] Writing only a few years after Napoleon's death, Clausewitz could only wonder whether "from now on will every war in Europe . . . have to be fought only over major issues that affect the people? Or shall we again see a gradual separation taking pale between government and people?" [100] Now that states had the moral and physical resources to propel warfare toward the absolute, the character of war would depend primarily on political judgment, leaving Clausewitz with a fully developed theory but little in the way of predictions.

The Trinity and Modern War

The evolution of warfare since Clausewitz's death in 1831 has done little to resolve his ambiguous conclusions. War remains either decisive or limited, although the two categories are not mutually exclusive, a point which Clausewitz makes in his supplementary notes but was unable to develop fully in the text. [101] A war can transition from one type to the other due to a change in political objectives or the momentum of combat. One side can utilize the whole of its resources against a fraction of the enemy's strength, or develop the capacity to switch from limited to decisive warfare through technological innovation and popular mobilization. In all its classifications and permutations, modern war has remained subject to a consistent rule: all wars bear the potential to hurtle toward the absolute, but upon doing so, the same trinitarian factors that drove the escalation will then arrest or reverse that escalation. The vast range of modern war can assume has not erased its essential differences from absolute war.

The most obvious historic approximation to absolute war is a "total war" featuring "deep underlying polarization of hostility" and threats to "the core territory of a major state," so that "normal restrictions on behavior and fighting go by the board." [102] Nevertheless, even when two sides draw on the full weight of their industrial and popular resources to pound the enemy into submission, two factors in particular preserve the qualitative difference from absolute war. The first is the uneven development of the trinity within and between the belligerents. Total war is often the unintended result of a failed bid for a quick and decisive victory, whereupon the political leadership must then expand the scope of its efforts and rouse the people to take up a struggle that has spiraled beyond its anticipated dimensions.[103] Instead of the steady and reciprocal escalation that characterizes absolute war, the combatants in a total war often struggle to align the disparities between their initially lofty objectives with the insufficiency of their tactical assets, replicating the standard problems of friction on a large scale.

For example, the First World War commenced with the failure of Germany's Schlieffen Plan and France's Plan XVII, both of which presumed a quick and decisive offensive. The course of combat then gave way to the "technical surprise" that victory would only come through mass production on the home front and relentless attritional pressure over an expanse far larger than the traditional battlefield. As leaders rallied their people to the grandiose causes of German *Kultur* or making the world safe for democracy, the soldiers "were killing each other without contempt or hatred . . . bound together by a mystical communion of fate"[104] amid shared horrors only they could understand. Even if one side manages to unite the leadership, military, and people in a common struggle, this is likely a luxury bought from the enemy's distinct inferiority. At the outset of the Second World War, both the Western Allies and Germany generally refrained from intentionally bombing one another's civilians, until the difficulties of conducting accurate raids against military targets at an acceptable cost led to each side ramping up attacks on civilians in order to break the will of the enemy population.[105] Once the Allied achieved air superiority, they incinerated entire cities such as Dresden to prove the inefficacy of Axis resistance and thereby expedite the inevitable surrender.[106] In the Pacific, the Japanese hardened their resolve as their capabilities deteriorated, until the twin shocks of the atomic bomb and the Soviet invasion of Manchuria impelled the Emperor and cabinet to surrender rather than expose the Home Islands to invasion.[107]

The second major difference from absolute war is the impossibility of achieving decisive results through combat alone. After both of the World Wars, the stability of the postwar environment and the likelihood of renewed hostilities depended far more on the resulting constellation of political forces than the outcome of the final engagements. The Imperial German Army succumbed to the parliamentarians of Weimar rather than Allied arms, and only the intractable divergence of French, British, and Soviet aims permitted Hitler to convert his revanchist fantasies into a viable strategic doctrine.[108] The devastation of Germany and Japan in 1945 was reversed within a decade as the United States helped turn its erstwhile foes into stalwart allies against the communist menace on their doorsteps. The prospect of nuclear war that has hovered over global politics since Hiroshima and Nagasaki has struck many observers as the realization of absolute war.[109] But as Herman Kahn argued, even in a nightmare scenario of all-out nuclear exchange, after which "the survivors envy the dead,"[110] human beings would likely resume political competition as soon as a sufficient degree of social organization permitted them to do so.

The continuous operation of the trinity prevented the total wars of the nineteenth and twentieth century from achieving the absolute, and in the Cold War produced an awkward amalgamation of two superpowers armed for total war and yet eager to keep their competition limited. Proxy battlegrounds such as Korea, Vietnam, Afghanistan, and Angola were pawns on a chessboard for the Great Powers while local players fought for total stakes among themselves.[111] The low yield of direct Third World interventions proved to many scholars that war was a crude and ineffective instrument for a modern superpower, and put forth "forceful persuasion" (also known as coercive diplomacy) as a more nuanced alternative. Rather than waste precious resources on behalf of admittedly limited objectives, a range of diplomatic and military tools, could produce greater results with much less expenditure, provided that one could accurately gauge the enemy's hierarchy of preferences and psychological makeup.[112]

The end of the Cold War has all but erased the distinction between local flareups and global confrontations, as "fault-line wars"[113] in the former Yugoslavia and then Syria again brought the U.S. and Russia to opposite sides of bloody ethnic and sectarian feuds. Countless local wars in which the Great Powers refrained from participating or take no interest have approached absolute war for their inhabitants, or at least retained the potential to do so, in the form of warlordism or ethnic cleansing. The Great Powers have refined measures of harassing and sabotaging one another with cyber capabilities that often leave no physical damage and offer a veneer of plausible deniability. Yet even as these innovations threaten to incapacitate an opponent in advance of an all-out assault, these measures are most likely to serve as a "blunt force measure in circumstances in which conventional force would risk retaliation."[114] Cyberwar a qualitative advancement in the conduct of war, but as with previous advancements, they are integrated within the political competition that generated it in the first place and determines the contours of its use.[115]

In wars among states, rebel factions, guerrilla armies, and private militias, reciprocity places a cap on escalation either by its presence or its absence. Adversaries may stop short of their full fighting potential for fear of enemy retaliation, resulting in limited war, or at a certain point may prove unable to match the enemy blow-for-blow. In the latter case, the inferior side either succumbs and grants the superior side a decisive victory or reverts to asymmetrical forms of warfare, seeking to draw the enemy past the "culminating point of attack" through evasion and attrition, causing their strength to "diminish day by day."[116] No contest between trinitarian combatants has ever featured a series of unidirectional escalations toward a climactic moment of decision. So long as each side has the capacity and will to harm the other, war has either proceeded well beneath the absolute or ended before the loser's will was completely and irrevocably broken.

Decisive and Limited War vs. Terrorism

Clausewitz's typology of limited and decisive war has often been compared to a boxing match.[117] A prizefighter can win on points with accurate punching, skillful defense, and ring generalship, or simply try to bludgeon an opponent into unconsciousness. Both strategies have their weaknesses: the technician may tempt a physically stronger opponent to walk through punches and force them into an unanticipated slugfest, and the brawler's pursuit of the knockout may expose them to a devastating counterattack. In any case, the fight invariably takes place in the shadow of the potential knockout and the fighter's response to the perceived risk. A winning fighter may coast on advantages or summarily dispatch a fading opponent, while a losing fighter may take desperate measures in the later rounds or try to minimize the amount punishment sustained and accept a loss in order to preserve their health for future bouts. As each adapts their strategy to the other round by round, they must also contend with fatigue, anxiety, the advice of trainers, and the roar of the crowd, all of which effects their ability to detect and exploit their opponent's mistakes under severe pressure. No match will proceed with mutual and symmetrical escalation toward a point of mutual, maximum expenditure concluding with a last-second knockout. The match will either conclude at the final bell due to both fighters displaying sufficient caution, or earlier on account of one fighter having achieved distinct superiority.

As a theorist of war, Clausewitz was exclusively concerned with the impact of the "new political conditions now obtaining in Europe"[118] on military and political institutions, but those same conditions planted the seeds of a new form of combat, the nature of which would not become fully apparent until decades after Clausewitz's death. Technological and political developments offered the possibility of breaking the Machiavellian cycle of symmetrical and reciprocal conflict. Terrorism does not seek victory through direct contact with enemy forces, where the logic of reciprocity is inescapable. Rather, it achieves its unique decisiveness through erasing all boundaries between the combatants and a target audience. Subjecting a people to an approximation of absolute war permanently discredits the notion of warfare as an extension of policy by other means and turns it into the central fact of political life.

There is no time for the prudential arrangement of political objectives, military capabilities, and popular attitudes when individuals understand themselves to be locked in a struggle for survival. For its enemies, continued resistance can only have the effect of hastening its formation, which becomes increasingly apparent as it escalates its own efforts. Whereas a conventional combatant can choose to back down and perhaps resume the effort another day, the enemy of a terrorist campaign realizes that their employment of force is ineffective only after they have completely lost the power to choose the continued pursuit or abandonment of their objective. Among the prospective members of the community, some will surely blame the terrorists for triggering the breakdown of social order, but as the trajectory of war bends ever closer to the absolute, their maintenance of perfect discipline amid the wreckage of the old system makes them the only agency capable of supervising the construction of a new one.

Returning to the analogy of war and boxing helps to illustrate the the particular character of terrorism. Rather than engage in a prizefight and choose between the style of a skilled boxer or power puncher, terrorism ignores Queensberry rules altogether and employs a method more akin to that of a professional wrestler. The fight doubles as a piece of gaudy theater, complete with an elaborately choreographed entrance into the ring, direct appeals to the audience, and a no-holds-barred style designed as much to hold the crowd's attention as harm the opponent. The purpose of a boxing match is to determine the superior fighter, while a professional wrestling contest is entirely a means to the end of pleasing the crowd, and so applause becomes the primary determinant of victory. Terrorism disabuses the audience of their respect for partial and reversible victories by decision or stoppage, and instead crowd to become complicit in transitioning toward a far more ruthless form of combat that promises more decisive results.

Some of the crowd may abhor the use of dirty tricks and braggadocio in a historically rule-bound arena, especially when that it blurs the traditional distinction between combatants and observers. Others will cheer the willful disregard of old restrictions that had too long reserved its laurels for a privileged few and feel little sympathy for spectators who at last suffered the kind of violence they had cheered from the safety of their front-row seats. Partisan of both will then take direct measures to prevent retribution against their hero, spilling the fight over into the bleachers and turning any notion of rules or restrictions into a bloody farce. Assuming that the traditional prizefighter still wants to win, there is no remaining option other than to dispense with pugilistic honor, but this renders victory impossible since it invalidates the legitimacy of referees to monitor conduct, judges to determine winners, and sanctioning bodies to confer titles. All that remains is for each to maximize their efforts and minimize their moral compunction while rallying their followers to do the same.

ABSOLUTE WAR IN HISTORY

The Republic of Friends

War, like society, has for so long been a part of the human condition that one can only speculate on its origins, requiring theorists such as Clausewitz to reconstruct a hypothetical state of nature to isolate the thing itself from its historical manifestations. By contrast, a theory of terrorism proceeds from a much more concrete historical foundation, as the concept can directly trace its inception to the period of *"La Terreur"* in 1793 and 1794 that marked the climax of the French Revolution.[119] This does not mean that terrorism emerged *sui generis* and fully formed or that the participants were conscious of having introduced a new form of warfare. As a historical point of origin, the Terror serves to identify the features that classify a new phenomenon and pinpoint the confluence of social and political forces that facilitated its emergence. The model would evolve considerably and always remain subject to circumstantial variation, but subsequent examples of terrorism will nonetheless exhibit the same fundamental tension between the promise of building a new community along rational lines and the activation of primordial passions in order to achieve it.

The Terror rejected the Clausewitzian understanding of war as a temporary and limited phase of political interaction. The revolutionary regime sought to overcome the limits of the trinity and achieve a complete synthesis of political objectives, military methods, and popular attitudes. Replacing the moral presumptions of the sovereign state with what Robespierre called "holy equality and the inprescriptable [sic] rights of man," would in turn generate a "high-minded devotion which sinks all private interests in the interest of the whole community."[120] The nascent Republic would transcend the conventional limits of war, creating "an army fit to represent a free people"[121] capable of enduring any sacrifice, achieving any task, and defeating any enemy. The motivation to achieve this lofty task would come from citizens who enthusiastically rallied to the flag of a regime that put aside the narrow interests of the state, the benefits of which were distributed narrowly, and proclaimed the universal goal of human betterment. Passion and reason would be fully in alignment, with a limitless capacity for escalation. Although this radical experiment barely lasted a year, it signaled that the Westphalian state system rooted in trinitarian warfare had spawned its own nemesis: a combatant that regarded absolute war not as a specter to avoid, but as the catalyst for realizing the full scope of its ambitions.

Like most revolutionary concepts, terrorism was not an entirely new phenomenon so much as the innovative use of existing ideas and structures. The ideological impulse behind the Terror reflects the "revolutionist tradition" of international theory. Martin Wight defines the revolutionists as:

"those who believe so passionately in the moral unity of the society of states or international society, that they identify themselves with it, and therefore they both claim to speak in the name of this unity, and experience an overriding obligation to give effect to it as the first aim of their international policies."[122]

Dating at least as far back as the early medieval dream of a unified *Res Publica Christiana,* revolutionism infuses politics with missionary zeal, seeking to tear down corrupt institutions to restore a sacred authority such as God, History, or the People. As Wight points out, revolutionism is "a series of disconnected illustrations of the same politico-philosophical truths," the different strains of which tending to reject one another's legitimacy. In order to assert its exclusive and universal claim, each new version of revolutionist doctrine is compelled to "deny its past, to try to start from scratch, to jump out of history and begin again"[123] the mission to redeem mankind, or at least the portion of it worth redeeming.

When taking the form of an actionable political program, revolutionism struggles with conflicting imperatives to convert the unbaptized and to avoid the contaminating influence of mainstream society. Similarly, the propagation of the doctrine depends on a combination of institutional rigor and individual spontaneity, the prerogatives of which are likely to interfere with one another. During the Reformation, John Calvin oversaw a repressive apparatus in Geneva while inspiring his followers in France to resist unjust authority in the name of individual conscience, forcing him to manage "the risks inherent in his own ideas."[124] Revolutionism also thrives on regular demonstrations of charisma even as its authority ultimately rests on the stability of bureaucratic structures and inviolable laws. A premodern society such as Calvin's Geneva simply could not marshal resources or build political structures corresponding with its proclaimed universality. It could either consolidate its authority within circumscribed limits or sustain prophetic urgency by eschewing all forms of authority above the righteous and dedicated individual. This trade-off between rational political direction and raw popular energy fits quite neatly within the categories of trinitarian calculation.

The capabilities and normative pretensions of the nation-state heralded the possibility of uniting political pragmatism with revolutionary urgency. France was among the first nations to develop the attributes of the modern state, and in doing so, it inspired a new generation of secular ideologues to seize this apparatus and convert it into a midwife of revolutionary transformation. Eighteenth-century developments in science and administration encouraged many in government and the academy that "the empirical gathering of data was the first step towards a society that could progressively free itself from poverty, ignorance and pain."[125] For the emergent middle class, frustration with the vestiges of feudal privilege and the promise of a more egalitarian future produced a paradoxical vision of rational social reform that would also restore mankind to a romantic natural condition. High levels of literacy and political consciousness among the public indicated the potential to "educate an entire people for happiness in and by liberty,"[126] actualizing Rousseau's dream of moral and political regeneration through the pure expression of the General Will.

The French Revolution made the community itself into the exclusive source of political legitimacy, spawning a myth of national destiny designed to "bind the masses emotionally and to arouse in them the politically effective expectation of salvation."[127] In practice, shared belief in the achievement of perfect equality only fueled disagreement over the proper methods of bringing it into existence. The ideal of the unified commonwealth was a cudgel for rival factions within the National Assembly to wield against one another in their battles over issues such as the expropriation of the nobility, the status of the monarchy, and the aristocratic *emigres* urging foreign monarchs to restore Louis XVI by force. The dominant Girondin faction attempted to break this stalemate by pushing for war against Austria to "rally public opinion behind the assembly and undermine the counterrevolutionary forces within France," as well as justify "more active efforts to suppress internal opponents."[128] After a disastrous start to the war, the dissident Montagnard faction seized on the emergency to press the radical internal measures which they had long argued as necessary for securing the Revolution at home. Lacking sufficient power in the legislature, they instead spurred on the lower-class Parisian *sans culottes* to take to the streets and demand prince controls, the execution of the royal family, and the establishment a republic under the complete control of a National Convention.[129] After French fortunes on the battlefield improved, the rivals briefly joined hands in a meeting of their ambitions, launching a campaign to "liberate Europe in six months and purge the earth of all tyrants,"[130] until peasant resistance to conscription left their already overstretched armies critically short of new volunteers.

By the summer of 1793, a series of military reverses and domestic insurrections turned the Convention against itself, with mutual recriminations of treachery crippling its ability to act as the crisis worsened.[131] The ascendance of the Committee of Public Safety and the commencement of the Terror sought to overcome the barriers that had historically forced a revolutionist doctrine either to moderate its aims in times of crisis or collapse entirely. Without the power to indoctrinate and command followers directly, revolutionists of the past could only implore unity of purpose among their far-flung followers and sympathizers. When this did not materialize, they had little choice but to adjust their doctrine in light of the circumstances and grudgingly accept the limits of status quo conventions and structures. Under the Jacobin dictatorship, it was finally possible for a revolutionist to apply the instruments of the state toward the fulfillment of a halcyon ideal. As Tocqueville argued, the aim of the Revolution was to destroy only those outmoded

institutions and practices that inhibited the central authority from implementing a "simple and more uniform" social order and thereby refining a purer
distillation of total equality.[132]

The architects of the Terror were remarkably candid about the role of
brutality in the formation of a society fully steeped in public virtue. Like
medieval monks who wore hairshirts or flagellated themselves to affix their
minds on the divine, terror was a salutary mortification of the body politic
that deprived the individual of any room for concerns beyond the collective
good. Robespierre proclaimed that terror was "nothing but prompt, severe,
inflexible justice . . . the general principle of democracy applied to the homeland's most pressing needs."[133] The perfection of domestic structures would
transform politics from a balancing act among competing goods into the
complete and unadulterated fulfillment of the popular will. A sufficiently
dedicated citizenry would have no need to choose between security and
revolutionary orthodoxy since they could attend to both in full. Once the
principle of popular sovereignty had been proclaimed, the only remaining
task was to eliminate all remaining impediments to its fulfillment. As Saint-
Just reported at the outset of the Terror, "since the French people made its
will clear, whatever is opposed to it is not part of the sovereign; whatever is
not part of the sovereign is an enemy."[134] A comprehensive and sustained
baptism of fire would distinguish the bearers of the sacred truth from the
"denatured"[135] souls incapable of living under righteous governance.

Absolute War and *La Terreur*

Robespierre and his colleagues were aware that the pronouncement of the
"Republic of Virtue" was a declaration of moral purpose and not a statement
of empirical fact. The Terror was deemed necessary precisely because a
horde of enemies within and without confronted the Committee "with a
superhuman task which they pledged to accomplish with honor and barbarism." Incapable of summoning the requisite virtue by their own efforts, the
people were crying out for a vanguard "to organize, in the midst of anarchy, a
violent minority government."[136] Terror would expose the hypocrites pursuing their own ends while outwardly professing the public good, and provide a
clear set of instructions for the mass of well-meaning citizens uncertain of
how to make a sincere and worthwhile contribution.[137] Only a small cadre of
the most fanatically devoted was sufficiently cohesive to articulate a coherent
ideological narrative and then demonstrate the necessary measures for making it a reality.

As soon as it moved from theory to practice, the notion of a "collective
and conscious choice to institute 'the Terror' as a system of government"
gave way to the reality of "an improvised set of responses to a shifting
situation"[138] without a clear defining purpose or hierarchy. Lacking the pow-

er to impose its will from the top down, the Terror intended to structure the choices of the masses so that they themselves became the primary agents of its implementation. The actual motivations of citizens would range from fear and opportunism to wholehearted devotion, but their aggregate complicity would project the image of complete social unity. The Terror would further validate its own necessity the more spies and traitors it unmasked, keeping any potential source of opposition off balance and progressively tearing down all barriers between the atomized individual and the wrath of the collective. To the coalition aligned against France, the Terror concealed its internal divisions behind a fearsome image of a people who had dispensed of every convention of military and diplomatic conduct, answering only to the call of "fire, steel, and patriotism."[139]

The Terror was effective to the extent that it brought the general crisis facing the country to the doorstep of every citizen, leaving no middle ground between collaboration and direct opposition. Its initial priority was to end the disputes over the conduct of the war, judicial powers, price controls, and dechristianization which continued to paralyze the efficient operation of government even after the establishment of the Jacobin dictatorship.[140] Although their decision-making primarily reflected the pressures of immediate necessity, the ideology of the Terror provided cover for various agencies to paper over their disagreements under the guise of a common purpose. Robespierre and Danton both expressed concerns that the universal conscription intended to produce a Nation in Arms would instead raise an armed mob that could promptly turn on the Committee. In the context of the Terror, it laid a stepping stone in the radicalization of the Revolution. The exigencies of war and mass conscription would infuse the army with badly needed manpower, purge the army of its lingering aristocratic habits, and direct the most fervent *sans culottes* away from Paris. It would also justify the formation of an administrative apparatus responsible for equipping this massive force and shield it from counterrevolutionary penetration.[141] Within weeks of proclaiming the *levee*, the Committee ordained that "terror is the order of the day," imposed state control over the economy, ordered the requisition of all usable materiel, and passed the Law of Suspects which granted Revolutionary tribunals near-unlimited powers of trial and execution.[142]

Logrolling one measure on top of another redirected the externalities of factional rivalry onto the public at large. So long as the threat of an aristocratic plot persisted, the Committee's *representants-en-mission* in the provinces and roving bands of *armees revolutionnaires* were fully empowered to investigate homes, confiscate property, and liquidate anyone deemed lacking in revolutionary enthusiasm. The individual's best defense against denunciation was to signal their own loyalty in every possible way, especially through the eager denunciation of others. While totalistic in its aims, the violence was usually selective in its application. In many departments far from the front lines or outside pockets of royalist insurrection, "the Terror barely lived up to its name."[143] Nonetheless, the perennial threat of state-sanctioned brutality and its legitimation through a garish series of proclamations and festivals crafted a public morality in which cruelty on behalf of the community was the height of virtue. The individual citizen may have complied only to minimize the risk of becoming its next victim, but even the most reluctant collaboration wore down psychological resistance to performing whatever the will of the people commanded.

The ambition to turn the entire republic into an armed camp far outstripped the administrative capacity of ad hoc coordination between Paris and the provinces, leading to rampant evasion of the draft, hoarding of supplies, and violence against government personnel.[144] But while implementation fell short of the soaring rhetoric of social regeneration, the Terror was successful in its immediate purpose of repelling the foreign invaders and suppressing domestic insurrection. The *levee* managed to integrate a massive influx of enthusiastic recruits with holdovers from the royal army, especially artillery officers such as a young Napoleon Buonaparte. Artillerists had been dismissed as a "useful auxiliary" under the old regime but had already proven the merits of the "scientific corps" against Coalition forces at Valmy and Jemappes, making them both necessary and politically reliable.[145] The sheer size of the army placed them far beyond the limits of their own logistical base, compelling them to "externalize their supply needs, imposing them upon conquered opponents or recently 'liberated' allies."[146] The junior officer's thirst for distinction, the volunteer's desire for patriotic service, the conscript's fear of the guillotine, and an unlimited license for all of them to requisition enemy and civilian stockpiles at will combined to produced an army uniquely well-suited for offensive warfare.

The Revolutionary Army scored a series of stunning victories against the Allies, conquered Belgium, and crushed royalist rebellions in the Vendee, Brittany, and Maine. The triumph of ragged conscripts and volunteers singing "La Marseillaise" while routing the polished and disciplined troops of the European monarchies was particularly formative experience for Clausewitz, who first encountered them at Valmy as a twelve-year-old standard-bearer. As he later noted in his "Political Declaration, "the king does not wage war against the king, nor the army against another army, but rather one people against another, and king and army are part of the people."[147] The full weight given to each component of the revolutionary trinity and their harmonized interaction laid the foundation for total war, but the critical element in the Terror's approximation of absolute war was the shift in its basic objective toward breaking the will of its own society to acceptance of theoretically unlimited escalation.

The Committee had long discarded the Girondin dream of exporting the revolution across Europe, opting to treat the war against the Coalition primarily as an opportunity to perfect the revolution at home. For Robespierre, the Allied conspiracy to "make us retreat into servitude" took the form of both invading armies and "all the cunning scoundrels they have in their pay" whose "main object is to set us at odds with each other." Complacency in the wake of a battlefield victory would be worse than a defeat, sapping vigilance while "the wretches who tear secretly at our entrails . . . still conspire unpunished!"[148] Mobilization against the external danger was only the first step in the truly decisive contest against the feudal remnants at home whose desperation would increase with the advancement of the revolutionary state. Given the presumption that "the terrible war, which liberty sustains against tyranny, [was] indivisible," the mere presence of Coalition forces in the field proved the existence of an aristocratic conspiracy within France itself, especially given their patent inability to defeat the army in battle. It stood to reason that Austrian, Prussian, and English designs on France would only cease when "there are no citizens in the Republic but republicans."[149] Any lingering sign of friction or resistance from without or within demanded still more brutal measures until the perfection of revolutionary virtue brought forth a condition of untrammeled peace and prosperity.

The Fall of Absolute War and the Rise of Total War

A successful approximation of absolute war must postpone its climactic moment until both sides have pushed one another to the utmost, so that whichever side can escalate still further thereby demonstrates its qualitative superiority. Unfortunately for the Jacobins, they lacked an adversary capable of sustaining the fight into the championship rounds, depriving the Committee of the time needed to firmly secure the home front. Competition among the members of the Coalition to maximize their own sliver of French territory and minimize the costs of acquiring it made concerted action against France impossible. For the Austrians and Prussians in particular, French victories did not encourage them to redouble their efforts, but instead to scale back and pursue expansion in the more amenable theater of Poland.[150] Meanwhile, the exigencies and disruptions of warfare provided countless opportunities for Dantonists, Hébertists, Enragés, and other factions to vie for position against each other through pet projects such as dechristianization, economic centralization, or a diplomatic breakthrough, all with the common aim of bolstering their own prestige to maximize their share of postwar leadership. Although the war presented a boundless opportunity for factional rivalry, it also compelled its moderation, lest the success of one group so thoroughly weaken the state as a whole as to render it vulnerable once again and too exhausted to repeat its previous successes.

The passing of the supreme emergency as a result of the victories of the *levee* brought those rivalries to a head before any one faction had come close to asserting superiority. Success on the battlefield ideally paved the way for the completion of the revolutionary project at home, but the aggregate effect of disparate wartime measures had pulled the state, army, and people in so many contrary directions as to make postwar reconciliation impossible without civil war. Robespierre could not appease public demand for a relaxation of the Terror without purging its most pitiless enforcers, a charge which could plausibly fall on practically any prominent figure within the government.[151] Meanwhile, the imposition of price controls and wage ceilings meant to curb runaway wartime inflation turned the *sans culottes* against Robespierre at precisely the moment he needed their support to take on his opponents Convention who understood that the end of the Terror required the end of Robespierre.[152] As François Furet argues, the Thermidorian overthrow of the Committee and the end of the Terror terminated the project of pure democracy that had animated the Revolution up until that point, which led the way for a "revolution of special interests"[153] to take its place. The exhaustion of revolutionary ideology as the lodestar of French politics left the succeeding governments of Convention (1794–1795) and the Directory (1795–1799) helpless to arrest an ongoing cycle of recriminations and reprisals between Jacobin Terror and the subsequent White Terror against Robespierre's followers and collaborators.

With royalists and Jacobins locked in a seesaw battle for control of the government, each looked to the army for deliverance against the other. The army had undertaken a permanent campaign footing to guard against the threat of a renewed Coalition offensive and to defend its own "strong vested interest in continued war"[154] through which it had acquired immense wealth and prestige. Various government officials adopted the military interest as their own, whether to claim a share of the spoils, keep charismatic generals away from Paris, or to ensure military support in the event of a *coup d'état* or popular uprising. The conquest of Italy, the establishment of "sister republics" in Holland and Switzerland, and Napoleon's 1798 Egyptian expedition had embodied the mystique of militant nationalism and universal service as other governing institutions fell into disrepute.[155]

By the time that Napoleon returned to Paris in November 1799 to install a military dictatorship, "all shades of political opinion could find something to support in the new regime."[156] Napoleon was a trinity unto himself: a popular hero with the personal loyalty of the army, whose dictatorship held the promise of both stability and enlightened social reform. In spite of the Terror's ultimate failure, it succeeded in its initial task of collapsing the distinction between politics and war. Turning popular sovereignty into an imperial project harnessed the logic of absolute war by using the prospect of limitless escalation to perfect the union of state and citizen. Open-ended war would indefinitely postpone the climactic struggle at home that would force a resolution to its intractable political decisions. As discussed above, the weakness in this strategy was that it shifted the emergency away from France and onto its enemies, restoring the principal of reciprocity to warfare. Prolonged exposure to Napoleon's model ensured that other states could eventually copy and utilize it to inflict a defeat no less comprehensive than the ones they had suffered.[157]

The Revolution's progression from idealism to terror to dictatorship has become one of the defining arcs of the modern nation-state, with different audiences each taking away a distinct set of lessons. For liberal democracies, the French example emphasized the need for institutional and normative restraints on the pure expression of popular will to prevent the citizenry from degenerating into the mob. For authoritarian regimes, it showed the possibility of reconciling popular support with centralized direction, provided the leadership could prudently navigate between the Scylla of revolutionary exuberance and the Charybdis of military reactionism. The lessons of the French example would prove to be most salient for ideologues aiming to succeed where the Revolution failed in the establishment of a new and idealized community. This impulse would take shape in two distinct forms: social engineering by a revolutionary party that had captured the power of the state, and dissidents aiming to carve out a new political community from the ground up.

For those who constructed utopia from a position of state power, the chief takeaway from their Jacobin forebears was to keep absolute war separate from real war. Making victory on the battlefield a precondition of social transformation forced the state to recalibrate its political priorities in light of enemy behavior and the uneven balance within its own trinity, inhibiting its unilateral progression toward the absolute. Revolutionary elements among the people would absorb the lesson that the state itself was too much a contingent product of history to serve as a proper vehicle for the assemblage of a fully harmonized trinity, which must form completely free from the bounds of traditional norms and institutions. The Jacobins outlined the concept of terrorism for generations to follow, but since they were painting on a blank historical canvas, they had little chance of gauging how their program would interact with a dynamic social reality. Subsequent examples of terrorism would both validate the basic objective of undermining civil society for the purpose of engineering a new community, and provide enough experiential lessons for later practitioners to combine their singular and uncompromising vision with a flexible and prudent strategy.

NOTES

1. Beatrice Heuser, *Reading Clausewitz* (London: Pimlico, 2002), 118.
2. Terence M. Holmes, "The Clausewitzian Fallacy of Absolute War," *Journal of Strategic Studies* 40 (2017): 2.

3. Richard Ned Lebow, "Clausewitz and Nuclear Crisis Stability," *Political Science Quarterly* 103 (1988): 81–110; Christopher Daase, "Clausewitz and Small War," in Strachan and Herberg-Rothe, *Clausewitz in the Twenty First Century*, 182–195; Thomas A. Drohan, "Bringing 'Nature of War' into Irregular Warfare Strategy: Contemporary Applications of Clausewitz's Trinity," *Defence Studies* 11 (2011): 497–516.

4. Grant Wardlaw, *Political Terrorism: Theory, Tactics, and Countermeasures* (New York: Cambridge University Press, 1989), 18.

5. Peter Paret, *Clausewitz and the State: The Man, His Theories, and His Times* (Princeton: Princeton University Press, 1985), 151.

6. Michael I. Handel, Introduction to *Clausewitz and Modern Strategy*, edited by Michael I. Handel (Abingdon: Frank Cass, 2004), 5–6.

7. Stephen J. Cimbala, *Clausewitz and Escalation:Classical Perspectives on Nuclear Strategy* (New York: Frank Cass, 1991), 199.

8. Smith, *On Clausewitz*, 86.

9. Clausewitz, *On War*, 76.

10. Ibid., 79.

11. Ibid., 77.

12. Ibid., 91.

13. Ibid., 82.

14. Ibid., 579.

15. Ibid., 582.

16. Ibid., 83.

17. Ibid., 78.

18. Ibid., 581.

19. Youri Cormier, *War as Paradox: Clausewitz and Hegel on Fighting Doctrines and Ethics* (Montreal: McGill-Queen's University Press, 2016), 121.

20. Clausewitz, *On War*, 593.

21. Ibid., 479.

22. Ibid., 228.

23. Eckhard Lubkemeier, "Building Peace Under the Nuclear Sword of Damocles," in *Nuclear Weapons in the Changing World: Perspectives From Europe, Asia, and North America*, eds. Patrick J. Garrity and Steven Maaranen (New York: Plenum Press, 1992), 229.

24. Jon Tetsuro Sumida, *Decoding Clausewitz: A New Approach to* On War (Lawrence: University Press of Kansas, 2008), 123–125.

25. R. Harrison Wagner, "Bargaining and War," *American Journal of Political Science* 44 (2000): 472.

26. Ian Roxborough, "Clausewitz and the Sociology of War," *The British Journal of Sociology* 45 (1994): 623.

27. Jan Willem Honig, "Clausewitz's *On War:* Problems of Text and Translation," in *Clausewitz in the Twenty-First Century*, eds. Strachan and Herberg-Rothe, 66–67.

28. Antulio J. Echevarria II, *Clausewitz and Contemporary War* (New York: Oxford University Press, 2007), 67.

29. Clausewitz, *On War*, 580.

30. Raymond Aron, *Peace & War: A Theory of International Relations* (New Brunswick: Transaction Publishers, 2003), 23–24.

31. Heuser, *Reading Clausewitz*, 27.

32. Clausewitz, *On War*, 120.

33. Ibid., 117.

34. Ibid., 115–116.

35. Ibid., 130–132.

36. Ibid., 187.

37. Ibid., 189.

38. Ibid., 102–104.

39. Ibid., 110.

40. Ibid., 122.

41. Ibid., 85–86.

42. Ibid., 80.

43. Ibid., 128.

44. Ibid, 78.

45. Ibid., 81.

46. Ibid., 84

47. Ibid., 87.

48. Ibid., 612.

49. Ibid., 382.

50. Ibid., 336–337.

51. Ibid., 585.

52. Ibid., 87.

53. Bernard Brodie, *Strategy in the Missile Age* (Princeton: Princeton University Press, 1965), 36.

54. Hew Strachan, "Clausewitz and the Dialectics of War," in *Clausewitz in the Twenty First-Century*, eds. Strachan and Herberg-Rothe, 43–44.

55. Colin M. Fleming, *Clausewitz's Timeliness Trinity: A Framework For Modern War* (Burlington: Ashgate, 2013), 58.

56. Clausewitz, *On War*, 81.

57. Ibid., 89.

58. Ibid., 94.

59. Ibid., 138.

60. Ibid., 608.

61. Ibid., 89.

62. Ibid., 90.

63. Ibid., 93.

64. Ibid., 606.

65. Ibid., 99.

66. Andreas Herberg-Rothe, *Clausewitz's Puzzle: The Political Theory of War* (New York: Oxford University Press), 140.

67. Van Creveld, *More On War*, 3.

68. Hugh Smith, "The Womb of War: Clausewitz and International Politics," *Review of International Studies* 16 (1990): 43.

69. Ibid., 51.

70. Carl von Clausewitz, "Notes on History and Politics (1803–1807)," in *Historical and Political Writings*, trans. and eds. Peter Paret and Daniel Moran (Princeton: Princeton University Press, 1976), 245.

71. Carl von Clausewitz, "Notes on History and Politics (1807–1809)," in *Historical and Politics Writings*, 268–269.

72. Niccolo Machiavelli, *The Prince*, trans. Harvey Mansfield (Chicago: University of Chicago Press, 1998), 89.

73. Clausewitz, "Notes on History and Politics (1807–1809," 269.

74. Carl von Clausewitz, "Letter to Fichte (1809)," in *Historical and Political Writings*, 282.

75. Alissa M. Ardito, *Machiavelli and the Modern State: The Prince, The Discourses on Livy, and the Extended Territorial Republic* (New York: Cambridge University Press, 2015), 182; Peter Paret, *Clausewitz in His Time: Essays in the Cultural and Intellectual History of Thinking About War* (New York: Berghahn Books, 2015), 104.

76. Paret, *Clausewitz and the State,* 172.

77. Gat, *A History of Military Thought*, 204.

78. Harvey Mansfield, *Machiavelli's Virtue* (Chicago: University of Chicago Press, 1998), 19.

79. Machiavelli, 66.

80. Paret, *Clausewitz and the State*, 368–369.

81. Clausewitz, *On War*, 585.

82. Ibid., 586.

83. Ibid., 594.

84. Ibid., 587.
85. Ibid., 586.
86. Hedley Bull, *The Anarchical Society: A Study of Order in World Politics* (New York: Columbia University Press, 2002) 151.
87. Clausewitz, *On War*, 590–591.
88. Ibid., 591.
89. Michael Howard, *War in European History* (New York: Oxford University Press, 2009), 82–84.
90. Paul W. Schroeder, *The Transformation of European Politics, 1763–1848* (New York: Oxford University Press, 1994), 395.
91. Clausewitz, *On War*, 583.
92. Ibid., 580.
93. Smith, *The Utility of Force*, 57.
94. Clausewitz, *On War*, 593.
95. Russell Weigley, *The Age of Battles: Decisive Warfare from Breitenfeld to Waterloo* (Bloomington: Indiana University Press, 1991), 536–538.
96. Howard, *War in European History*, 85–86
97. Clausewitz, *On War*, 479–480.
98. Philip Bobbitt, *The Shield of Achilles: War, Peace, and the Course of History* (New York: Anchor Books, 2002), 547–548
99. Henry Kissinger, *A World Restored: Metternich, Castlereigh, and the Problem of Peace, 1812–1822* (Boston: Houghton Mifflin, 1973), 226.
100. Clausewitz, *On War*, 593.
101. Ibid., 69.
102. John A. Vasquez, *The War Puzzle Revisited* (New York: Cambridge University Press, 2009), 278–279.
103. Kalevi J. Holsti, *The State, War, and the State of War* (New York: Cambridge University Press, 1996), 34–35.
104. Raymond Aron, *The Century of Total War* (Boston: Beacon Press, 1954), 22–26.
105. Ward Thomas, *The Ethics of Destruction: Norms and Force in International Relations* (Ithaca: Cornell University Press, 2001), 128–131.
106. Lawrence Freedman, *The Evolution of Nuclear Strategy* (New York: Palgrave Macmillan, 2003), 16.
107. Robert A. Pape, *Bombing to Win: Air Power and Coercion in War* (Ithaca: Cornell University Press, 1996), 122–123.
108. A.J.P. Taylor, *The Origins of the Second World War* (New York: Touchstone, 1996), 71–74.
109. Stephen J. Cimbala, *The Politics of Warfare: The Great Powers in the Twentieth Century* (Philadelphia: Penn State University Press, 2010), 81.
110. Herman Kahn, *On Thermonuclear War* (New Brunswick: Transaction Publishers, 2010), 40.
111. Odd Arne Westad, *The Global Cold War: Third Interventions and the Making of Our Times* (New York: Cambridge University Press, 2007), 180–185.
112. Alexander L. George, *Forceful Persuasion: Coercive Diplomacy as an Alternative to War* (Washington, D.C.: U.S. Institute of Peace Press, 1991), 43–46.
113. Samuel P. Huntington, *The Clash of Civilizations and the Remaking of World Order* (New York: Penguin, 1996), 252–254.
114. Adam P. Liff, "Cyberwar: A New 'Absolute Weapon'? The Proliferation of Cyberwarfare Capabilities and Interstate War," *Journal of Strategic Studies* 35 (2012): 408–409.
115. Bradley A. Thayer, "The Political Effects of Information Warfare: Why New Military Capabilities Cause Old Political Dangers," *Security Studies* 10 (2000): 80–85.
116. Clausewitz, *On War*, 528.
117. W.B. Gallie, *Philosophers of Peace and War: Kant, Clausewitz, Marx, Engels, and Tolstoy* (New York: Cambridge University Press, 1978), 59–60.
118. Clausewitz, *On War*, 609.

119. Gerard Chaliand and Arnaud Blin, "The Invention of Modern Terror," in *The History of Terrorism: From Antiquity to ISIS*, ed. Gerard Chaliand (Oakland: University of California Press, 2016), 95.

120. Quoted in Eli Sagan, *Citizens & Cannibals: The French Revolution, the Struggle for Modernity, and the Origins of Ideological Terror* (Lanham: Rowman & Littlefield, 2001), 495.

121. Alan Forrest, "*La Patrie en Danger:* The French Revolution and the First *Levee en Masse,*" in *The People in Arms: Military Myth and National Mobilization Since the French Revolution*, eds. Daniel Moran and Arthur Waldron (New York: Columbia University Press, 2003), 16.

122. Martin Wight, *International Theory: The Three Traditions* (Leicester: Leicester University Press, 1996), 8.

123. Ibid., 12.

124. Michael Walzer, *The Revolution of the Saints: A Study in the Origins of Radical Politics* (New York: Atheneum, 1976), 64–65.

125. Simon Schama, *Citizens: A Chronicle of the French Revolution* (New York: Alfred A. Knopf, 1989), 182.

126. Francois Furet, "Rousseau and the French Revolution," in *The Legacy of Rousseau*, ends. Clifford Orwin and Nathan Tarcov (Chicago: University of Chicago Press, 1997), 179.

127. Eric Voegelin, "The Political Religions," in *The Collected Works of Eric Voegelin, Vol. 5: Modernity Without Restraint* (Columbia: University of Missouri Press, 2000), 64.

128. Stephen M. Walt, *Revolution and War* (Ithaca: Cornell University Press, 1996), 66.

129. Ibid., 76.

130. Timothy Tackett, *The Coming of the Terror in the French Revolution* (Cambridge: Harvard University Press, 2015), 249.

131. Ibid., 270–275.

132. Alexis de Tocqueville, *The Old Regime and the French Revolution* (New York: Anchor Books, 1983), 19–20.

133. Maximilien Robespierre, "On the Principles of Political Morality That Should Guide the National Convention in the Domestic Administration of the Republic," in *Virtue and Terror*, ed. Slavoj Zizek (London: Verso, 2007), 117.

134. Quoted in Dan Edelstein, *The Terror of Natural Right: Republicanism, the Cult of Nature, and the French Revolution* (Chicago: University of Chicago Press, 2009), 213.

135. Ibid., 168.

136. Arno J. Mayer, *The Furies: Violence and Terror in the French and Russian Revolutions* (Princeton: Princeton University Press, 2000), 561.

137. Steven B. Smith, "Hegel and the French Revolution: An Epitaph for Republicanism," in *The French Revolution and the Birth of* Modernity, ed. Ferenc Feher (Berkeley: University of California Press, 1990), 230.

138. Marisa Linton, *Choosing Terror: Virtue, Friendship, and Authenticity in the French Revolution* (New York: Oxford University Press, 2013), 189.

139. Howard, *War in European History*, 80.

140. Linton, *Choosing Terror,* 185–186.

141. Owen Connelly, *The Wars of the French Revolution and Napoleon, 1792–1815*. New York: Routledge, 2006), 42.

142. Georges Lefebvre, *The French Revolution, Volume II: From 1793 to 1799* (New York: Columbia University Press, 1964), 68.

143. Schama, *Citizens*, 786.

144. Alan Forrest, *Conscripts and Deserters: The Army and French Society During the Revolution* (New York: Oxford University Press, 1989), 33.

145. Gunther E. Rothenberg, *The Art of Warfare in the Age of Napoleon* (Bloomington: Indiana University Press, 1978), 106.

146. Theda Skocpol and Meyer Kestnbaum, "Mars Unshackled: The French Revolution in World Historical Perspective," in *The French Revolution and the Birth of Modernity*, ed. Ferenc Fehér (Berkeley: University of California Press, 1990), 24.

147. Quoted in Karen Hagermann, *Revisiting Prussia's Wars Against Napoleon: History, Culture, and Memory* (New York: Cambridge University Press, 2015), 132.

148. Maximilien Robespierre, "On the Principles of Revolutionary Government," in *Virtue and Terror*, ed. Zizek, 100–105.

149. Quoted in Sagan, *Citizens & Cannibals*, 357.

150. Walt, *Revolution and War*, 97–98.

151. Peter McPhee, *Robespierre: A Revolutionary Life* (New Haven: Yale University Press, 2012), 212–213.

152. Florin Aftalion, *The French Revolution: An Economic Interpretation* (New York: Cambridge University Press, 1990), 156.

153. François Furet, *Interpreting the French Revolution* (New York: Cambridge University Press, 1981), 74.

154. Schroeder, *The Transformation of European Politics*, 138.

155. Forrest, "La Patrie en Danger," 13.

156. Martyn Lyons, *France Under the Directory* (New York: Cambridge University Press, 1975), 233.

157. Mlada Bukovansky, *Legitimacy and Power Politics: The American and French Revolutions in International Political Culture* (Princeton: Princeton University Press, 2002), 208–209.

Chapter Three

The Strategy of
State-Directed Terrorism

The term "state terror" typically refers to a regime's systematic use of violence to strike fear into a segment of the population under its control. Such measures include, but are not limited to, the use of a secret police or semi-private militias to suppress dissidents, the ethnic cleansing of a minority group, or indiscriminate violence against an occupied civilian population in wartime.[1] Scholars of state terror are careful to distinguish it from the "political terrorism" of the non-state variety, given that the state has far greater resources at its disposal and is thus able to inflict a far more severe condition of terror on its victims.[2] Despite these obvious differences, the semantic distinction has had the unfortunate consequence of isolating the phenomenon of terrorism from the workings of the state. Even if one state lambasts another's repressive measures or sponsorship of non-state militants, they are careful not to ascribe the label of terrorism onto the behavior of the state itself, in part for fear that similar accusations will then be hurled at themselves or their allies. This in turn promotes the assumption that the statesman and the terrorist, aside from both being political actors, operate from entirely different frameworks of decision-making, and thus can learn nothing from one another than how best to defeat them.

State terror is fully explicable within a Machiavellian understanding of international politics as a perpetual struggle among states for relative power. Regardless of the morality or wisdom of such actions, they follow the standard logic of war by which one side imposes its will over an enemy with presumptively identical motives. Yet as with any other warlike measures, the effects of state terror are necessarily incomplete, as it no less difficult to physically annihilate one's foes through repression than to obliterate another state in wartime. The state that seeks a truly decisive outcome must go

61

beyond the limits of Machiavellian competition and restore warfare to its original state of logical perfection. Since this is not possible within the bounds of interstate or even intrastate warfare, the state can only approximate a condition of absolute war against itself, with the result of a fully mobilized and unquestionably obedient citizenry. The achievement of this ideal, or at least the appearance thereof, can then return to the conventional battlefield free from the bounds of friction and reciprocity.

The state that undertakes such a campaign is likely to merit the description of a "rogue state" acting entirely outside the bounds of international society.[3] This description not only tends to reduce the causes of political violence to the quirks of leadership personality, regime type, or culture,[4] it also ignores the extent to which terrorism attempts to restore the original truth of warfare prior to the corrosive influence of politics. A state-directed terrorist campaign reveals the full extent of the tension between the desire to overcome the limits of the state system while still attending to the realities of interstate competition prior to the moment of triumph. The Soviet Union under the rule of Josef Stalin provides the archetypical example of this paradox.

The Soviet Union set the paradigm for state terror much as Napoleon did for modern war, similarly refining its methods to their apex and spawning a host of imitators around the world. The geopolitical significance of the Soviet Union subjected the regime to constant international pressure, including a war for national survival with Nazi Germany and prolonged security competition with the United States. The U.S.S.R. also demonstrates the possibilities and limits of transitioning from terror to a comparatively normal form of politics and diplomacy. The duration of the Soviet experiment, its unparalleled successes, and ultimate collapse each provide the standout example for subsequent practitioners of state-directed terrorism, thus making it a fitting template by which to compare contemporary cases.

CLAUSEWITZIAN STRATEGY AND REAL WAR

"The Principal Moral Elements"

In order for war to be a continuation of policy by other means, there must be relative certainty that the formulation of policy will in fact continue after the war concludes. A state may face severe threats to its interests or sovereignty, but if it reaches the point whereupon its actual existence hangs in the balance, it has left the boundaries of war and can either fight to the death or submit to its fate. Strategy takes shape within these extremes, where there is both the active use of military power and a political purpose regulating its exercise. The strategist directs the conduct of a war or makes plans in peacetime that advance or defend a flexible set of interests, which in turn requires that the leadership retain the capacity to redefine the objective in accordance with changes in the tactical, strategic, or political environment. Clausewitz defines strategy as the use of "the engagement in terms of its possible results and of the moral and psychological forces that largely determine its course."[5] The strategist upholds the principles and standard operating procedures that coordinate the campaign, assesses the salient facts of experience, and realigns tactical assets to fit new realities.

The nature of strategy derives from the elements of military and political decision-making that compose the environment of real war. Clausewitz assumes a fully realized system of political entities who are all familiar with one another, capable of drawing on a quantifiable pool of material and human resources, and possessed of physical space in which to deploy them. The statesman articulates the political motivation for the war, the tactician brings forces directly to bear against enemy resistance, and the strategist governs the undefinable space between the capital and the battlefield. This space exists because a single engagement is not sufficient to accomplish the political objective, turning the chain of command into a feedback loop between the source of intellectual guidance and the instrument of its practical application.[6] Strategy abstracts from the tangible purpose of the individual engagement, such as the "capture of certain geographical points or the seizure of undefended provinces," and evaluates this "isolated advantage" in terms of the "overall result"[7] of the campaign. No less importantly, it links the political objective to the "sum total of the phenomena of war"[8] as they unfold and interact in reality. As Colin Gray describes it, strategy "is neither military power *per se* nor political purpose," but rather "the use that is made of force and the threat of force for the ends of policy."[9] Although the instruments of strategy are military in nature, their effectiveness can only be judged on political grounds.

Clausewitz famously comments that "in strategy everything is very simple," since it requires neither the political wisdom of statesmanship nor the detailed, technical knowledge of tactics, only that there be a reasonable connection between them. The difficulty behind this theoretically simple proposition arises from the multitude and mutability of variables that result from the convergence of politics and tactics, the absence of a clear standard of right and wrong action, and the severe consequences of either acting or failing to act.[10] Clausewitz's understanding of strategy gives preeminence to the moral factors that are necessary for clear thinking and resolute decision-making under conditions that compel a "rapid, only partly conscious weighing of the possibilities."[11] At every level of command, the virtues of soldiery amount to the "courage to accept responsibility, courage in the face of a moral danger,"[12] ranging from the general who orders an assault against a fortified position down to the private who charges into enemy fire. The main difference is that as the burdens of responsibility increase, virtue becomes "less a matter of personal sacrifice and increasingly [a matter of concern] for the safety of others and for the common purpose."[13] Whereas the private learns to be bold through a habituated response to immediate physical danger, the general must possess the boldness born of deliberate choice and pursuit of a rationally defined objective in the face of unpredictable and ever-changing circumstances.

For any strategist, the criterion of "genius" is the extent to which their own qualities of boldness and intellect translate to the architectonic management of those same qualities over the army as a whole. Much of Clausewitz's description of genius suggests an innate tendency that "will not yield to academic wisdom" and "is above all rules,"[14] since its qualities are difficult to detect in advance and impossible to pass on through instruction. Although genius ultimately manifests itself through a unique combination of talent and circumstance, Clausewitz insists that states and armed forces can institutionalize the habits of genius through regularized instruction and experience, thereby reducing the dependence of virtue on the whims of fortune within the armed forces and society as a whole.

Developing an organizational culture of genius centers on the paradoxical task of habituating them to think creatively and act spontaneously. The only "lubricant that will reduce [the] abrasion"[15] of friction is combat experience, but no amount of experience in the junior ranks can provide an adequate foundation for the unique burdens of supreme command. To redress this deficiency, theory first establishes that "every level of command has its own intellectual standards, its own prerequisites for fame and honor." These range from the "outstanding intellect" of the commander to the practical wisdom of the staff officer to the exemplary courage of the platoon sergeant.[16] Having identified the most desirable qualities for each primary role within the campaign, the next step is to screen candidates for advancement by routinely cycling them through the parade ground, war colleges, and the front. Fittingly, a model of this system first appeared in Clausewitz's native Prussia. With a patriotic citizenry primed for mass mobilization, a general staff rigorously trained in the operational sciences, and a high command that honed the ideal of the "creative battle,"[17] the trinity took a distinct shape. Cultivating successive generations of strategists requires a pedagogy attuned to both the evolving character of the task and the fixed moral disposition required for adapting to those changes with the proper mixture of equanimity and creativity.

Clausewitz's program of strategic education appears to favor a clear distinction of people, army, and state, which he emphasized precisely because he recognized the weakening of the traditional barriers between these three agencies. The popularization of war demands that the strategist achieve a more ambitious integration of "the skill of the commander," the "experience and courage of the troops, and their patriotic spirit."[18] Armies of the past often took on the singular genius of a great leader such as Alexander or

Gustavus Adolphus, but in post-Napoleonic warfare, it is equally important that the leaders themselves personify the national struggle. The modern state can only "hope for a strong position in the world" by educating its people "in the spirit of boldness,"[19] but in doing so it becomes increasingly difficult to insulate political calculation and military professionalism from the elemental force of popular will.

Once a government shares with its people the moral authority to wage war, it has irrevocably lost its monopoly on the power to define the national interest or conduct warfare exclusively in accordance with the preferences and expectations of statesmen and commanders. The logistical difficulties of managing a mass army across an extended battlefield shifted emphasis from rigid discipline to the raw emotional forces that keep, in the words of Barry Posen, "these dispersed, scared, lonely individuals risking their own lives, and cooperating to take the lives of others."[20] In a system of nation-states, strategy becomes fully three-dimensional, since popular energy is no longer a passive instrument of political and military calculation, and is in fact the only leg of the trinity with the capacity to impose its will unilaterally on the other two. As the domestic politics of states become more fully trinitarian, they are likely to disrupt the system-wide symmetry of means and ends that had characterized "wars in which policy was based on the comparative size of regular armies." Clausewitz warned that as soon as governments become "conscious of these resources, we cannot expect them to remain unused in the future."[21] This new reality compounds the initial problem of strategic formulation. In addition to reconciling the state's political and tactical objectives, the strategist must also weigh the conduct of the war against its likely effect on public opinion, and find a way to harness popular energy to political direction while reserving the capacity to unleash the fury of the masses.

Terrorism attempts to capture the advantages of modern, popular warfare and isolate them from the shackles of traditional political calculation. Modern communication techniques opened up avenues for direct competition over the loyalty of a public audience, who with sufficient motivation and access to weaponry could mount a direct military challenge against political and military elites. The idealized community of terrorist propaganda stands in stark contrast with conventional states whose arbitrary borders, diverse populations, and byzantine political structures reflect the accumulated baggage of past wars and diplomatic compromises. The campaign itself serves as the incubator of a fighting force which is both a product of rational design and fully in line with the passions of its prospective members, rendering it morally preferable to the petty squabbles of dynastic princelings and elected demagogues. Consequently, there is no need to accept the normative limits of warfare that have moral standing only because they advance the interests of the status quo powers. The inherent rightness of the objective justifies any escalation that advances its interests, since escalation is tantamount to the cultivation of perfect military virtue.

Strategy in a terrorist campaign uses violence and propaganda to align the ideal of the synthesized trinity with its prospective members between the ideal of the community and its prospective members. The gap closes to the extent that a target audience adopts the model of relentless escalation that the architects of the campaign put forth. Whereas the conventional strategist must refine and even dilute qualities of courage and boldness in line with logistical and political limits, the terrorist has no concern outside the campaign itself. Escalation is the automatic answer to every form of friction, whether it be stiff enemy resistance, operational inefficacy, or popular apathy. The closer that the campaign approximates the ideal of absolute war, it renders itself increasingly immune to reciprocity from a conventionally trinitarian opponent, in which each component has a character apart from the others and interests beyond a single campaign. Sooner or later, the terrorist campaign will expose fissures among a conventional arrangement political leadership, armed force, and public, each of whom will weigh their interests in the present conflict with broader political considerations and place limits on their willingness to escalate. The primary task of the terrorist is to break down the psychological and practical resistance to escalation and guide that process past the point beyond which the enemy cannot travel, rendering all subsequent resistance ineffective or counterproductive.

The Concentration of Forces

On War differs from countless other military treatises in that it gives far greater attention to streamlining the process of strategic formulation than enumerating the facets of an effective strategy. As Lawrence Freedman states, "[Clausewitz's] stress was on the limits of strategy, the constraints that make it unwise to try to be too clever,"[22] not principles of tactical success that commanders should seek to apply to the battlefield. Book Three, called *On Strategy in General*, devotes its first seven chapters to the moral and organizational facets of an army. He then turns his attention to critiquing widely accepted principles of battlefield success, including numerical superiority and the achievement of surprise. Clausewitz regards it as "seriously misunderstanding our argument, to consider numerical superiority as indispensable to victory,"[23] and dismisses the element of surprise or the use of deception as a "tactical device" that "can rarely be outstandingly successful."[24] Each of these dismissals are riddled with qualifications and exceptions, but they reflect Clausewitz's overall conception of strategy as the art of distinguishing the essential from the nonessential and keeping sight of the former under enormous physical, intellectual, and moral stress.

The outcome of a battle may end up hinging on objective factors of space, time, resources, and numerical mass, and from time to time a surprise maneuver or clever stratagem may exploit a critical weakness at exactly the right moment. In general, however, the capable strategist enjoys neither the luxury to devise grand plans nor the reasonable expectation that such plans will succeed simply on account of their superior design. Amid the relentless push and pull of competing forces, "stern necessity usually permeates direct action to such an extent that no room is left for such a game."[25] The "energy, forcefulness, and resolution of the commander" means nothing if the costs of achieving surprise on the battlefield diminishes the strength of the army, distracts from more pressing strategic assets, or if the enemy refuses to play along with their assigned role. The utility of surprise depends on the "relationship established between the two sides,"[26] and so an army capable of indulging in stratagems likely does so from a position of considerable superiority.

All other things being equal, the effectiveness of a strategy derives from its attending to the mundane skills of implementation more thoroughly and more consistently than the enemy. There is no need for creativity because any strategic option is simple in and of itself: to attack, hold firm, or withdraw, to commit or hold back reserves, to reinforce or abandon a critical point, to suspend or resume a campaign. The choice between these options is never unequivocally right or wrong, and the merits or drawbacks of each only become fully evident in the wake of the enemy's reaction, of which preliminary assessments are at best probabilistic. Whatever the ultimate decision, the skillful strategist must "ensure that no part of the whole force is idle,"[27] and keep the far-flung components of an armed force operating as a harmonious whole. Strategic wisdom is no less evident in conducting maneuvers and preserving morale than it is at the moment of victory.

The one exception to Clausewitz's habit of dismissing strategic principles is the concentration of forces at a decisive moment of the campaign. As Michael Handel notes, the principle of concentration is "so central to the intricate relationships of his concepts and insights that Clausewitz uses uncharacteristically emphatic language to ensure that its role is properly understood."[28] In general, Clausewitz argues that "the best strategy is always to be very strong; first in general, and then at the decisive point . . . there is no higher and simpler law of strategy than that of keeping one's forces concentrated."[29] Achieving "relative superiority" in the engagement "is much more frequently based on the correct appraisal of [the] decisive point . . . which leads to appropriate disposition of the forces . . . and the courage to retain the major part of one's forces united."[30] The decisive point may reveal itself through the interaction of physical forces with the laws of time and space. The fighting strength of an army, the quality of its weapons and the morale of its soldiers will achieve an optimum point of effectiveness, or vulnerability, based on the duration of the engagement, its ability to adapt to the terrain, and the proximate availability of reserves.[31] Pinpointing and exploiting the enemy's vulnerabilities "gains in absolute significance with the importance of the defeated force, and consequently the possibility of recouping such losses at a later encounter also becomes less likely."[32] Since war unfolds as a chain of linked engagements, a single encounter is decisive to the extent that it shapes the subsequent engagement in one's favor and threatens the adversary with the prospect of a climactic engagement that they have little hope of winning.

While the decisive engagement consists of "the lengthy interaction of mutually destructive forces,"[33] its importance stems chiefly from its psychological effects. An army is defeated only when "the feeling of having been defeated . . . runs through the ranks down to the very privates," a self-fulfilling prophecy "leav[ing] a vacuum which is filled by a corrosively expanding fear which completes the paralysis." Accordingly, a major aspect of achieving victory is targeting and disrupting the enemy's primary sources of confidence, exposing their hidden weaknesses, turning courage into despair and demonstrating the "palpable fact that the enemy is stronger."[34] Yet even this seemingly ironclad rule is contingent upon a host of other factors. The decisive point does not come into being unless the enemy concentrates its own forces to the extent that their defeat would entail a major setback. The "fear and indecision native to the human mind" and "imperfections of human perception and judgment"[35] may cause combatants to shrink away from the climactic battle or fail to discern it coming into being. Other aspects of the nature of war, such as the general superiority of the defensive, may in some circumstances outweigh the principle of concentration, and "where the impetus of interest is slight . . . governments will not want to risk much." For any of these reasons, one or both sides may settle into "a state of rest and equilibrium"[36] in which both sides renounce positive objectives and instead probe for momentary advantages while waiting for more favorable conditions.

Despite the various conditions that affect its real-life value, the concentration of forces at a decisive point is the guiding principle of strategy because it supplies the only outcome that represents a permanent ideal for all combatants. The prospect of the decisive engagement is the common thread running through the infinite variabilities that result from two sides each using force to impose their will. Combatants must hope to have at least the potential to strike a decisive blow and must regard the enemy's ability to do the same as a worst-case outcome. Although war does not trend inexorably toward the decisive point, the prospect of the decision fixes the character of war in terms of its relative immediacy or absence.

It is certainly possible for war to settle into "nothing more than armed neutrality, a threatening attitude meant to support negotiations" provided that both sides conventionalize their mutual reluctance to face the test of battle.

From that point forward, reciprocity will hold to the extent that each side remains willing to confine its objectives within conventional parameters and perceives its adversary as willing to do the same. There are ample political and humanitarian reasons to "turn war into something half-hearted," but the strategist must not regard them as anything other than a reprieve from "the real, authentic art of war."[37] Even if a state has no reason for risking a decisive engagement, it cannot limit itself to "half-hearted policies and shackled military policy," if only to guard against the sudden emergence of an enemy "who, like the untamed elements, knows no law other than his own power."[38]

The emergence of popular warfare, with its permanent risk of escalation, increases both the costs of the decisive engagement and the likelihood that one state can force others to share in the risk. The frightful prospect of a campaign that risks the fortunes of the state on the battlefield exposes the "vagaries" of reducing strategy to scientific principles that "expressed the higher functions of the intellect"[39] and equated military skill with the avoidance of bloodshed. Strategy faces its ultimate test against an enemy who is capable of maximizing the resources of a nation and is unwilling to accept voluntary restraints upon their full expression. This does not mean that popular warfare culminates in a single, winner-take-all trial of strength, although the destructive capabilities and rapid mobilization of modern armaments have beguiled countless leaders with the prospect of a quick and decisive victory.

With rare exceptions, two comparably armed and motivated combatants require several engagements for the superiority of one or the other to become evident.[40] Modern armies can endure so long as there is physical space in which to operate, a material base from which to keep them in the field, and the support of politicians and the public. Across a long series of battles, the strategic advantage ultimately goes to whichever side is better able to reassemble "the fragmented results" of each engagement back into "a single, independent whole"[41] before the enemy can do the same. Several moments of decision take place on the tactical level, but the cumulative effects of successive decisions will eventually determine whether one side is either in a position to deliver a paralyzing blow or at least able to avoid such a blow indefinitely.

Under the conditions of modern, popular warfare, strategy extends the principle of concentration beyond the physical cohesion of armies to include the full range of assets that make up a nation's fighting strength. Maintaining an effective connection between policy, public opinion, and military capabilities amid a relentless cycle of accumulated tension and spasmodic violence elevates the principle of concentration to a prerequisite of national survival. The strategist endlessly reassembles order from chaos, counteracting the rapidly unfolding and disruptive effects of the modern campaign on emotional resolve, organizational efficiency, and political willpower. The destruction of enemy forces and occupation of territory gives way to repairing the dispersion and demoralization suffered in the course of the engagement. Just as a wrestler may apply too much pressure against their opponent and thereby throw themselves off balance, tactical victories that ignore the cumulative effects of battle on the fighting spirit of soldiers and sentiments of civilians on both sides are laying the groundwork for strategic defeat.

Terrorism at first glance seems an ill-suited to adopt Clausewitz's principle of concentration. The adoption of terrorism generally presupposes the inability to inflict or even credibly threaten a decisive defeat through conventional means. A terrorist campaign almost never culminates with direct contests of strength, and is extremely unlikely to result in complete dominance over the enemy, as it is far more likely to suffer the decisive blow than to administer it. Deprived of the means that Clausewitz regards as necessary for victory, terrorism rearranges the basic dynamics of warfare in order to achieve a more perfect form of military virtue and decisiveness than would be possible for any conventional force. A terrorist campaign does not even attempt to achieve a decision over the military forces of an external enemy. Rather, the decisive moment occurs within its own target audience, as its prospective members make an irrevocable break with their existing trinitarian arrangement and pursue a condition of absolute war until they have perfected the logic of war or suffer complete collapse in the attempt. With no fixed battlefield or objective means of identifying enemies, every individual is thrust into an absolute condition wherein they must redouble their efforts to survive or will surely perish at the hands of those with greater skills and fewer scruples.

A conventional army emphasizes concentration at the point of decision, because the solitary soldier is plainly insufficient to the task. A terrorist campaign breeds combatants who shed every other aspect of themselves, especially fear and empathy, and seek a complete overlap of martial and individual virtue. As a result, it can achieve a distinct military advantage over any external opponent through dispersion rather than concentration. Increasing public participation in the process of communal formation entails not one climactic moment of decision, but a decision for each individual, which then have to be preserved against the risk of backsliding or penetration. vast and fluid social network that can recruit followers, ensure compliance, and mitigate the effect of setbacks.

Once that network is in place, it is ideally suited to negate the risk of absorbing a decisive blow from the external enemy. The persistent and limitless disruption of enemy concentration is only possible when enough agents have enough motivation and wherewithal to identify and target potential points of concentration before they coalesce. As the campaign drives the enemy to intensify their efforts, the community must approach the ideal of universal and permanent mobilization to keep the enemy off balance and demonstrate the impossibility of bringing their forces to bear in a climactic engagement. The indefinite postponement of the decisive battle is itself decisive insofar as the community transforms itself into an absolute combatant and nullifies not merely the prospect of an enemy victory, but their very opportunity of bringing it about through battle.

THE THEORY OF STATE-DIRECTED TERROR

Real War Within States

The moment of a decision is a necessarily relative concept. A battle, operation, or war may leave one side completely incapacitated, but this condition endures only so long as the balance of resolve and capability remains squarely on the side of the victor. Once a defeated state recovers or a victorious one enters into a relative decline, the mere potential of renewed hostilities is sufficient to invalidate the result of the original decision. The conclusion of a campaign may give way to a more comprehensive program of political and cultural assimilation, like a migratory Gallic tribe that accedes to Romanization following a disastrous battle with Caesar's legions. But while much of history has featured higher forms of civilization absorbing less advanced societies, the conditions of modern politics have rendered this wholesale transferral of popular loyalty considerably more difficult. National communities rooted in territoriality, a collective desire for self-determination and a system of education and cultural dissemination can regularly reproduce loyal members, even without the structural advantages of a state. [42]

When the national principle sparks conflicts within states, the results tend to replicate the same fundamental dynamics as interstate warfare. Dominant social groups routinely utilize "compulsory state-controlled primary education, state-organized propaganda, official rewriting of history, [and] militarism" [43] to marginalize politically undesirable peoples, or employ ethnic cleansing to expel or exterminate them. Such efforts often succeed in thwarting the political ambitions of a separatist movement, but in doing so they "tend to increase the quest of oppressed ethnic groups to have their own independent states." [44] Repression that begins with a unilateral application of state power against a victim utterly incapable of reciprocity can often have the unintended consequence of strengthening a group's collective self-consciousness and eagerness for combat. Indiscriminate brutality tends to empower the most radical elements within the movement and encourage foreign sponsors who are either sympathetic to the cause or eager for an opportunity to embarrass a rival. Like interstate war, the outcome will depend on the relative capabilities of the combatants and the "balance of interests and forces that extend beyond the state," [45] such as regional powers and global public opinion. And as is also the case with conventional wars, these internal conflicts end with results that are both relative and reversible.

Intrastate conflict is firmly within the domain of real war, albeit in a potentially severe form, so long as the contest is over relative advantages in wealth, territory, and support of key social actors. The relative fortunes of competing factions will reflect their relative political coherence, military skill, and willingness to continue the fight. Each successive engagement with domestic and foreign enemies brings forth a new strategic environment and with it a moment of decision for each combatant to disarm, negotiate a settlement, pursue a decisive victory, or dig in and hope to stave off further losses. The contest must draw to a close eventually, whether one faction successfully imposes a monopoly of legitimate violence, a stalemate codifies the inconclusive results of the battlefield, or prolonged struggle leads to a total collapse of social order. No matter how conclusive the outcome, the potential conflict will reemerge as soon as more than one entity is capable of operating on a trinitarian basis.

State-directed terrorism is the attempt to impose a unilateral and permanent settlement to the struggle for power within a state by orchestrating the wholesale destruction of civil society and generation of a new one entirely and unerringly subject to a single authority. The initial imperative for such a campaign derives from a radical incompatibility between a regime's legitimizing principles and its security requirements. State-directed terrorism is most likely when a regime seizes power on the basis of an ideological claim that belies its actual levels of public support. Ideology is a uniquely valuable supplement for traditional props of authoritarian rule such as the army, tribal consanguinity, or public acceptance of emergency rule in a crisis. A monistic ideology positing a "universally true and exhaustive system of ideas"[46] serves as an infallible standard of action that regulates every single aspect of political life. Its highly specified political terminology and strict moral categories break down a complex amalgamation of social groups into a single mass and erode the social barriers separating the state from the atomized individual.[47]

A regime's ability to enjoy the benefits of its ideological claim depends upon the degree to which the public accepts it as an authoritative guideline for political life, whether they do so out of sincere conviction, fear, or as a convenient guise for furthering other interests. Maintaining a plausible connection between formal orthodoxy and political reality requires an ongoing process of doctrinal revision and public reeducation, setting off an internal debate that poses the scientific reasoning of the doctrine against the conflicting exegesis of its interpreters.[48] Advancing an ideological claim in the public imagination will trigger disagreement among the leadership over strategy and, even more importantly, the authority to interpret the political ramifications of the guiding doctrine. For example, one faction may recommend a "scholastic reinterpretation of the texts" to meet the needs of "pragmatic policy formulation" instead of relying on a "fixed ideology [that] limits its choices too much." Another will point to "the fact that a simplified and vulgarized version of the ideologies has been central to the indoctrination" of the masses, which "makes it difficult to abandon certain policies"[49] without compromising the foundation of regime legitimacy. The scope of debate within the regime must accommodate the inevitable competition among its members for office and honors without dividing the ranks so thoroughly as to compromise group solidarity.

In an atmosphere of contested ideological authority and intra-regime competition, a sudden outbreak of domestic insurrection or foreign invasion exposes the leadership to perceptions of weakness among dissidents and charges of treason from within the ranks. A crisis threatens to deprive the regime of its singular ability to define events in accordance with its overarching narrative. Even in the most totalitarian dictatorship, a crisis necessitates power-sharing among institutions in order to optimize the exploitation of resources and sharing of information. The urgency of immediate action forces the regime to accept the risk that subordinates will later use their newfound privileges to "credibly threaten a rebellion,"[50] to protect themselves against the retraction of those privileges or to secure additional ones. A regime facing a genuine challenge to its rule no longer enjoys that exclusive "access to power positions, spoils, and privileges"[51] necessary for maintaining loyalty among subordinates. This leaves the regime with the painful choice between addressing the crisis by delegating authority it may be unable to recover or preserving its own power monopoly at the cost of undermining its ability to resolve the crisis at hand.

An atmosphere of crisis deprives the ideologically motivated and internally divided regime of a stable trinity. Faced with the paramount necessity of using violence to ensure its survival, the regime cannot guarantee the support of the people, the loyalty of the armed forces, or the unanimity of the political leadership. A state in this position is too weak to brutalize its people into submission, too unpopular to rally public support for a crusade against a foreign enemy, and too riddled with factional rivalries to secure a uniform baseline of action. The more that the crisis escalates, the more likely it is to expose the limits of its ideological pretensions and reveal the true scope of its power as a function of the resources under its control, the discipline of its forces, and the genius of its commanders, any or all of which may be severely compromised.

The regime may choose to engage its enemies in a kind of conventional war with the hope of eventually seizing and holding onto a sufficient degree of power for as long as possible. In the vast majority of cases, the best that it can hope for is to achieve "tinpot" status, forced to allocate its resources toward the satisfaction of fickle friends and suppression of determined rivals with no hope for claiming the loyalty of the public at large.[52] If the regime is unable or unwilling to accept this partial and uncertain outcome, then its only alternative is to turn war from a symmetrical contest of strength and will into a consummate act of political theater, complete with a stirring climax and definitive resolution. The regime must subject its own society to the appearance of absolute war, crafting a narrative of open-ended escalation to clear away every vestige of resistance and then refashion an entirely new trinity in its own image.

Absolute War Within States

State-directed terror is a *coup d'etat* in reverse, with the state overthrowing its own citizenry and replacing it with one more amenable to its preferences. The Jacobins commenced their version of absolute war in their moment of supreme emergency, with enemy armies marching on Paris and insurrectionists in the countryside ready to link arms with them. The severity of the crisis lent plausibility to the rampant paranoia of *La Terreur*, at the cost of circumscribing the leadership's freedom of action within strict bounds of objective political and military necessity. The Committee could not fight an external war and remake society at the same time, as the requirements of one called for modifications to the other. The lesson for subsequent examples of state terrorism was to maximize the moral atmosphere of crisis while keeping its political ramifications under the regime's exclusive direction. Rather than let the crisis reach full maturity and then rally the citizenry to meet it, the regime (or an ambitious faction within it) can deliberately incite or exacerbate a crisis to which it can then present itself as an agent of deliverance. It is then free to wage war on its own citizenry at a time and in a manner of its choosing, against an enemy utterly incapable of offering effect resistance. This enables the regime to wage, or at least appear to be waging, a theoretically perfect war linking a utopian objective with an increasingly militarized citizenry toward a complete and irreversible victory over its former self.

An approximation of absolute war first requires a political objective that gives lifts all normative restrictions on hostile intentions. The regime accomplishes this by positing an existential clash between the loyal followers of an emerging community and an external enemy bent on snuffing it out and reducing its people to servitude. This narrative maximizes its political impact when it is in fact a vastly exaggerated account of political reality, and may even be a complete fiction. If there actually was a vast and monolithic enemy implacably bent on some combination of invasion, subversion, and conquest, this would place the state in a condition of real war with partisans of each faction scrambling for relative advantage. The actual enemy is the lone individual, against whom the regime seeks the decisive victory of breaking their will to resist. When there is in actuality a scattered plethora of competing domestic and foreign interests with uncertain dimensions and ambitions, wrapping them all in a mantle of a Manichaean struggle gives the regime a qualitative advantage in forming points of concentration while keeping enemies isolated from one another. The regime may not have the power to compel obedience, but it can use the inherent advantages of sovereign power to subject all of society to a common condition of insecurity from which only the regime and its loyal fighters will be able to recover.

Carl Schmitt, who would later lend his philosophic and legal expertise to the exercise of state terrorism in Nazi Germany, famously defined the sovereign as the one "who decides on the exception."[53] Under normal circumstances, including conventional warfare, the sovereign performs what appears to be the opposite role of upholding the rules and punishing violations. Schmitt's definition finds the other limits (and thus the most authentic form) of sovereignty in conditions under which the rules have broken down, which clarify who is capable of deciding "whether there is an extreme emergency as well as what must be done to eliminate it."[54] By declaring a condition of all-out ideological warfare, the regime willfully abandons any pretense of ruling in accordance with the law, or any other objective standard, and will henceforth base its exercise of power entirely on the political criterion of friendship and hostility. While formally remaining within the framework of legal statutes and judicial pronouncements, there is no logical correlation between crime and punishment, nor is there intended to be one. The laws serve only to give full scope to the exception, so that guilt and innocence, and by extension life and death, is nothing other than an expression of raw power. Incapable of coercing everyone, the regime must nonetheless prove itself to be capable of targeting anyone.

There is of course nothing new about governments abusing the laws for their private advantage. What distinguishes state-directed terrorism from other forms of corruption and tyranny is that it shares this theoretically pure form of sovereign power with its people. Clausewitz's depiction of absolute war begins with the presumption of a community united only in its hostile intent against its enemy. State-directed terrorism approximates this condition in reality by equating civic identity with relentless hostility against anything that would compromise the process of communal formation. It necessarily falls short of the ideal insofar as the regime cannot expect every citizen to increase their personal commitment and improve their combat skills until the achievement of total victory. Such an outcome is not even desirable, as it would eventually direct the regime onto a course of aggression abroad, which would replace the theatrics of absolute war with the vicissitudes of real war. Instead of building a singular and perfectly harmonious trinity, the regime grants each citizen a fraction of the sovereign power, who then wield it with the primary aim of preventing the rest of that power from turning on them. As official propaganda proclaims an epic clash of forces approaching a fiery climax, this merely provides a blanket of legitimacy to innumerable wars among individuals for whom the stakes are absolute.

Bringing the pressures of war down to the level of the individual restricts the whole of strategic calculation into a stark choice of maximum effort or certain death, which gradually phases out every social fact inconsistent with the ubiquitous reality of war. Society itself becomes a providing ground for citizens to demonstrate their willingness to abandon all other loyalties and scruples beyond their own survival. But before this condition degenerates into a war of all against all, the regime steps in and introduces structures which compel participation as a means of maximizing one's own share of the sovereign power. Building an apparatus of repression first makes citizens fearful of succumbing to the hostile intentions of others, and then encourages them to take hold of the apparatus of repression and redirect it in a more favorable direction, especially when they can expect to earn plaudits for doing so. These structures arrange the community into a kind of trinity, but in a strictly hierarchical form, with each level based on distinct methods of linking personal security to the interests of the regime.

At the bottom of this hierarchy are those equipped only with primordial violence, a basic will to survive and desire to harm enemies but with no direct access to the instruments of repression or corridors of political influence. This mass of isolated citizenry has two non-exclusive avenues for satisfying the survival impulse which animates every facet of their social life. The first is participation in mass political activity such as political parties, demonstrations, and other vehicles of indoctrination, if only to take shelter within the crowd and thereby minimize the risk of direct engagement. The second is various forms of low-level collaboration, such as monitoring and reporting of suspicious activity or issuing denunciations. Such methods may avert suspicion or negate potential threats, but they also have uncertain consequences based on how the information is received and evaluated in comparison with similar reports from others. Such discretion falls to the security services, who represent a middle tier of the regime which preserves itself through its direct control over the instruments of political violence. Whether this power is principally lodged within the army, the secret police, radical student organizations, or a haphazard amalgamation among various agencies, their mission is to instigate and then direct war against the enemy of the moment. These organizations are distinct from conventional militaries in that they are not simply responsive to their political masters.[55] Whatever the individual motives of their agents, their existence and continued activity become ends unto themselves, making them the regime's last line of defense and the most likely instrument of its demise should political directives impinge too closely upon their privileges.

The regime is eminently Clausewitzian in its insistence on strict political control over the use of deadly force and the passion of the masses, although the leadership follows a much more literal version of politics than the typical trustees of the national interest. Control over the levers of state does nothing to reduce their fundamental vulnerability with respect to the bureaucracy and the masses, either or both of whom may decide to turn on them at any moment. Regime elite operate within a permanent security dilemma vis-à-vis one another, in which the ideological mandate for ruling belongs to all of them as a collective and thus to none of them in particular. This leaves open the permanent possibility of one faction seizing on the governing doctrine to advance its own power, the threat of which causes a "giant struggle under the carpet" in which "domestic groups with varying preferences compete for influence over policy."[56] Depending upon the shape and the severity of this threat, elements of the regime may elect to wage war against itself, taking the risk of drastic short-term instability in order to reshuffle the deck and secure their long-term position relative to their rivals. Alternately, a charismatic leader may look to bypass factional rivalry with direct appeals to popular support, building a cult of personality that elevates them above the fray of intra-regime competition.[57]

A strategy of dividing society along a trinitarian hierarchy and turning each against the other can succeed in practical terms of keeping the regime in power. The regime may never actually produce a fanatically loyal citizenry with no trace of dissent or incompetence, but it may elevate a cadre of loyalists who are sufficiently well-armed and motivated to keep the rest of the population in check or even mobilize their active compliance when necessary. This type of victory, however stands in tension with the formal premises of the war, which promises a smashing victory against a vast international conspiracy. A regime that features a balance of power among its governing factions and settles into an essentially conventional position on the international chessboard is nonetheless composed of distinct and essentially hostile factions which each retain the potential to escalate against their most pressing threats. All states have to reserve the capacity for vicious internal struggle, but the state that has secured power through terrorism compounds this tension by reserving the capacity to escalate against itself. The ultimate test of the regime's viability is its ability to tailor its dual penchant for escalation to the objective needs of internal and external security.

Ideally, the regime would reconcile its security needs through perpetual mobilization at home and subversion abroad, thereby concentrating its own forces while disrupting the enemy's likely points of concentration. Provoking instability abroad helps to channel popular outrage against a convenient enemy, which in turn limits the scope of factional rivalry, while cultivating a fully mobilized and fanatically loyal citizenry capable of deterring retaliation. The difficulty with achieving this strategy in practice is that a disruption in the balance of power abroad is likely to intensify competition within the state. The threat of war or security competition raises the value of subordinates with diplomatic and military expertise, which may not be readily available if those agencies are staffed with loyalists due to bureaucratic rent-seeking or a dictator's fear of capable subordinates.[58] A favorable military position depends in one way or another on effective diplomacy, if only to disrupt the formation of a hostile coalition, which places the regime in the undesirable position of having to negotiate and compromise among a variety of competing interests. Furthermore, whipping up public sentiment against an external enemy requires periodic demonstrations of its malfeasance, the most compelling proof of which would be revelations of treason at the highest levels of government. In every aspect of its domestic politics, the salience of the regime's narrative conflicts with its own institutional solidity.

Foreign policy likewise requires a careful alignment of propaganda with real political consequences. The regime necessarily views international relations through the prism of war. Even if the prospect of a decisive victory remains a figment of propaganda, the regime must maintain complete freedom of action to suppress potentially existential threats. This prohibits wholehearted participation in a conventional system of mutually agreed upon principles and rules, but it also counsels against a posture of outright hostility. A regime that spreads terror beyond its borders and weakens the conventions of state sovereignty may suddenly find itself claiming those protections in vain against an enemy even better positioned to capitalize on the resultant instability. An expansionist grand strategy may exacerbate internal imbalances as the military and other vested interests press for additional opportunities to "advance their parochial interests in the guise of the general interests of the whole society."[59] A relentlessly confrontational foreign policy makes it more difficult for regime leaders to assess the costs of their action with respect to both international and domestic audiences. Leaders who are liable to punishment from their subordinates may find themselves under pressure to make threats to satisfy a hawkish clique, only to bear the exclusive responsibility for backing down. Leaders immune from such concerns place the regime in an acute condition of moral hazard, where even the most disastrous measures cannot elicit the political will and capacity to oust those responsible.[60]

State-directed terrorism is itself a transient phase of political activity, but the regime that employs it to secure power has indelibly fixed its own society in a condition of war against itself. Just as it competes with its neighbors for relative advantage, the mandate of rule will continually pass in and out of the hands of rival factions and charismatic leaders. Unlike the state which can almost always assume its national existence even in the wake of a catastrophic defeat, the regime lives in the shadow of its potential destruction, which necessarily phases out barriers to escalation as that prospect approaches reality. Given the extraordinary risks involved, the regime may elect to move toward a conventionalized system of relative advantage in both diplomacy and domestic politics to the extent that other states become invested in (or at least accustomed to) its continued existence. As long as the regime must hold terror in reserve as the guarantor of its security, it must still retain the potential to approximate the absolute form of war. Ultimately, the purpose of absolute war is not to actually achieve a decisive victory, although the promise of such may motivate many of its combatants. Rather, its purpose is to make war such a pervasive condition of social and international life that the willingness to escalate frees itself from the constraints of politics and resumes its theoretical property as the key to victory. In such a conflict, the advantage naturally falls to whomever has the fewest scruples, the weakest attachment to the status quo, and the most experience in fighting for survival.

STATE-DIRECTED TERRORISM IN ACTION

The Roots of Bolshevik Terrorism

There is an oft-noted connection between Clausewitz and Marxism, which is not surprising given that Marx and Engels emerged from the same German intellectual tradition of Hegelian idealism that had produced Clausewitz a generation earlier.[61] The main difference between them is that Clausewitz's dialectical comparison of absolute war and real war produces an ongoing, dynamic interchange of theoretical principles and material forces. For Marx and Engels, dialectical materialism is an inexorable progression toward the full realization of a theoretical ideal. As they explained in their 1848 "Manifesto of the Communist Party," the ascendance of industrial capitalism had laid bare the moral pretensions of the ruling class and "left remaining no other nexus between man and man than naked self-interest."[62] The globalization of bourgeois society would soon divide all of humanity into a self-conscious proletarian mass and the increasingly desperate forces of reaction.

The resulting struggle to control the means of production would turn absolute war from an abstract template into the climax of mankind's historical evolution, with Engels in 1887 predicting "a universal war of unprecedented force, unprecedented scope" resulting in the "collapse of the old states and all their vaunted wisdom."[63] In order to precipitate this outcome, the communist revolution would "never cease, for a single instant," to militarize workers all over the world, nor would it fail to make use of every available weapon against an enemy whose total annihilation had been ordained by History itself. The "revolutionary movement against the existing social and political order of things"[64] represented such a perfect form of warfare that its results would be sufficiently decisive to end war itself.

The Bolshevik seizure of power in November 1917 dispelled any lingering faith in this imminent cataclysm. Despite hopes that the Petrograd coup against the fledgling Russian Republic would light the powder keg of world revolution, the workers of Europe instead clung to the false consciousness of nationalism and democratic socialism. Lacking influential friends beyond their borders and suddenly confronted with the enormous difficulty of applying Marxist theory to an overwhelmingly agrarian Russia, over which they exercised only partial control, every aspect of Soviet politics became a form of combat. The disappointment of their ideological expectations and the prospect of warfare at home and abroad directed the Bolsheviks toward intellectual sources beyond those of the Marxist canon. Lenin, who had read and commented on Clausewitz during his exile in Switzerland, cited him to justify a flexible understanding of war as the continuation of socialist politics by other means, which required a realistic appreciation of the correlation of forces rather than slavish obedience to doctrine.[65]

Confronting a vast array of opponents composed of monarchists, anticommunist leftists, and ethnic irredentists, along with intermittent intervention of Western powers, theoretical innovation was a prerequisite for regime survival. Leon Trotsky's Military Commissariat eschewed the communist orthodoxy that called for an all-volunteer force that adopted the model of the *levee en masse* and called for a purely class-based warfare against property owners.[66] Instead, he drew the majority of commanders from the old Tsarist army, filled the ranks with conscripted peasants, and honed an attritional strategy of defending interior lines while hoarding grain, coal, and oil, which favored traditional military discipline over Party loyalty. After his rivals, the ideologically fervent "Red Commanders," championed a disastrous offensive into Poland in 1920, Trotsky denounced "all attempts at building an absolute revolutionary strategy."[67] Following the Bolshevik victory in the Civil War, Lenin followed in the footsteps of Trotsky's ideological flexibility with his "New Economic Policy" of tolerating free enterprise in the countryside, the Bolsheviks proved willing to appropriate bourgeois means in defense of socialist ends.

Lenin's pragmatism was a function of both the extraordinary circumstances of the Civil War and his own unassailable prestige. After his death in 1924, no other leading Party member could so openly flout communist doctrine without drawing accusations of heresy. Nor was collective rule among theParty elite a realistic model of governance given the vast differences of opinion regarding the proper means of communizing Russia and exporting the revolution abroad. In order for anything to happen at all, someone would have to perform Lenin's role as *primus inter parres*, guiding debate and casting the deciding vote when necessary. But while Party luminaries such as Trotsky, Grigoriy Zinoviev, and Nikolai Bukharin recognized the need for "a new political chief and interpreter of its ideological doctrine,"[68] none could cede prominence to the other without threatening their own position. The collective leadership attempted to square the circle with a posthumous "cult of Lenin" that cited his flexibility as a model for subsequent action while giving all credit to the deceased founder, but this unsurprisingly failed to mute the struggle for power among those claiming to best approximate the Leninist model.[69]

The need for decisive leadership was particularly acute given the dissonance between the Party's experience as a centralized, conspiratorial organization and the need for winning public acceptance for its rule. The vast majority of the population had "accepted the Communists precisely to the extent that . . . they did not socialize the countryside," but none among the leadership could propose a *modus vivendi* without being "seen as cowards"[70] lacking the nerve to push a recalcitrant peasantry into socialism. As Left and Right factions emerged to argue the respective merits of crash industrialization and cooperative gradualism, Stalin proved a useful ally for each precisely because he lacked the stature or intellectual plaudits to make his own bid for prominence. As General Secretary of the Party, which was a modest office before his tenure later made it synonymous with head of state, Stalin could credibly represent the average Soviet bureaucrat loyal to the state rather than any individual. Stalin's penchant for cruelty, which was well-known long before he had the power to give it full scope, was rebranded as praiseworthy "vigilance"[71] so long as it was turned against potential dictators like Trotsky or Bukharin.

Stalin's signature program for overcoming the gridlock of the Left-Right debate was the "General Line" of rapid industrialization and collectivization of agriculture, which selectively borrowed from both sides to discredit whoever appeared to be in the ascendant. To the extent that terror was necessary to achieve this purpose, Stalin had an existing apparatus on which to rely. In September 1918, the Bolsheviks formally declared a state of "Red Terror" calling for indiscriminate repression of landowners, merchants, Mensheviks, and other potentially "socially dangerous"[72] persons. Once the moment of supreme emergency had passed, the various agencies of repression born amid the chaos of the Civil War continued to exercise their powers, but as much for the sake of competing with one another as to protect the state against class enemies. With respect to the network of labor and concentration camps that had sprung up to house prisoners of war and victims of the Red Terror, "control over [these] penal institutions would remain in constant flux. Responsible institutions would be endlessly renamed and reorganized as different bureaucrats and commissars attempted to gain control over the system."[73] This bureaucratic infighting also resulted in erratic relations between the Soviet state and the outside world. A shared commitment to waging the "anti-imperialist struggle" did little to resolve the split between the diplomatic and trade agencies looking westward for economic assistance and the agents of the Comintern conducting agitprop and espionage against those same governments.[74]

Partisans of both "peaceful coexistence" and "the world revolutionary process" agreed that ultimate triumph would have to await the inevitable crisis of capitalism, when the ranks of the proletariat would become sufficiently numerous and desperate to achieve class consciousness. Their disagreement stemmed from the question of whether to wait out the conflagration behind the fortress of a strong Soviet state or accelerate it through revolutionary agitation.[75] Both of these approaches followed Lenin insofar as they offered an essentially Clausewitzian understanding of Marxist doctrine as a flexible response to emerging political realities. By 1929, Stalin had outmaneuvered the factions and earned the status of de facto *vozhd'* (leader). Having laid sole claim to Lenin's mantle, he proceeded to replace the Clausewitzian conception of politics as the push and pull of competing forces with a unidirectional mission that was guaranteed to triumph by virtue of superior reasoning and passions. Stalin's Five-Year Plans collapsed the distinction between the consolidation of the Soviet state and the worldwide triumph of socialism by turning the countryside, rather than capitalist Europe, into the main theater of the anti-imperialist struggle. The obliteration of an independent peasantry was at once a test of the Party's ability to break the last vestiges of internal resistance and an imperative to match the industrial and military capacity of its European rivals, lest it fall victim to the "capitalist encirclement."[76]

Stalin would later dismiss Clausewitz as the "representative of the hand-tool period of warfare," and that in the new "machine age" socialists must move beyond old theoretical doctrines lest they "want to be left behind by life."[77] A supporter of the Red Commanders during the Civil War, Stalin had long argued for a distinctly Marxist military science "subordinate to party politics, not to policy in the Clausewitzian sense." The core assumption of Marxist strategy was that technological advancement combined with ideological enthusiasm would enable a communist army to overcome the limits of friction, taking the fight to the enemy while securing the rear against counterrevolutionary subversion.[78] Following Marx and Engels, Stalinist military theory moved beyond Clausewitz only to find itself back at his starting point of absolute war. The doctrines of mobile combined-arms units probing deep into enemy territory, which leading Soviet military theorist Mikhail Tukhachevsky (later a victim of the purges) had developed after the Civil War, were to be applied to society at large. As Geoffrey Roberts explains, "the solution to social and economic problems was typically seen in terms of squads of vanguard workers using shock tactics to root out and destroy entrenched enemies holding back the implementation of party policy."[79] Workers were organized into "shock brigades" charged with rooting out "shirkers" and "loafers," while Komsomol members poured into the countryside to confiscate the property of "kulaks" (wealthier peasants) and force them onto *kolkhozy* (collective farms).[80]

When substantial elements of the peasantry resisted these measures, whether through open revolt or passive resistance such as slaughtering their own cattle, this lent substance to Stalin's insistence that capitalist agents had infiltrated the countryside to sabotage the advancement of the socialist utopia.[81] To counter the rampant threat of "wreckers," all Soviet workers were called upon to adopt the "Stakhanovite" ideal of superhuman productivity, which turned work itself into a form of combat. Labor was the ultimate expression of loyalty, as the individual furnished the raw materials necessary for the survival of the state and embodied the socialist ideal of efficiency and progress. In a similar vein, the vast expansion of the Gulag system stemmed from the imperative that "no one had the right not to engage in socially useful labor," making labor camps a morally praiseworthy corrective for "social parasites" in need of additional direction to achieve proletarian consciousness.[82] The all-consuming demand for the Promethean transformation of society, combined with the pervasive threat of capitalist sabotage, made collaboration a condition of survival for both the bureaucrat and the ordinary citizen. Regional party secretaries throughout the Union routinely "unmasked" their associates as conspirators, "an obvious way for local leaders to expel troublesome critics and subordinates while appearing to be zealous."[83] For the average Soviet worker and peasant, "failure to unmask" a traitor was itself treason, extending the Stakhanovite ethos to every facet of social interaction lest the slightest slacking of vigilance betray one's own lack of revolutionary virtue.[84]

The apex of the *Ezhovshchina* (known in the West as "the Great Terror") in 1937–1938 directed the struggle to the ranks of the Party itself. The murder of Leningrad Party boss Sergei Kirov in December 1934 appeared to validate the existence of a "terrorist organization" whose ability to kill a major official proved that the threat was growing and that it had sympathizers among the Party elite. The need for retaliation drew Stalin to the "Old Bolsheviks" whose history of opposing collectivization, as well as their continued contact with the exiled Trotsky, made them a fitting demonstration that all non-Stalinists were enemies of the people who would not hesitate to kill if they were not killed first.[85] A cycle of denunciation, show trial, and execution proceeded to cut down a host of Party luminaries, each time to the rapturous applause of their erstwhile colleagues. By the time that the Terror turned its focus onto the Party elite, ordinary Soviet citizens had become sufficiently well-versed in the jargon of denunciation to bring down unpopular officials and managers.[86] Terror was most effective when it operated "as a form of popular political justice, generated as much by pressure from below as it was by policy from above."[87] Although the pool of potential victims was theoretically unlimited, terror unfolded as a series of individual outbursts against a rotating list of groups "isolated by their social groups or their peers, not by the political police."[88] Since each iteration of terror featured the masses turning on a suspicious individual or group, the regime was able to build a mass culture around the expectation of a rapidly escalating confrontation between good and evil, with each bout of bloodshed bringing the imminent triumph ever closer.

Stalinist Terrorism vs. Real War

Terror proved effective in disrupting any potential locus of anti-Stalinist activity and eliciting active public support for the regime, but it proved increasingly difficult to parse the political utility of absolute war from its tendency for self-perpetuation. As the rise of Nazi Germany presented the Soviets with a quintessential nemesis, the prospect of a fascist plot to destroy the revolution took on still greater immediacy, demanding correspondingly harsh measures to root out its agents. While the increasing threat of real war reinforced the short-term necessity of absolute war, it also raised the question of its its long-term consequences for Soviet security. The German threat could provoke speculation among lingering dissidents that "a foreign invasion would unsettle Stalins's rule and provide an opportunity for a return to power."[89] Equally dangerous was the prospect of the army seizing control during a war, or in the imminent expectation of one, with the promise of a more effective national defense. These twin dangers called for accelerated purges of the Party and military to eliminate any alternative source of crisis leadership, at the cost of decimating "what was arguably the most talented group of general staff officers in the world."[90]

The risks of this approach were not lost on Stalin. An indefinite continuation of internal warfare would deprive the Soviet Union of the wherewithal to shape its fate on the international stage, and halting terror too soon would expose the regime at its moment of critical vulnerability to the wrath of the persecuted. In order to square the circle of internal and external security, Stalin had to postpone war long enough to exterminate the last vestiges of opposition and then rebuild the state in his image. He could then frame the conclusion of the purges as preparation for the next stage of the climactic showdown with the capitalist powers. As the Great Terror reached its climax, with the evisceration of the officer corps and the few surviving members of Lenin's original Central Committee, Stalin probed for any possible diplomatic opening that would counter or at least redirect the fascist menace.

For the better part of the 1930s, People's Commissar for Foreign Affairs Maxim Litvinov moved the U.S.S.R. toward a revival of the Triple Entente with France and Great Britain.[91] The Soviet Union joined the League of Nations in 1934, lifted the ban on foreign communists entering into "popular front" coalitions the following year, signed mutual assistance treaties with France and Czechoslovakia, and intervened on behalf of Republican forces in the Spanish Civil War. Yet each of these measures met with frustration and failure: the League's commitment to collective security failed each of its most critical tests. France proved unwilling to defend either its own Rhineland occupation or the Czech Sudetenland against German aggression, and Franco's victory in 1938 was a fittingly tragic conclusion to a war that featured savage infighting among pro and anti-Soviet factions within the Republican camp.[92] These setbacks appeared to demonstrate the fallacy of a conventional foreign policy in a system that was once again on the brink of total war. Rather than conduct diplomacy and strategy along Western lines, Stalin chose to export a condition of absolute war even as his domestic terror campaign was winding down. By expediting the destruction of the European order, the Soviet Union would drag the other powers down to its own level of weakness, after which Soviet advantages in mass mobilization and sheer ruthlessness would give it a qualitative advantage in a struggle without technological or normative limits to escalation.

The signature piece of this shift in Soviet strategy was the signing of the Molotov-Ribbentrop Pact with Germany in August 1939, after which the word "fascist" promptly vanished from Soviet propaganda and German communists who had sought refuge in the U.S.S.R. were sent home by the thousands to their likely doom. The separate peace with Hitler has struck many observers as a standout example of old-fashioned *realpolitik* trumping ideology,[93] but this interpretation conflates the means with the ends. Whereas the diplomacy of the Age of Absolutism permitted flexible alliances for the sake of preserving the balance of power, the Nazi-Soviet pact was a diplomatic act of terrorism against the status quo by the two powers with, as Stalin later put it, "a common desire to get rid of the old equilibrium."[94] The subsequent collaboration between the totalitarian powers in the dismemberment of Poland sent an unmistakable signal that European politics would henceforth subscribe to no laws or conventions other than the rule of armies and secret police.

Once Hitler transitioned from *sitzkrieg* ("phony war") to *blitzkrieg* in the West, Stalin would carve out a sphere of influence in the Baltic, Eastern Europe, and the Balkans, granting him a resource base with which he could complete the modernization of the Red Army.[95] As Germany and the Allies wore each other down in an attritional struggle, Stalin would at last make good on his 1925 prediction that in the next inter-imperialist war, "we will not be able to idly stand by. We will have to take part, but we will be the last to take part so that we may throw the decisive weight onto the scales, a weight that should prove the determining factor."[96] The First World War had so shaken the foundations of imperialism that the Tsarist empire crumbled, leaving the door wide open for the Bolshevik seizure of power. The Second World War would repeat that same victory on a grander scale, dividing Europe into those under Soviet domination and those incapable of contesting it, without the Soviets even having to directly engage in the fighting until they were fully ready. Having inured themselves to the pain of absolute war and then spread it abroad to those who were incapable of similar fortitude, the Soviets would liberate themselves from the bounds of reciprocity on the world stage just as they had in their war against themselves.

The chief flaw of this grand design was that the onset of absolute war was strictly contingent on a fixed sequence of outcomes which the U.S.S.R. was ill-equipped to bring about by its own efforts, and yet could hardly expect to occur without their direct intervention. Stalin sought territorial expansion to gain a buffer zone for the likely resumption of competition with Germany, the outward projection of Soviet power tended to exacerbate its internal weaknesses. Stalin looked to secure his Baltic front by making the same kind of demonstration in Finland that Hitler had in Poland, until stiff Finnish resistance revealed the full impact of the purges on the Red Army's operational effectiveness. Stalinist military doctrine "had long stressed aggressive counterattack, decentralized command, and organizational flexibility, but within such a rigidly hierarchical political despotism, only the first principle was realized in practice." The extraordinarily high costs of Soviet territorial gains indicated to German observers that the Red Army was a "colossus of clay"[97] incapable of standing against a peer competitor.

Soviet forces along the Polish-Ukrainian frontier were liable to these same weaknesses, this time in ways that Germany could directly exploit. In the period between the signing of the Pact and the German invasion, the Red Army undertook a massive increase in manpower, industrial output, mechanization, and construction of new fortifications along the new German-Soviet border. The General Staff had paid careful attention to the problem of maximizing the economic potential for war, but "authoritarian centralization did not guarantee that those in the economic front line would be able to adapt to war, or that those at the center would be able to tell them how best to do so."[98] Similarly, the concentration of troops at the likely point of contact was intended to tie down an initial invasion until reinforcements could mount a counterattack, but this was a product of decades-old doctrinal orthodoxy rather than tactical realities. After Germany demonstrated the full potential of its *blitzkrieg* against France in June 1940, Stalin was at last forced to directly confront a peer squarely within the dynamics of real war, in which the Soviets were at an acute disadvantage.

As the Germans made their offensive intentions increasingly obvious in the spring of 1941, Soviet forces were trapped between their tactical disposition and strategic expectations. In the months before the invasion, Soviet military planners devised a posture of "aggressive defense" that would disrupt German preparations with hit-and-run attacks while keeping the bulk of the Red Army in reserve, to strike only after the Wehrmacht had overextended itself. This otherwise sensible strategy required a degree of tactical coordination far beyond the experience of the young and inexperienced officers who disproportionately survived the purges. Furthermore, the vast scale of the theater and the fluidity of the modern battlefield was sure to paralyze even the most intrepid commander when any hint of independent action would alert the NKVD counterintelligence operatives assigned to every border unit.[99] There was no way for Stalin to counter the threat without revealing the weakness of the Soviet position and precipitating the German attack, leaving him with the unenviable option of hoping that Hitler was merely probing for weaknesses before turning back to fight the British. On the night of June 21, with the German onslaught a few hours away, the Kremlin acknowledged the possibility of imminent surprise attack before warning its units "not to respond to any provocative actions that might result in serious complications."[100] The Soviet expectation that they could reap the benefits of absolute war at the end of a lengthy historical process on a lengthy timetable left them vulnerable to the one other state with its own plans for absolute war, and with a much shorter timetable.

Absolute war seems a fitting description for the Eastern front of the Second World War, as its totalitarian principals fought on a greater scale, with a higher proportion of of resources, and with more systematic cruelty than at any time before or since.[101] Yet not even this apotheosis of modern warfare exhibited both sides engaged in symmetrical escalation toward a climactic decision. German advantages in mobility, firepower, and tactical skill quickly evaporated over the immense distances of the Soviet frontier, as vehicles broke down, ran out of fuel, or upon the onset of winter, froze to the ground. The atrocities of the S.S. *Einsatzgruppen* enabled the Soviet government to rally the population against the invader, especially given their willingness to elevate traditional Russian nationalism and the Orthodox church alongside Marxism-Leninism.[102] Instruments of Soviet terror such as the Gulag and NKVD turned their attention toward the thoroughly conventional goals of sustaining war production and instilling military discipline. With a production base shielded behind the Ural mountains, badly needed supplies from American Lend-Lease, and inexhaustible manpower, Soviet forces were better able to absorb the lessons of experience and fine-tune new doctrines with fresh soldiers and equipment.[103] The war against Germany accomplished the objectives of the Terror by validating Stalin's leadership at home and demonstrating Soviet martial prowess to the world, but even this decisive victory was relative, since the Soviets were not the only claimants to the spoils.

Stalin was no less interested than the Western Allies powers in the construction of a stable postwar system. The incalculable costs of the war, the public's yearning for a return to normalcy after years of suffering and privation, and the vast superiority of the United States all counseled against confrontation, yet those same factors also prohibited full Soviet compliance with the premises of the Atlantic Charter and United Nations. The traumatic experience of the war made it necessary to "keep Germany enfeebled and to extend the Soviet borders to the lie of 1941," secure "a glacis of 'friendly states'" along its western frontier, and build a network of enclaves from Manchuria to the Mediterranean.[104] Stalin attempted to square the circle by paying lip service to national self-determination and democracy while using using personal diplomacy with the British and Americans to secure a free hand on his side of the "Iron Curtain." A revival of traditional *realpolitik* would affirm his acceptance of the basic international order while reserving the right to take all necessary steps in defense of the Soviet position within that order. From a position of strength, the Soviets could gradually scale down the armed forces and allocate resources to domestic recovery, providing a textbook example of a "peaceful transition to socialism"[105] that other European states could adopt as a model, all while deterring Western encroachment.

Effecting the transition to domestic stability and international respectability required that the regime maintain a bulwark against capitalist subversion and an "incomprehensible spirit of resistance and complete ignorance"[106] among their new subjects. The massive bureaucracy that sprang from war and occupation maintained itself principally through divisions between the beneficiaries of repression and its victims. In Germany, the Soviet Military Authority oversaw the systematic dismantling of industry and forced extraction of skilled workers, both as a reward for the exhausted Red Army and a policy of preventing Germany's economic revival.[107] In Poland, the only institution that offered upward social mobility was the secret police, which ultimately spoiled the initial occupation policy of tolerating private business, a free press, and democratic politics.[108] Where the Soviets lacked the direct power to suppress opposition, such as Turkey and Iran, their demands for territory and basing rights resulted in humiliating withdrawals. These setbacks confirmed the necessity of preserving strict control over the empire, resulting in the coup against Czechoslovakia's democratic government, the rejection of the Marshall Plan, and the Berlin Blockade.

Victory in the Second World War consolidated the community which Stalin had forged through terror, but the narrative of socialist harmony barely concealed the rifts within its empire. Soviet politics were too rigid to reconcile its grand strategic vision of cooperation and stability with the "interplay of often contradictory impulses from different officials and agencies" and so policy evolved "haphazardly rather than by design."[109] "Socialist imperialism" wedded the interests of regime elites to the preservation of the Stalinist apparatus, and thereby averted a struggle for power within the regime that would have left it vulnerable to American predation. In addition to the consolidation of totalitarianism in Eastern Europe, this also gave rise to an expansionist impulse, especially among representatives of ethnic minorities eager to carve out personal domains over their respective national populations.[110] Security competition with the United States was both a consequence of this arrangement and a cause of its perpetuation for the proceeding forty years. Stalinist terror was successful in building a new Soviet community, but that community could only justify its existence by remaining in the shadow of absolute war.

NOTES

1. Jeffrey A. Sluka, "State Terror and Anthropology," in *Death Squad: The Anthropology of State Terror* (Philadelphia: University of Pennsylvania Press, 2000), 1–45.
2. Richards, *Conceptualizing Terrorism,* 116–117.
3. Kelly P. O'Reilly, "Perceiving Rogue States: The Use of the 'Rogue State' Concept by U.S. Foreign Policy Elites," *Foreign Policy Analysis* 3 (2007): 295–315.
4. S. Alexander Haslam, Stephen D. Reicher, and Michael J. Platow, *The New Psychology of Leadership: Identity, Influence, and Power* (New York: Psychology Press, 2011), 179–181.
5. Clausewitz, *On War*, 177.
6. Ibid., 181.
7. Ibid., 182.
8. Ibid., 183.
9. Colin S. Gray, *Modern Strategy* (New York: Oxford University Press, 1999), 17.
10. Clausewitz, *On War*, 178.
11. Ibid., 192.
12. Ibid., 102.
13. Ibid., 190.
14. Ibid., 184.
15. Clausewitz, *On War*, 122.
16. Ibid., 110–111.
17. Cathal J. Nolan, *The Allure of Battle: A History of How Wars Have Been Won and Lost* (New York: Oxford University Press, 2017), 257.
18. Clausewitz, *On War*, 186.
19. Ibid., 192.
20. Barry R. Posen, "Nationalism, the Mass Army, and Military Power," *International Security* 18 (1993): 84.
21. Clasuewitz, *On War*, 220.
22. Lawrence Freedman, *Strategy: A History* (New York: Oxford University Press, 2013), 86.
23. Clausewitz, *On War*, 197.
24. Ibid., 198.
25. Ibid., 203.
26. Ibid., 200–201.
27. Ibid., 213.
28. Michael I. Handel, *Masters of War: Classical Strategic Thought* (New York: Routledge, 2001), 276.
29. Clausewitz, *On War*, 204.
30. Ibid., 197.
31. Ibid. 207–209.
32. Ibid., 211.
33. Ibid., 205.
34. Ibid., 254–255.
35. Ibid., 217.
36. Ibid., 221.
37. Ibid., 218.
38. Ibid., 219.

39. Ibid., 215.

40. Geoffrey Blainey, *The Causes of War* (New York: Free Press, 1988), 113.

41. Clausewitz, *On War*, 206.

42. Ernest Gellner, *Nations and Nationalism* (Ithaca: Cornell University Press, 2006), 72.

43. Benedict Anderson, *Imagined Communities: Reflections on the Origin and Spread of Nationalism* (New York: Verso, 2006), 104.

44. Benjamin Miller, "The State-to-Nation Balance and War," in *Nationalism and War*, eds. John A. Hall and Siniša Malešević (New York: Cambridge University Press, 2013), 81–82.

45. Donald L. Horowitz, *Ethnic Groups in Conflict* (Berkeley: University of California Press, 2000), 230.

46. Jaroslaw Piekalkiewicz and Alfred Wayne Penn, *Politics of Ideocracy* (Albany: State University of New York Press, 1995), 26–27.

47. Hannah Arendt, *The Origins of Totalitarianism* (New York: Houghton Mifflin Harcourt, 1994), 323.

48. Raymond Boudon, *The Analysis of Ideology* (Chicago: University of Chicago Press, 1989), 32–33.

49. Juan J. Linz, *Totalitarian and Authoritarian Regimes* (Boulder: Lynne Rienner Publishers, 2000), 77.

50. Carles Boix and Milan W. Slovik, "The Foundations of Limited Authoritarian Government: Institutions, Commitment, and Power-Sharing in Dictatorships," *The Journal of Politics* 75 (2013): 300–316.

51. Beatriz Magaloni, "Credible Power-Sharing and the Longevity of Autocratic Rule," *Comparative Political Studies* 41 (2008): 9.

52. Ronald Wintrobe, *The Political Economy of Dictatorship* (New York: Cambridge University Press, 2000), 47.

53. Carl Schmitt, trans. George Schwab, *Political Theology: Four Chapters on the Concept of Sovereignty* (Chicago: University of Chicago Press, 2005), 5.

54. Ibid., 7.

55. Milan W. Slovik, *The Politics of Authoritarian Rule* (New York: Cambridge University Press, 2012), 159.

56. Helen V. Milner, *Interests, Institutions, and Information: Domestic Politics and International Relations* (Princeton: Princeton University Press, 1997), 12–13.

57. Roger Eatwell, "The Concept and Theory of Charismatic Leadership," *Totalitarian Movements and Political Religions* 7 (2006):153.

58. Alexei V. Zakharov, "The Loyalty-Competence Tradeoff in Dictatorships and Outside Options For Subordinates," *The Journal of Politics* 78 (2016): 464–465.

59. Jack Snyder, *Myths of Empire: Domestic Politics and International Ambition* (Ithaca: Cornell University Press, 1991), 31.

60. Jessica L. Weeks, "Autocratic Audience Costs: Regime Type and Signaling Resolve," *International Organization* 62 (2008

61. Azar Gat, "Clausewitz and the Marxists: Yet Another Look," *Journal of Contemporary History* 27 (1992): 364.

62. Karl Marx and Friedrich Engels, "Manifesto of the Communist Party," in *The Marx-Engels Reader*, ed. Robert C. Tucker (New York: W.W. Norton, 1972), 337.

63. Quoted in Jacob W. Kipp, "Lenin and Clausewitz: The Militarization of Marxism, 1914–1921," *Military Affairs* 49 (1985): 184–185.

64. Marx and Engels, "Manifesto of the Communist Party," 362.

65. Donald E. Davis and Walter S.G. Kohn, "Lenin's 'Notebook on Clausewitz,'" in *Soviet Armed Forces Review Annual Vol. I*, ed. David R. Jones (Gulf Breeze: Academic International Press, 1977), 193.

66. Mark Von Hagen, "The *Levee en Masse* from Russian Empire to Soviet Union, 1874–1938," in *The People In Arms*, eds. Moran and Waldron, 178.

67. Earl Ziemke, "Strategy For Class War: The Soviet Union, 1917–1941," in *The Making of Strategy: Rulers, States, and War*, eds. Williamson Murray et al. (New York: Cambridge University Press, 1994), 503–508.

68. Roy Medvedev, *Let History Judge: The Origins and Consequences of Stalinism* (New York: Columbia University Press, 1989), 111.

69. Robert C. Tucker, *Stalin as Revolutionary, 1878–1929: A Study in Leadership and Personality* (New York: W.W. Norton, 1973), 310–311.

70. Robert Conquest, *The Great Terror: A Reassessment* (New York: Oxford University Press, 2008), 16.

71. Simon Sebag Montefiore, *Stalin: Court of the Red Tsar* (New York: Vintage, 2003), 55–56.

72. Paul R. Gregory: *Terror by Quota: State Security from Lenin to Stalin* (*An Archival Study*) New Haven: Yale University Press, 2009), 109.

73. Anne Applebaum, *Gulag: A History* (New York: Anchor Books, 2003), 12.

74. Adam B. Ulam, *Expansion and Coexistence: Soviet Foreign Policy, 1917–1973* (New York: Preager, 1974), 138.

75. Jon Jacobson, *When the Soviet Union Entered World Politics* (Berkeley: University of California Press, 1994), 29–30.

76. Stephen Kotkin, *Stalin, Volume I: Paradoxes of Power, 1878–1928* (New York: Penguin Books, 2014), 684.

77. Quoted in Gat, "Clausewitz and the Marxists," 377.

78. Ziemke, "Strategy for Class War," 512–513.

79. Geoffrey Roberts, *Stalin's Wars: From World War to Cold War, 1939–1953* (New Haven: Yale University Press, 2006), 72.

80. Hiraoki Kuromiya, *Stalin's Industrial Revolution: Politics and Workers, 1928–1931* (New York: Cambridge University Press, 1988), 236–237.

81. Lynne Viola, *Peasant Rebels Under Stalin: Collectivization and the Culture of Peasant Resistance* (New York: Oxford University Press, 1996), 206.

82. David Lloyd Hoffman, *Stalinist Values: The Cultural Norms of Soviet Modernity, 1917–1941* (Ithaca: Cornell University Press, 2003), 31.

83. John Arch Getty, *Origins of the Great Purges: The Soviet Communist Party Reconsidered, 1933–1938* (New York: Cambridge University Press, 1987), 145.

84. Wendy Z. Goldman, *Inventing the Enemy: Denunciation and Terror in Stalin's Russia* (New York: Cambridge University Press, 2011), 64.

85. Robert W. Thurston, *Life and Terror in Stalin's Russia, 1934–1941* (New Haven: Yale University Press, 1996), 28–30.

86. Sheila Fitzpatrick, "Signals From Below: Soviet Letters of Denunciation," *The Journal of Modern History* 68 (1996), 862–866.

87. Richard Overy, *The Dictators: Hitler's Germany, Stalin's Russia* (New York: W.W. Norton, 2004), 213–214.

88. Alfred J. Rieber, "Stalin as Foreign Policy-Maker," in *Stalin: A New History*, eds. James Harris and Sarah Davies (New York: Cambridge University Press, 2005), 144.

89. James Harris, *The Great Fear: Stalin's Terror of the 1930s* (New York: Oxford University Press, 2016), 145.

90. Alfred J. Rieber, "Stalin as Foreign-Policy-Maker," in *Stalin: A New History*, eds. James Harris and Sarah Davies (New York: Cambridge University Press, 2005), 144.

91. Henry L. Roberts, "Maxim Litvinov," in *The Diplomats, 1919–1939*, eds. Gordon Craig and Felix Gilbert (Princeton: Princeton University Press, 1981), 364.

92. Burnett Bolloten, *The Spanish Civil War: Revolution and Counterrevolution* (Chapel Hill: University of North Carolina Press, 1991), 503–509.

93. Gabriel Gorodetsky, *Grand Delusion: Stalin and the German Invasion of Russia* (New Haven: Yale University Press, 1999), 13.

94. Quoted in Timothy Snyder, *Bloodlands: Europe Between Hitler and Stalin* (New York: Basic Books, 2010), 115.

95. Roberts, *Stalin's Wars*, 39.

96. Quoted in Andreas Hillgruber, trans. William C. Kirby, *Germany and the Two World Wars* (Cambridge: Harvard University Press, 1981), 73.

97. Stephen Kotkin, *Stalin, Volume II: Waiting for Hitler, 1929–1941* (New York: Penguin, 2017), 748–749.

98. Mark Harrison, *Soviet Planning in Peace and War, 1938–1945* (New York: Cambridge University Press, 2002), 49.

99. Overy, *The Dictators*, 492–493.

100. David E. Murphy, *What Stalin Knew: The Enigma of Barbarossa* (New Haven: Yale University Press, 2005), 211–215.

101. Chris Bellamy, *Absolute War: Soviet Russia in the Second World War* (New York: Alfred A. Knopf, 2008), 16–19.

102. Steven Merrit Miner, *Stalin's Holy War: Religion, Nationalism, and Alliance Politics, 1941–1945* (Chapel Hill: University of North Carolina Press, 2003), 87–88.

103. Richard Overy, *Russia's War: A History of the Soviet War Effort, 1941–1945* (New York: Penguin, 1998), 192.

104. Vladimir Pechatnov, "The Soviet Union and the World, 1944–1953," in *The Cambridge History of the Cold War*, eds. Melvyn P. Leffler and Odd Arne Westad (New York: Cambridge University Press, 2012), 92.

105. Peter Ruggenthaler, *The Concept of Neutrality in Stalin's Foreign Policy, 1945–1953* (Lanham: Lexington Books, 2015), 34.

106. Quoted in Krystyna Kersten, *The Establishment of Communist Rule in Poland, 1943–1943* (Berkeley: University of California Press, 1991), 286.

107. Norman Naimark, *The Russians in Germany: A History of the Soviet Zone of Occupation, 1945–1949* (Cambridge: Harvard University Press, 1995), 170.

108. Anne Applebaum, *Iron Curtain: The Crushing of Eastern Europe, 1944–1956* (New York: Anchor Books, 2012), 68.

109. Vojtech Mastny, *The Cold War and Soviet Insecurity: The Stalin Years* (New York: Oxford University Press, 1996), 19.

110. Vladislav Zubok, *A Failed Empire: The Soviet Union in the Cold War From Stalin to Gorbachev.* Chapel Hill: The University of North Carolina Press, 2009), 9–10.

Chapter Four

Strategy and Non-State Terrorism

Non-state terrorism exhibits the same basic strategic logic as state-directed terrorism. Both types of campaigns aim to trigger a continuous process of escalation that compels increasing levels of public participation among a target audience, which facilitates the formation of a new and thoroughly militarized community under the exclusive direction of the organization. Escalation renders the organization immune from reciprocity as events appear to validate its narrative of heroic struggle and inevitable triumph in the minds of allies, enemies, and observers. A tightly organized and ideologically motivated cohort willing and able to push society toward a condition of absolute war creates the ideal training ground for further indoctrination in its avowed cause and methodology. In its ideal form, terrorism forms a virtuous circle in which escalation increases the group's effectiveness, rendering it capable of further escalation and still greater effectiveness.

Although the strategic blueprint for both types of terrorism is fundamentally similar, the strategic environment for non-state terrorist campaign is in many respects similar to conventional warfare. While state-directed terrorism construes or at least exaggerates an external threat as a means of domestic mobilization, the non-state terrorist campaign must actually compete with a specific external enemy. Non-state terroris thus assumes the basic structure of a duel, and the campaign reproduces the strategic conditions of a conventional campaign to the extent that each side is seeking to inflict a decisive victory upon the other. The critical difference is that a conventional force that risks a decisive engagement exposes its forces to comparable dangers, a risk that a terrorist campaign can almost never afford to undertake. Whether contending directly with a state that holds sway over the organization's target audience or deterring its allies from coming to its rescue, the organization must compel its adversary to accept a total outcome even as it retains the capacity to reverse that outcome.

The idea of an enemy voluntarily acceding to a decisive defeat flouts the Clausewitzian logic of war, in which outcomes are partial so long as each side retains some degree of agency. The terrorist campaign resolves this apparent contradiction by conducting its own campaign in accordance with the pure theory of war while keeping its enemy within the bounds of friction, convention, and political calculation. Since the political objective of the idealized community can be achieved through sufficient degrees of popular mobilization, victory does not require the enemy's utter defeat. It only requires that the enemy remain incapable of severing the nodes by which the organization binds an ideology and target audience to its leadership. Even if the enemy continues to escalate its own efforts, the formation of the community through an approximation of absolute war presents a *fait accompli* that does not depend upon its formal acknowledgment in order to become a reality.

The decision to undertake terrorism often springs from a preexisting campaign, such as an insurgency or guerrilla army, which may utilize terrorism alongside more conventional tactics or terminate terrorism and revert to other forms of fighting and bargaining. Terrorism however is not merely a variety of non-state political violence like insurgency or guerrilla warfare, but rather an attempt to launch an asymmetric war toward an absolute condition which clears the space for a complete fusion of warfare and politics. Lacking the military assets to engage the state in direct battle, a terrorist campaign instead deprives the state of its legitimacy by engaging in symbolic violence on behalf of a morally superior alternative. Non-state terrorist campaigns fall into two categories: "state-makers," who utilize terrorism as a means of entering the family of nations, or "state-wreckers," seeking to replace the state with a utopian government for their designated community.

While state-builders traditionally represent themselves as guerrilla fighters aspiring to legitimate diplomatic status, state-wreckers have sought to inspire imitators through a personal example of righteous vengeance and self-sacrifice. The Irish Fenians and Russian *narodniks* ("populists") stand as respective attempts to carry out the strategy of state-building and state-wrecking in their pure form, the failures of which prompted a continual process of both tactical innovation and mutual learning between the two models. Twentieth-century cases including the Zionist campaign against Mandatory Palestine, the Algerian *Front de Libération Nationale*, the Provisional Irish Republican Army, the Palestine Liberation Organization, the West German *Rote Armee Fraktion*, and the Islamic Resistance Movement (Hamas) demonstrate how non-state terrorist campaigns have learned to incorporate the strategy and personality of state-building and state-wrecking and tailor it to their particular audience. Establishing both the blueprint of terrorism and its method of change will permit an analysis of contemporary terrorism as a form of warfare and the likely course of its development.

THE ORIGINS OF NON-STATE TERRORISM

Rebels, Outlaws, and Terrorists

Non-state terrorism belongs to a long tradition of actors who have stood apart from or rebelled against the conventions of the international system, and relied upon fear to advance their political objectives. Practically every society throughout history has faced at least the prospect of revolt by slaves, colonial subjects, peasants, or any restive underclass seeking a "renegotiation" of the social contract through armed struggle, from the Peasants' Revolt of medieval England to the Arab Spring.

Empires ancient and modern have contended with insurgencies that use asymmetric or clandestine violence to render their homeland ungovernable for a foreign occupier. For example, many scholars of terrorism have traced the roots of terrorism roots back to the Zealots and *Sicarii* ("dagger-wielders") of first-century Judea who assassinated agents of the Roman occupation and their Jewish collaborators.[1] Premodern regimes that governed through networks of cities and fortresses tended to leave large swaths of ungoverned space within their realm, creating a vacuum in which dissatisfied or hostile actors could evade or harass the central authority. The *hashishin* of medieval Persia and Syria, a breakaway sect of Ismaili Shi'a who preyed upon the Seljuk empire and Crusader kingdoms, are frequently cited as a precursor to contemporary Islamic terrorism.[2] Additionally, there have always been bandits, from the Barbary Pirates to the Neapolitan Camorra, who had sufficient numbers and influence to achieve an ersatz political status and demand the respect and even acquiescence of local officials who would otherwise prefer to shun or suppress them.

A formal typology of non-state political violence will not mesh neatly with the complexities of political reality. An organization may engage in criminal activity to fund its political objectives, engage in politics to protect its criminal enterprises, or make a full transition from insurgency to political legitimacy, as it reevaluates the plausibility of its objectives against its menu of tactical options.[3] The Zealots initially sought a restoration of local autonomy, with an expectation of broad-based public support encouraging them to strike in broad daylight and then disappear into the crowd. Once Rome proved willing to destroy Jerusalem rather than let it fall into enemy hands, the Zealots transitioned from an insurgency into a suicide cult.[4] The *hashishin* aspired to spreading their millenarian message through a mixture of proselytization and force, until the difficulty of coordinating their disparate networks favored a policy of concentration within an isolated pseudo-state that made it easier to retain and indoctrinate their followers. While boasting a reputation for staging daring assaults, the maintenance of discipline favored strict adherence to ritualistic violence rather than effective political action.[5] Colombian drug kingpin Pablo Escobar personified the wide range of possibilities for a violent non-state actor. His career ran the gamut of political activity, including winning a seat in the Chamber of Representatives, to sponsorship of left-wing guerrillas to put pressure on the government, to terrorist tactics including car bombings and the destruction of a civilian airliner.[6]

Rebels, outlaws, and insurgents have typically defined themselves "in reaction to the *raison d'être* of the dominant constitutional order, at the same time negating and rejecting that form's unique ideology but mimicking the form's structural characteristics."[7] In a patchwork system of empires, kingdoms, and small republics, the heterogeneity of the international system generated an equally diverse array of rebels seeking to replace one model of rule with another and outlaws who stood outside the authority while mimicking its conventions. The nation-state, by contrast, earns its legitimacy by filling the entirety of its territory with a monopoly on legitimate violence, and by the same logic, the concept of the nation-state has established a universal standard for the political structures and moral purposes of international society.[8] Of course, plenty of nation-states fail to live up to that ideal, and feature civil wars or insurgencies in which multiple parties can compete for territory and other assets. In contrast to these updated variants of asymmetric warfare, terrorism is a "strikingly modern" method of challenging the powers that be. With the advent of "destructive and portable weaponry, the mass media, literacy, and secular ideologies,"[9] it became possible to fight for the hearts and minds of peoples in a contest that all but negated traditional military advantages. For the would-be rebel or outlaw who chafes under the authority of the state and yet cannot escape it, terrorism resolves this paradox by offering a template by which to reject the conventions of international society while promising a more authentic fulfillment of their underlying moral claim.

Terrorism and the National Principle

Since the American and French Revolutions, the doctrine of national self-determination has consistently inspired revolutionary change against avowedly hierarchical systems, especially as social conditions fostered the rise of mass political activity. Industrialization and mass communication promoted the "political mobilization of large segments of the population," resulting in ideologies that combined populist demands for social reform with "an elite construction of a coherent political worldview."[10] A nation may divide along socio-economic and ideological lines, or struggle to define the precise boundaries of its ethnic and religious character, but the establishment of a nation-state generally presupposes a people with sufficient self-awareness to effect a prevailing union of culture and politics.[11]

Once a regime has secured the loyalty (or at least the compliance) of the nation, this tends to dampen the possibility of subsequent revision, leaving the would-be revolutionary with few options. The public at large is unlikely to countenance violent protest if the state lowers barriers to peaceful collective action, since dissenters can converge "around the corporate bodies and voluntary associations whose established position and real power enables them to gain advantages within the institutional framework of the state."[12] Even in the absence of legitimate avenues of protest, a *coup d'etat* would still fail the test of popular legitimacy, giving way to a revolving door of strongmen who can exploit popular outrage to overthrow the leader only to find themselves similarly vulnerable. Only a massive and sustained outburst of popular rage is sufficient to effect a genuine transfer of legitimate power within a nation-state, which depends on the development of a "collectivist conception of rationality"[13] that elevates the expected public goods of revolution over the significant risks of protest for the solitary individual. As Tocqueville argued in his analysis of the American republic, "the majority of citizens do not see clearly what they could gain by a revolution, and they feel at each instant and in a thousand ways what they could lose from one." Only the most extraordinary conditions can displace the typical focus on the "pursuit of well-being"[14] and infuse a people with revolutionary consciousness.

The triumph of the nation-state in Europe similarly dampened its own penchant for revolutionary urgency on the world stage. Throughout the nineteenth century, liberalism became the linchpin of a "system of international relations that combined stability with elasticity, security with progress," so that an ideology which had begun with a "theoretical attack on the foundations of international society was becoming the new orthodoxy."[15] In the immediate aftermath of the Napoleonic wars, direct opposition between monarchic legitimism and liberal nationalism led to a "cold war"[16] between absolutist Prussia, Russia, and Austria and the constitutional monarchies of France and Britain, until the former proved incapable of sustaining a united front. After the Crimean War shattered the Holy Alliance, archconservative Russia learned to isolate Slavic nationalism from liberal reformism, mirroring the proto-authoritarian nationalism of Bismarck and Napoleon III.[17] Once the national principle had converted its erstwhile enemies, it was free to cast the international system in its image. Nation-states would uphold the basic logic of a Machiavellian system, competing for relative gains and negotiating the tension between sovereign power and popular legitimacy.[18] Nonetheless, they would generally shore up the common basis of their legitimacy, creating a system of "organized hypocrisy"[19] that restricted membership to those that formally upheld the principle of popular sovereignty even when they violate its normative substance.

The apparent triumph of Enlightenment principles as a basis of both domestic legitimacy and diplomacy exposed the dilemma at the heart of its project. The idea of a "sovereign people"[20] presumed a singular and authentic nation whose collective existence in fact resulted more as a result of historical accident than any consciously held or commonly affirmed purpose. The presumption of a reasonable basis for social order generates two forms of internal challenge. One is a group that seeks to escape the domination of a rival nation and establish an equal place for itself on the world stage. The other rejects the conventional structure of the nation-state as an insufficient vehicle for the character and aspirations of the people they claim to represent. The first is likely to base their opposition on a claim to a more "organic"[21] nationalism against the prevailing concept of the nation as a voluntary and contractual association of rational individuals. The second is likely to uphold a cosmopolitan ideal which regards the nation-state as either a catalyst for a more utopian alternative form of organization or an impediment to be overcome as quickly as possible. In both cases, they are pushing back against the "constructed image of sameness"[22] that artfully conceals the grievances of the dispossessed beneath a veneer of homogeneity.

Terrorism results from an equal mixture of anguish and optimism. Frustration with political conditions and prevailing sentiments leads to the conclusion that the ruling powers have perverted the ideals of liberty and equality and pulled the wool over the majority of the people, leaving only the revolutionary whose alienation grants them freedom from self-deception. The yawning gap between an intense desire for transformative social change and its minimal influence generates feelings of alienation and angst worthy of a Dostoevsky protagonist. A sense of righteous rage will take on an especially bitter tinge if one has witnessed or taken part in a revolutionary movement only to have it fall short of expectations as members die, go to prison, or lose faith in the cause.[23] The omnipresence of the nation-state and the permeation of the bourgeois culture that so often follows in its wake phases out the alternatives to conformity by sanctifying the interests and tastes of the masses. This fixes knowledge and morality on exclusively empirical grounds, since nothing can be good or true that is beyond the comprehension of the general public. The resultant inability to conceive or act upon a higher purpose than personal gratification means that, as Nietzsche describes it, "insofar as we believe in morality, we pass sentence on existence."[24] Pessimism slips into nihilism when "all one has left is the repudiated world, and one adds this supreme disappointment to the reasons why it deserves to be repudiated,"[25] conflating the faculty of moral judgment with an urge toward self-destruction.

Disgust with modernity causes an existential crisis for the individual, but it ironically furnishes hope that a societal condition of rage and despair will eventually render the masses open to a shift in consciousness. The disjuncture between the egalitarian premise of the nation-state and the likely reality of inequality guarantees the existence of a disaffected audience amenable to calls for dramatic upheaval. The prospective members of the promised meritocracy will fall short of their expected station and suspect the workings of a hidden oligarchy rigging the system in their favor. This "alienated young man of promise, who appears in all modernizing countries . . . articulates a profound sense of inadequacy, and tries to draw an ambitious blueprint to overcome it." Initially, they may be confident that fellow members of the "educated minority" will have arrived at the same conclusion and that the "illiterate majority"[26] will defer to their leadership.

If the public is surprisingly resistant to spontaneous mobilization, this provides additional evidence of an elite conspiracy to suppress the popular will. Violence then becomes both a practical necessity and a morally praiseworthy act in and of itself, on the basis that anything which is harmful to society is good for the individual. The use of violence then enables the underground movement to leverage mass media, the principal binding agent of modern society, into a tool for disseminating its own counter-narrative.[27] The police can disrupt a meeting of subversives or toss their press into a river, but it cannot disabuse the public of its fascination with seemingly senseless violence or its desire to understand the motivations of its perpetrators. Such actions signal to the disaffected that their private anguish is in fact a universally felt malaise, and that all it takes is one concerted push to actualize a new and more authentic vision of communal identity. The terrorist aims to resolve the essential paradox of the nation-state by articulating a rational plan for a community, the precise shape of which unfolds through each of its members professing and demonstrating their total commitment. Once the masses achieve self-awareness, their irrepressible voice will drown out the elites whose tenuous position hinged entirely on their ability to distract or deceive the people from their true interest. On its own, the wrathful spirit of the nihilist would find a virtuous end only in self-destruction. When that same spirit grafts itself upon the nation, it becomes a catalyst of communal purgation and rebirth.

THE THEORY OF NON-STATE TERROR

State-Directed Terrorism and Non-State Terrorism Compared

Both state and non-state terror share the basic basic ambition of shaping a new political community over which the architects of the campaign can then claim undisputed leadership. The justification for this community stems from a universal ideology that professes a morally superior alternative to prevailing structures. Lacking access to, or the patience for, conventional means of attracting a target audience or defending it against external forces, "the terrorist will slash through [the] Gordian knot"[28] of politics and turn warfare into a pure contest of brute force. An approximation of absolute war shakes the masses out of their individualistic stupor into a stark awareness that any deficiency in public spiritedness is a critical liability against an enemy implacably dedicated to their destruction. In both sets of cases, the perception of absolute war is more important than its literal achievement. The prospect of the climactic showdown serves mainly to expedite popular mobilization to the point where no enemy could hope to prevail in such an engagement. The purpose of terrorism is to smash an existing trinity and reconstitute a new one through a fixed sequence, in which a condition of primordial violence adopts a model of perfect military discipline in order to attain an ideal political end-state.

The key difference between the two types of terrorism is the specific nature of the victory that each is seeking. In the case of state-directed terrorism, a regime turns to terrorism for the simple goal of staying in power, which forces it to work within the parameters of the state system even as it challenges or ignores its prevailing norms. It cannot refashion society in its image unless it has sufficient control over the army, police, and other bureaucratic agencies that it seeks to purge. While cultivating mass support for its ideology is the highest form of security, it can also expect some measure of public support from ingrained habits of patriotism and the presumption of the state as the guarantor of law and order. Even if it plunges its own society into chaos or engages in subversion beyond its borders, the regime can still enjoy many of the privileges of sovereignty, including a monopoly of legitimate force, control over mass media, and a network of formal and informal diplomatic relations. None of these assets are a guarantee against overthrow or invasion, but since the regime is seeking stability in spite of its disruptive means, most citizens and foreign statesmen will most of the time prefer the devil they know over the unforeseeable alternative.

A hybrid status as an ideological vessel and sovereign state permits the regime to define success in relative terms. A revolutionary agitator with few sympathizers abroad can declare success every day that it persists against the presumed antagonism of the status quo powers. It can tailor its ideological message to justify practically any conceivable foreign policy measure, and thereby take part in an essentially conventional sequence of war and peace. But while the regime can become a fully fledged member of international society, it can never fully discard the instruments of terrorism without exposing its ideational monopoly to a potentially fatal challenge. Nor will it always have the luxury to moderate or escalate the use of terrorism at a moment of its choosing. Shoring up a standard trinity of people, army, and government, and focusing on the demands of real war almost always represents a welcome change from the apocalyptic urgency of absolute war to competition for relative stakes. The main danger of this transition is the sudden emergence of a threat to the regime's legitimacy that again draws the regime into a condition of war that pits that trinity against itself. A regime that used terror to consolidate power can never fully escape the dilemma of guarding against future instability through the deliberate undermining of its own social fabric.

A non-state terrorist campaign faces a much more formidable barrier to victory, as it is seeking to acquire rather than hold a position of power, against an enemy wielding the assets of the modern state and enjoying the presumptive loyalty of its citizens. As Martha Crenshaw states, terrorism emerges when "discontent is not generalized or severe enough to provoke the majority of the populace to action against the regime . . . [terrorism] may thus be a sign of a stable society rather than the symptom of fragility and impending collapse."[29] The non-state terrorist campaign must undertake a complete transformation from underground cadre to mass political movement with no means of gauging public support in advance. It must then cultivate public support through means that undermine public order and are likely to invite retaliation that it cannot directly absorb without collapsing. A state-directed terrorist campaign perfects a victory that began with the seizure of power, while the non-state terrorist lacks the ability to assemble its forces until after it has already declared war. All terrorist campaigns depend upon other states for their affirmation, which is of course easier to gain when one already enjoys the trappings of sovereignty. A non-state campaign may choose to appropriate the features of a sovereign state to boost its legitimacy, but cannot do so without undermining its cohesion as a revolutionary underground. Failing to manage the delicate balance between fear and respectability can ruin the prospects of an otherwise powerful and popular organization.

However formidable the obstacles to complete victory may be, the organization can avoid defeat as long as it exhibits the potential for escalation or burrows deeply enough within political structures to achieve a degree of institutional solidity. The effective use of terrorism gradually reduces its own necessity by compelling the enemy to accept what they once held to be intolerable and demonstrating to a target audience that the dream has become a reality. From that point on, it can accommodate itself to more conventional political channels by claiming to have appropriated them on behalf of their revolutionary ambitions. The exact point at which the campaign can plausibly declare victory, and the best means of reaching it, depends upon its ability to construe a narrative of absolute war from the conditions of an actual duel with an enemy that it cannot defeat outright. It must introduce a form of combat that a conventional force cannot control without undermining the basis of its own legitimacy, while reserving the power to reward compliance with its demands. The campaign must escalate just enough for the enemy to still be able to make a rational calculation to submit before the momentum of combat deprives it of the power to choose.

Genius and Non-State Terror

At first, the disparity between the scope of a terrorist campaign's ambition and their disadvantage in numbers, capabilities, and reputation will strike most observers as despicable, absurd, or both. The dismal fate of most non-state terrorist campaigns, which on average collapse after a period between five and nine years,[30] indicates that the public's reticence is entirely reasonable, since the means of terrorism will most likely fail to achieve the ends. Although the odds of outright victory will remain prohibitive throughout the campaign, the campaign can profit from this expectation and use the strength of its opponent to its own advantage in the manner of a judoist or a matador.[31] Every time the state fails in the attempt to use brute strength to stomp out a patently inferior foe, it signals either its own incompetence or that the campaign enjoys greater public backing than expected. Every time that the campaign defies the expectation of its impending defeat, it dares its enemy to intensify their efforts at the risk of still greater humiliation until its lack of moral and political capital nullifies its advantage in capabilities. Since legitimacy is the primary objective of a terrorist campaign rather than any concrete gain, the enemy's loss of face is automatically to their benefit as long as they have trained the public to focus its attention on the contest.

Provoking a superior power, evading the force of its wrath, holding the public interest, and promoting a desired interpretation of events in the public consciousness imposes a high standard of genius within a terrorist campaign. Maximizing the effectiveness of terrorist violence and propaganda requires that each member of the organization, in Clausewitzian terms, "completely immerse his personality in the appointed task."[32] Whether it operates through a pyramidical hierarchy or a network of semi-autonomous cells, there is precious little middle ground between "the smooth harmony of the whole activity"[33] and disaster. A chain of command in a conventional army endures because it can generally assume the safety of its leadership and noncombat personnel, while every single participant in a terrorist campaign is potentially subject to death, imprisonment, or betrayal at a moment's notice. The precariousness of the organizational structure and the consequent need for adaptability at all levels of command prohibits a neat classification of virtues and skills among tacticians, strategists, and political decision-makers. Accordingly, the full burden of genius fall directly on all participants. The vulnerability of each part, and the risk of disruption in any quarter undermining the whole, demands that each component intuitively understand how to achieve a "harmonious combination of elements, in which one or the other ability may predominate, but none may be in conflict with the rest."[34]

The acute sensitivity of a terrorist campaign extends to its public perception. The errors of terrorist campaigns are "more consequential than a comparable error by a state," not only because it is liable to a devastating counterblow, but also because its brand must remain unblemished if expects to convince followers and sympathizers to undertake enormous risks on its behalf. As Audrey Cronin points out, a state enjoys a sufficient "degree of immortality in the international system" to regard its own existence as an end unto itself, while a terrorist campaign is an avowedly provisional means of achieving the end of forming a new community. "Governments are expected to be hypocritical; terrorist [campaigns] cannot afford it."[35] Any conspicuous failure to interpret the strategic environment correctly, implement the right tactics, or anticipate the political ramifications of their actions threatens to rupture its professed union of word and deed. If the internal logic of the campaign becomes divorced from external perceptions, the cause may appear to be better served by a different group, different methods, or lose its appeal altogether.

Such a standard of perfect organizational genius is all the more difficult to achieve, given the particular constraints under which a terrorist campaign operates. Recruitment alone can never determine whether or not a prospective terrorist possesses "great strength of character, as well as great lucidity and firmness of mind," and can be trusted to "follow through steadily, to carry out the plan, and not to be thrown off course by thousands of diversions." Only the test of battle reveals the extent of genius, and before it has the chance to gain combat experience, incompetence may prevent the campaign from ever developing the habits of professionalism that it needs to draw competent recruits. To make matters worse, terrorists experience forms of friction that prohibit a proper search for potential geniuses. In any military organization, expecting every member to "possess the combination of qualities needed to make him a greater than the average commander"[36] is illogical on its face. Adding the problems of a limited recruiting pool, uncertain access to training, and frequent turnover further diminishes the likelihood of attracting, holding, and effectively utilizing the most capable combatants.

The nature of a terrorist campaign also restricts the exercise of the intellectual qualities necessary for genius to flourish. Terrorist commanders are unlikely to enjoy sufficient access to their own forces to make accurate assessments of their overall capabilities and morale.

The inherent risks involved in essential noncombat tasks such as disseminating propaganda, acquiring supplies, and collecting intelligence covers the entire organization in a dense fog of war. A persistent state of imminent danger tends to favor innovation in immediately useful combat skills rather than a comprehensive education in moral courage and prudential judgment. Even if a campaign were to populate itself entirely with geniuses, this would actually prevent any of them from realizing their intellectual and moral po-

tential. A genius on the battlefield or in the command tent is no less susceptible to "deep anxiety" than the ordinary soldier, but manages to overcome it
through an awareness of "all those who, directly or indirectly, have entrusted
[them] with their thoughts and feelings, hopes and fears."[37] A collection of
geniuses would lack the basis of comparison that elevates one over the others, and that distinction must be clear in order for the lesser intellect to
accede to the leadership of the genius. If everyone was equally convinced of
their own superiority, then each would accept only their own authority.

Terrorist campaigns are of course not entirely composed of geniuses, but
the likely limits on command and control make them radically dependent on
the skill of each individual. This can be particularly problematic for strategy,
as the willingness to partake in a terrorist campaign often reflects intense
personal motives that do not easily enfold within a broader organizational
schema. Assuming that the campaign successfully inculcates a spirit of total
devotion, the conflation of the group and the individual can work both ways,
with each projecting their own unique experiences and cognitive biases onto
the whole. The prospect of advancing a righteous mission "contributes to
consolidating psychosocial identities at a time of great societal instability and
flux," but shared commitment to a cause does not automatically translate into
organizational effectiveness. People who exhibit "greater-than-normal reliance on the psychological mechanisms of externalization and splitting"[38] are
just as likely to exhibit those qualities against one another as a common
enemy.

The socialization of recruits seeks to minimize this friction through a
process of "redefining oneself as a new or reborn person, often involving a
renunciation of the past . . . taking on the new faith as a more or less totalistic
wave of life."[39] At the same time, it cannot be so successful in indoctrinating
its recruits that it saps them of the initiative that they will surely need in the
field. Terrorist campaigns have a distinctly trinitarian problem in which its
fluid operational model admits a necessary tension between passion and
political supervision. As Louise Richardson states, "philosophical or political
aspirations are of greater interest to the leadership of the movements, while
followers are more attracted by the nearer-term appeal of revenge, renown,
and reaction . . . it is this success that appeals to disaffected youths seeking a
means of rapid redress."[40] A decentralized structure may be necessary for
evading detection, but under such conditions lower-ranking, less experienced
members eager to prove their mettle are much more likely to kill civilians,
often to the chagrin of their politically savvier leaders.[41] On the other hand,
the imposition of strict political control is likely to prompt open disagreement between principals and agents, especially as lower-ranking members
accumulate the prestige of combat experience with which they can challenge
the senior leadership.[42]

Not even the most brilliant commander will ever strike a perfect balance between the political utility of attacks and the urge among its membership to commit them. The conflicting preferences of its members inhibit the organization from simply positing stable objectives that it can advance through alternating phases of coercion and negotiation. Shared commitment to the formation of a new community through violence and propaganda may be strong enough to commence a campaign, but it is also vague enough to prohibit a fixed and concrete set of grievances and demands.[43] In contrast to the conventional genius who finds the prudent middle ground within the trinity, the genius of terrorism is the maximization of passion within its target audience and political calculation outside of it. Attacks serve as "costly signals" that "provide credible information to the audiences whose behavior they hope to influence."[44] No terrorist campaign is capable of achieving absolute war in the purely Clausewitzian sense of amassing enough strength to break the will of an enemy. Rather, it approaches the absolute by triggering a cycle of action and reaction among enemies, prospective supporters, and interested observers. Public perception of the organization as implacable and ruthless compels each audience to configure their own behavior around the certainty of future terrorism.[45] The prospect of inevitable escalation leaves enemies susceptible to instruction on the course of action necessary to avoid the pain of absolute war and makes supporters all the more eager to claim a share of its benefits.

Non-State Terrorism and the "Diplomacy of Violence"

There is considerable overlap between the strategy of non-state terrorism and what Thomas Schelling referred to "the diplomacy of violence," also known as coercive diplomacy. Like coercive diplomacy, terrorism is an alternative to brute force or a "contest of strength" in which the the stronger combatant overcomes the weaker and seizes an objective from them directly. Coercion relies on "the power to hurt" rather than the power to take, compelling desired behavior through the threat of violence, especially "violence that can still be withheld or inflicted, or that a victim believes can be withheld or inflicted."[46] Terrorism also shares in Schelling's description of a contest of "endurance, nerve, obstinacy, and pain," a "dirty, extortionate, and often quite reluctant [process of] bargaining"[47] that, when compared to the historical record, appears fully consistent with many widespread and even accepted features of modern war. In Schelling's understanding, terrorism is a variation of conventional warfare that results from one side's inability to resort to brute force.[48] Their adaptation of a pure strategy of pain puts the most shocking and disturbing features on full display, but this represents a difference in degree rather than kind from other types of combat.

This interpretation misses a critical difference between the role of pain in each strategy. Coercive diplomacy rests on the premise that both sides would prefer to avoid pain, and resort to it only as a grim necessity. As Schelling points out, "violence is most purposive and most successful when it is threatened and not used. Successful threats are those that do not have to be carried out." The fact of the enemy's suffering "gives us little or no satisfaction compared with what he can do," and the success of a coercive strategy depends upon "finding a bargain" in which the costs of compliance is less than that of continued obstinance. While inflicting pain may be the only effective means of changing the adversary's calculus, its direct effects are entirely negative for those on the giving end no less than the receiving end. Inflicting pain erodes the commonality of interest that makes a coercive threat credible. If the enemy's pain "were our greatest delight and our satisfaction his greatest woe, we would just proceed to hurt and frustrate each other."[49] Mutual destruction of value not only reduces incentives for compliance, but also risks inflicting so much damage that compliance is no longer physically possible.

Terrorists similarly use violence as a means of psychological conditioning, but few if any organizations have achieved their objectives as a direct result of the pain they were able to inflict. The organization almost certainly lacks the unity of purpose and range of capabilities to issue a demand, reward compliance, and raise the costs of noncompliance as part of a logical sequence of deterrence or compellence.[50] Neither the specific demands nor the actions of terrorism can become predictable without diminishing the shock factor which provides terrorists with their distinct tactical advantage. For terrorists, pain is not a tool for eliciting a desired response, but a means of reconfiguring politics itself to fit their narrative of existential struggle and inevitable triumph. As Albert Bandura points out,

> "the victims are incidental to the terrorists' intended objectives and are used simply as a way to provoke social conditions designed to further their broader aims. Third-party violence is especially socially terrorizing when the victimization is generalized to the civilian population and is unpredictable, thereby instilling a widespread sense of personal vulnerability."[51]

The pain that results from a terrorist attack and any subsequent retaliation is a universal language with which terrorists can communicate simultaneously to each of their various audiences. There is no way to guarantee that the audience will respond in a desired fashion, but a sufficient degree of pain ensures that there will at least be a reaction. An audience that meets an attack with revulsion, anger, or sympathy signals where it is most likely to fit within the campaign's narrative, supplying the campaign with the information to tailor subsequent actions that push them further toward a desired position. So long as the campaign is driving the process of action and reaction, it can break down a complex set of interests and sympathies into an unequivocal binary of friendship and hostility. From there, the experience of inflicting and absorbing pain reinforces that dichotomy still further, wearing down the mere possibility of politics outside the exclusive categories of victory or defeat.

Pain is most useful insofar as it reduces each audience's confidence in the utility of conventional restraints on the use of force. If the attackers leave a clear path for retaliation, then the aggrieved state can simply utilize its police or military forces to satisfy public demands for safety without compromising its institutions.[52] If instead the attackers provide no clear target for retaliation, or become embedded within their target audience that any retaliation would disproportionately affect civilians rather than members of the organization, then the state faces a severe dilemma. The state can either refrain from retaliation and compromise its monopoly on legitimate violence, or engage in a brutal crackdown which undermines its claim to be the guarantor of law and order. Either way, the terrorists' target audience will recognize that the state is unable to protect them, making "the aggrieved public more inclined toward extremism because the opportunity costs of violence are lowered."[53] The weakening of conventional barriers accelerates the process of moral disengagement, feeding a mutual willingness to inflict greater suffering with fewer pangs of conscience. Each subsequent act of belligerence reinforces the antagonism of the warring sides, encourages the adoption of increasingly radical means, and compels the masses to view one another through the prism of their own unimpeachable virtue and the other's immutable evil.[54]

As the passions of its target audience align with the political objectives of the campaign, the reason and passion of the state become increasingly contradictory. The primordial desire to punish wrongdoing is likely to "evoke feelings of dishonor and humiliation rather than fear or submission"[55] and galvanize support for terrorism rather than deter it. Even if the state recognizes that retaliation is counterproductive, refusing to keep up the pace of escalation would amount to a humiliating concession to an enemy that it had previously regarded as a hateful gang of fanatical outlaws. It cannot defend the status quo except through means that destabilize it further, prompting another agonizing choice between causing still greater instability or squandering the value of previous sacrifices. Within the organization's target audience, the breakdown of norms and institutions only reifies the "politicized social identity"[56] by which members recognize one another in terms of a shared grievance expressed through symbolic violence. As long as the organization continues to demonstrate its viability, its intended public confronts the prospect of indefinite escalation. This in turn enhances the organization's ability to mobilize resources, expand its tactical portfolio, advertise its own effectiveness, and draw greater levels of support.[57] Its application of a pure theory of war exposes the vulnerabilities of organizational and emotional friction that inhibit all conventional entities while exhibiting its own immunity to such frailties.

NON-STATE TERRORISM IN PRACTICE

State-Makers and State-Wreckers

War is extremely resistant to classification, as its objectives depend entirely on the peculiarities of circumstance. Every major innovation in military technology and politics scrambles the relationship between them, leaving only general lessons on the dangers of unintended escalation or the difficulty of terminating a war as easily as commencing it. [58] The basic objective of non-state terrorism is always the formation of a new community through violence and propaganda, and is thus more likely to feature recurring patterns of behavior that extend across technological, cultural, and methodological differences. Scholars have divided the history of non-state terrorism into four types, each based on prevailing ideological motivations, characteristic tactics, and the ways in which they reflected broader international trends. [59] David Rapoport's model of the "four waves" has proven the most influential, positing a chronological progression of anarchist, nationalist, New Left, and religious waves, each of which tend to last about a generation. [60] Marc Sedgwick offers an adapted chronology that more closely links global ideological trends to particular sources of inspiration, arriving at a classification of Italian, German, Chinese, and Afghan waves that overlap chronically and range between forty and one hundred and twenty years. [61] Tom Parker and Nick Sitter challenge the notion of separate and successive waves with a concept of four "strains," socialist, nationalist, religious, and exclusionist, which overlap in time and are distinguished by both the titular ideology and their tactical mirroring of one another. [62]

The main weakness for each of these approaches is that none of them properly identifies the common thread running through each of their subcategories, so that they offer versions of terrorism without defining the thing itself. The approximation of absolute war identifies the common end-point and methodology of terrorist campaigns, which then provides a basis of comparison through which to separate one period of terrorism from another, parse the differences among contemporaneous groups, and identify the trends that reoccur in some groups and not others. All terrorists seek the approximation of absolute war in order to shape a new political community, the main difference being the relationship between character of the proposed community and international society. The two types of communal formation that they may pursue are "state-making" and "state-wrecking." A terrorist campaign seeks either to shape a new a people for entry into the existing international system or clear away the authority of the state to create space for an idealized form of popular association based on a non-national criteria such as class, religion, or a cosmopolitan ideal.

Both forms of absolute war advertise themselves as professing superior fidelity to the prevailing sentiments of world public opinion. Terrorism forces international society to view itself in a funhouse mirror, twisting the avowed guardians of law and order into terrorists and terrorists into noble freedom fighters. The adoption of brutal and shocking methods is not a sign of barbarism or psychosis, but an untainted commitment to eliminate all impediments to the fulfillment of widely desired social change, especially when compared to the hypocrisy and baneful compromises of the status quo. State-makers presume the ability to precisely define the physical and demographic boundaries of a nation, and therefore serve as a more authentic model of the nation-state than the self-appointed gatekeepers of international order. State-breakers look instead to the promised benefits of life within an orderly system of states, such as individual freedom and social equality, and insist that the actual fulfillment of those ideals requires the destruction of the state. In both sets of cases, acts of terror double as moral education, instructing the target audience in the insufficiency of existing structures and the efficacy of philosophically informed violence in achieving personal and political fulfillment.

State-makers typically build off of an existing tradition of popular protest or asymmetric warfare, which can fill in many of the informational gaps that would otherwise prevent a campaign from gauging its tactical prowess or popular support in advance. The transition to terrorism often seizes on a seminal event, whether a local incident such as a government atrocity or a global turning point like the end of a major war. A heady atmosphere enables them to convert a latent desire for reform into a sudden embrace of revolutionary violence in the expectation of dramatic results. Launching onto the scene at the peak of public outrage and international attention can cement an external perception of the organization as a government-in-exile whose regrettable adoption of terrorism is meant to shake the world out of its indifference to their eminently reasonable aims. Its military wing will represent itself as a guerrilla army whose unconventional tactics are simply a prudent response to power disparities, while its political wing courts the favor of governments and other powerful actors in order to to ensconce its presence on the world stage.

State-wrecking is similarly predicated on blurring the moral differences between its own actions and those of the state, but rather than aspire to the status of the state, they seek to drag the state down to the level of the terrorist. State-wreckers do not emerge *ex nihilo*, and most likely drift to terrorism as a consequence of disillusionment in alternative methods, but they are unable to translate their grievance into a political program that the status quo powers could accede to even if they wished to do so. Isolated from society and doubtful of the prospects for revolutionary change, the state-wrecker wages a solitary war against an overbearing system for the sake of demonstrating their complete personal liberation from all external constraints, especially manmade law and morality. Rather than advance a specific agenda, the purpose of violence is to prove that ruling institutions reflect nothing more than the selfish will of their beneficiaries. In this understanding, all systems ultimately rest on a foundation of coercion and have concealed that fact only to the extent that they have lulled their people into semi-conscious compliance. The majority of people will initially view acts of rebellion with horror and disgust, but over time the allure of self-assertion through violence will give rise to a new community of truly free individuals.

The Shared Origins of State-Making and State-Wrecking

The emergence of non-state terrorism in the latter half of the nineteenth century introduced the model of the state-maker and the state-wrecker in their purest possible form. In both cases, "it is easy to discern echoes of the ethos behind the French Revolution."[63]

Aspiring revolutionaries across Europe cherry-picked aspects of Jacobin doctrine, from the Nation in Arms to the maximum fulfillment of the Rights of Man, and used them to rally popular sentiment against an inegalitarian social order. The adoption of terrorism in particular reflected a combination of optimism regarding the emergence of genuine popular consciousness and despair over the refusal of entrenched elites to accept their fate. The revolutions of 1848, Russia's defeat in the Crimean War, and the gathering of Irish expatriates in North America under the republican banner each suggested a a fragile system on the brink of collapse. Yet each of these events proved to have limited long-term impact. Peaceful reformism such as Alexander II's liberation of the serfs had failed to dislodge fundamental iniquities, and attempts at direct incitement of the masses left revolutionary forces exposed to repression, as in the failed 1867 Fenian Uprising or the 1871 Paris Commune.

Sensing an imminent victory that was just out of reach, the adoption of terrorism made a virtue out of necessity. Rather than rally the masses to confront the state directly, an elite vanguard would sacrifice themselves and tie down the state in endless warfare to rupture bit by bit the cracks in its edifice until they burst open, leaving the path wide open for the people to assert themselves without opposition. The primary form of linkage between the terrorists and the people they claimed to represent was the myth that emerged from the aggregation of their actions, the propaganda justifying them, the response of authorities, and sensational media coverage along every step. The self-representation of the terrorist as lonely, righteous, and doomed was a creative effort to mold the archetypical hero of the age and a practical response to past failures. During they heyday of classical liberalism and Romanticism, the terrorist sought to embody both John Stuart Mill's model of *homo economicus* and the gloomy Byronic hero who "knew himself a villain, but he deem'd/The rest no better than the thing he seem'd." Violence was a utilitarian means of bringing about the greatest good for the greatest number in the quickest possible time, at the cost of their own suffering and near-certain condemnation within their lifetime.

The pioneering example of state-making was the Fenian campaign and it adoption of terrorism in the early 1880s. Groups such as *Clann na nGael*, United Irishmen, and the Irish Republican Brotherhood regarded themselves as the continuation of a long tradition of guerrilla warfare against British rule. After having failed to provoke a popular uprising, *Irish World* editor Patrick Ford declared in 1875 that

> "we should oppose a general insurrection in Ireland as untimely and ill-advised. But we believe in action nonetheless. The Irish cause requires Skirmishers. It requires a little band of heroes who will initiate and keep up without intermission a guerrilla warfare—men who will fly over land and sea like invisible beings."[64]

From 1881 to 1885, Fenian operates conducted a series of dynamite attacks in Britain itself, primarily against barracks and railway stations, with the intention of creating a facsimile of war despite acute shortages in personnel and materiel. Using time-delay explosives so that the perpetrators could escape prior to the blast, this "cumulative effect strategy"[65] would either make average British soldier and traveler feel the high costs of occupation, prompting either negotiation or an indiscriminate retaliation that would at last trigger the long-hoped-for mass insurrection. Recruitment, financing, and propaganda took place primarily in the United States with the intent of placing it beyond the reach of British police, especially the Special Branch which formed in 1883 in direct response to the dynamite campaign.

While each of these features would become permanent trademarks of nationalist terrorism, the Fenians would prove to be more of a lesson to absorb and improve upon than a model for imitation. Police surveillance and organizational ineptitude inhibited the flow of support from ringleaders in New York and Boston to the operatives in the field, harming morale and leaving the bombers isolated and exposed. As Niall Wheelman points out, "arrests and long prison sentences also resulted form the lack of material support provided to the dynamiters during their missions and while awaiting trial."[66] The campaign also failed to move the needle within the broader ranks of the Irish nationalist movement, since neither the leaders nor rank-and-file were integrated within the Irish population and so Fenians actions and the British reaction were alike remote from their experience. Within Ireland itself, "urban guerrilla warfare was imagined not as a replacement, but as a complement to other methods of political agitation praised by land reform agitators, the Irish Parliamentary Party and the wider nationalist movement in general."[67] The halting of the dynamite campaign in 1885 coincided with reforms in the British voting system turned the Home Rule movement into a potent political force. As soon as other avenues emerged for the Irish nation to negotiate its political standing, terrorism was more a hindrance than a help.

The Fenian campaign commenced only a few weeks prior to the assassination of Tsar Alexander II in March 1881, which signaled the rise of state-wrecking terrorism. This act inspired an outbreak of anarchist violence across Europe and the Americas, including the assassination of heads of state in France, Austria, Spain, Italy, and the United States, generating widespread fear of "a mighty international conspiracy undermining the entire established order."[68] The architects of the Tsar's demise, *Narodnaya Volya* ("People's Will"), had formed from the clubs of radical *narodniks* which had cultivated widespread support among the upper crust of the Russian intelligentsia before falling under the watchful eye of the Third Department.[69] Desperate to strike a decisive blow before falling into the dragnet, the group focused their efforts almost entirely on the assassination of the Autocrat. Killing the "Tsar Liberator" would smash the sanctified aura of the autocracy and usher in a far more perfect revolution at much lower cost than the glacial pace of state-sponsored reform which left the oppressive structure of the regime intact. As *Narodnaya Volya* leader Vera Figner later wrote,

> "the destruction of the absolutist form of government was the most vital aspect of our program, the part that had the greatest importance to me. I really didn't care whether the regime was replaced by a republic or a constitutional monarchy. The crucial thing was that conditions be created under which people could develop their capacities and apply them to the benefit of society."[70]

When the organization finally succeeded in killing the tsar in March 1881, it became evident that "the means they had chosen to achieve their goal . . . limited the spread of their ideas among the intelligentsia, and that the people would never understand their actions without this."[71] Unable to cultivate the social conditions that justified their operational imperative, its leadership soon fell victim to the newly formed *Okhrana* and the *agents provocateurs* it had managed to insert within the revolutionary ranks.[72]

Like their Jacobin forebears, the Fenians and Russian *narodniks* attempted to replicate a model of absolute war wholesale, leaving them incapable of adjusting when events failed to align with expectations. Both presented a model of the thoroughly militarized individual who had subjected their entire passion and reason to the destruction of an enemy, whose escalation would succeed only in prompting the emergence of a community whose entire membership would replicate the example of the heroic individual. As nineteenth-century Russian anarchist Sergei Nechaev wrote in his "Catechism of the Revolutionist," the terrorist must have "no personal interests, no business affairs, no emotions, no attachments, no property, and no name. Everything in him is wholly absorbed in the single thought and the single passion for revolution." No hint of scruple or sentiment can interfere with with the central task of finding "the surest and quickest way to destroy the whole filthy order."[73]

The pure models of state-making and state-wrecking both assumed that their example would be sufficient to induce mass participation while operating within distinct, isolated cadres whose existence, and ultimate fate, had practically no direct bearing on the welfare of their avowed community. A strategy of absolute war would not survive its first contact with reality unless it could first instruct their target audience in the character of the struggle and then compel them to take part to ensure not just their political future, but their immediate survival. This would necessitate a selective integration of the state-making and state-breaking models, which had each proved themselves insufficient on their own. A successful campaign would require both a discernible set of objectives, the satisfaction of which would reduce the need for terrorism, and an ethos of pure destruction that would tear down the status quo and leave their target audience with little choice other than to adopt their example. For example, the assassination of the Archduke Franz Ferdinand and his wife at the hands of Serb nationalist Gavrilo Princip in June 1914 specifically targeted the chief advocate of Slavic co-equality within the Dual Monarchy. The outrage surrounding his murder dispelled any prospect of the moderate political solution he had advocated in life.[74] Vienna would seek revenge against Belgrade, forcing the Serbs to rise up as a nation or face obliteration.

For most of the twentieth century, the most successful linkages of organization and audience occurred primarily within the camp of the state-makers, who had learned to direct the locus of terrorism onto their own target audience as much as on their external enemies. Hitler's *Sturm-Abteilung* terrorized the interwar German public into a state of fervent impatience with the Weimar Republic and helped him win mainstream acceptance of the Nazi program.[75] Nationalist insurgencies in China and Vietnam explicitly held up terrorism, particularly punitive acts against noncompliant members of their own prospective community, as the first stage of revolution, to be followed by guerrilla attacks and then conventional warfare.[76] Other efforts were not so able to effect such a complete transition from subversive violence to statehood, leading them to integrate the objectives of the state-maker with the methodology of the state-wrecker.

The Convergence of State-Making and State-Wrecking

In the immediate wake of the Second World War, anti-colonial movements in India, Indonesia, Kenya, and dozens of other states from the newly designated "Third World" were poised to seize upon the prevailing sentiments of the era and advance the cause of national self-determination. With the charter of the United Nations confirming the nation-state as the sole legitimate form of political organization, colonial subjects and other victims of systemic oppression could represent themselves a more authentic embodiment of the charter's ideals than its authors, who particularly in the case of Britain and France were often the ones holding them in bondage. Should the colonial powers continue to betray their own professed ideals and resist the call for national self-determination, then nothing would exemplify the fact of emerging nationhood more vividly than a people in arms united against a foreign oppressor.[77] Referring to Algeria's struggle against France, Frantz Fanon celebrated "the important part played by the war in leading [the people] toward consciousness of themselves . . . we have realized that the masses are equal to the problems which confront them."[78] However, a moral claim alone would not prove sufficient should the ruling power value its possession more than appeasement of world public opinion. With no hope of defeating their enemy in combat or building a state through political agitation, insurgent groups would have to adopt terrorism to demonstrate their claim to viable statehood, threatening to punish the obstinance of their enemies and the outside world with a credible threat of absolute war.

The two foundational examples of this phase of terrorism are the various Zionist movements which helped establish the State of Israel in 1948, and the *Front de Libération Nationale* (FLN) which led the struggle against French colonialism in Algeria and has dominated Algerian politics ever since their victory in 1962. By the end of the Second World War, the Jews of the Palestinian Mandate had already developed a capable network of paramilitary organizations to defend against Arab riots, facilitate illegal Jewish immigration, and prepare for a possible Axis invasion. During the war, the Haganah ("the Defense") helped suppress the attempts by its more radical offshoots, the Irgun ("National Military Organization") and Lehi ("Fighters for the Freedom of Israel") to take advantage of British weakness, opting instead for collaboration in the expectation of a favorable settlement after the war.[79] When the postwar Labour government reneged on its promise to relax strict quotas on Jewish immigration for fear of inflaming Arab sentiment, even after the revelation of the Holocaust, the three groups aligned in their strategic purpose while continuing to pursue different tactics. The Haganah would represent itself throughout as the incipient military and police force of an emerging Jewish state, while the Irgun and Lehi directed attacks against British forces and Arab civilians so as to make the territory ungovernable.[80]

Algerian nationalists likewise gained traction immediately after the Second World War, when the successive defeats of the French to the Germans and then the Vichy to the Allies permanently smashed the myth of colonial superiority. In 1954, less than six months after the French defeat at Dien Bien Phu, the *Front de Libération Nationale* commenced its armed campaign with a leadership almost entirely composed of French army veterans. Standing in the way of their repeating the Viet Minh's success were the million-plus European *colons* who dominated the economic and political life of Algeria and had the voting power to wreck any parliamentary coalition in the metropole that even hinted at colonial reform.[81] The twin objectives of the FLN were to establish themselves as a concrete, unified representative of Algerian national consciousness and then threaten both the French and the *colons* with a complete collapse of social order should their claims go unacknowledged. By 1956, the FLN had introduced its signature tactic of dressing women in European garb to sneak them past checkpoints and plant bombs in cafes, theaters, and other targets populated with civilian *colons*. The certainty of retaliatory violence between the two communities would leave France with a painful choice between restraining the *colons* and risk a political backlash or watch the colony descend into anarchy.

Neither movement had a hope of winning through military means. Zionist attacks on British targets, while shocking, would never be enough to to inflict unacceptable damage or impose unmanageable costs. British raids on Jewish settlements and weapons caches crippled the Haganah's military capability, and the Irgun's bombing of the King David Hotel in July 1946 soured public opinion even among Zionist circles. Within ten months, the alliance of the Jewish Resistance Movement was over, and each group once again went their separate ways after less than a year of active cooperation.[82] The French were similarly successful in suppressing the armed campaign of the FLN and its guerrilla wing, the *Armée de Libération Nationale.* By 1958, the French army had reduced the flow of weapons and fighters from Tunisia and Morocco to a trickle and expelled the ALN outright from Algiers through the systematic use of torture to uncover FLN safe-houses and official toleration of *colon* vigilantism.[83]

External political support partially offset losses on the battlefield, with the United States and Soviet Union finding rare common ground in support of both both the Zionists and the FLN. Widespread sympathy for Zionism in the wake of the Holocaust combined with growing anti-colonial sentiment led to the formation of United Nations Special Committee on Palestine, which recommended partition in September 1947. Revelations of French brutality in Algiers and French incursions into Tunisia bolstered the political status of the FLN, which opened up offices in Washington, D.C., New York, Cairo, and Moscow.[84] In order to leverage these assets into a strategic victory, both movements had to extend the threat of disaster to their own people no less than enemies and observers. Even during its periods of truce with the British, the Haganah focused its efforts on the *Aliyah Bet* campaign of "boat propaganda," alternately smuggling refugees and deliberately damaging or sinking ships packed with Holocaust survivors to the severe embarrassment of the British authorities.[85] Meanwhile, the Irgun and Lehi continued to provoke retaliations from both the British and the Arab population, with the former becoming less and less interested in policing the latter. All of this combined to place the broader Yishuv population in a condition of existential crisis, forcing them to mobilize on behalf of Eretz Israel or face annihilation at the hands of an enraged majority while the departing Mandatory authorities looked on from their ships.

The FLN similarly focused its efforts on the "systemic victimization of civilians in an attempt to control the population." In the first two years of the war, the FLN killed more than five times as many Muslims as Europeans, whether for suspected collaboration with colonial authorities, affiliation with rival nationalist groups, or engagement in activities that the FLN had banned simply to exert dominance, such as smoking.[86] Martha Crenshaw offers a vivid description of how "compliance terrorism" wore down popular resistance and indifference:

> "FLN terrorism had an ambiguous connotation to Algerians. It was both acceptable and unacceptable. Both the ordinary Algerian and the leader were afraid of FLN violence, for which the surest remedy was to join the threateners. At the same time, the resentment and fear of these potential victims were tempered with the realization that violence agains them would be justified to their fellow Algerians. Thus to fear were added feelings of shame and dishonor."

Joining or at least collaborating with the FLN was one surefire way of alleviating this unease, which the FLN then redirected into violence against the colonial population as a means of both raising the costs of occupation and reasserting communal pride.[87]

Militarizing their own population still did not place either Zionists or the FLN in a position of parity with the colonial powers. Its full political value became evident when it led to the comparable militarization of their local opponents, the metropole would cede its own power of decision and let events on the ground take their course. By the time that the British formally terminated its Mandate in May 1948, the population of the newly declared State of Israel finally found itself in the climactic struggle for which the Zionist movements had been preparing them. The Israelis proved far more capable than their Arab enemies in effecting the transition to real war, inflicting a stunning defeat on an enemy that was numerically superior but unaccustomed to the demands of modern warfare and riven with internal strife.[88] The 1948 war was the first of many demonstrations of Israeli prowess in holding (and later, conquering) territory, but it would also demonstrate that Arab losses in conventional war simply pushed them to adopt the same tactics that had expelled the previous colonial power in Palestine.

In Algeria, a prolonged military stalemate gradually exposed the differences between Paris's increasing skepticism regarding the value of Algeria and the elements within the colonial population and army for whom *Algérie Française* was the core of their identity. As peace talks between President de Gaulle and the FLN began in March 1961, the diehard officers of the *Organisation Armée Secrète* (OAS) unleashed a furious burst of terrorism against Muslims and moderate French. Mimicking many of the FLN's tactics, the OAS aimed to spoil the negotiations through random brutality and militarize the *colons* enough to threaten Paris itself with a putsch if it continued to bargain away their position.They ultimately succeeded only in encouraging de Gaulle to accelerate the timetable of Algerian independence. Left to the mercy of the Algerian population hardened by eight years of war and flush with the prospect of imminent victory, the *colons* promptly discovered after a year of terrorism that they had commenced a march toward absolute war that they they were ill-equipped to finish. [89]

The success of these nationalist movements appeared to confirm the ideal model of terrorism as combining the ends of state-making with a capacity to utilize the tactics of state-wrecking as needed. The most prominent examples of movements seeking to replicate this model were the successive iterations of the Irish Republican Army and the various groups gathered under the umbrella of the Palestine Liberation Organization. The IRA, which had inherited the Fenian mantle in the 1919–1921 Irish War of Independence, tried to initiate a classic rural insurgency through its "Border Campaign" of 1956–1962. Operating independently of Catholic population centers in order to spare outnumbered civilians from retaliation by Protestant mobs and militias, the raiders were an easy mark for both the Northern Royal Ulster Constabulary and the southern Gardai. [90] By 1969, a disillusioned, Dublin-based IRA gave way to the Belfast-based Provisional IRA, focused principally on mobilizing the persecuted Catholics of Northern Ireland against the Stormont government, whose Protestant majority proved as hostile to parliamentary reform as the Algerian *colons*. Replicating the FLN's success would therefore demand a steady uptick of violence, forcing London either to accede to the formation of a unite Irish republic or else watch as Ulster's two communities plunged into absolute war.

The triumph of Jewish nationalism was of course a catastrophe for Palestinian nationalism, the prospects of which grew dimmer with each attempt and failure of Arab arms to defeat Israel on the battlefield. Israel's victory in the Six Day War of June 1967 deprived the PLO of a sanctuary within Palestine itself. It then proceeded to lose its sanctuary in Jordan in the 'Black September' battles of 1970, leaving them with a tenuous base in a crumbling

Lebanese state that left them vulnerable to both Israeli retaliation and Syrian manipulation.[91]

Their difficulties in waging a local struggle promoted the PLO to conduct a genuinely international terrorist campaign, with its affiliates staging guerrilla raids from Lebanon while also conducting a series of hijackings and bombings in Africa and Europe, most notably the kidnapping and eventual murder of eleven Israeli athletes and coaches at the 1972 Summer Olympics in Munich.

Many of these operations featured collaboration between the PLO and Marxists such as the the West German *Rote Armee Fraktion,* the Japanese Red Army, and Venezuelan professional revolutionary Ilich Ramírez "Carlos the Jackal" Sánchez. This alliance indicated a deepening integration between state-making and state-wrecking. Incapable of threatening absolute war in Palestine itself, the PLO could not foment the imminent crisis that would force Israel to accede to their demands or face unacceptable costs. Recapturing a sense of momentum toward a decisive moment required linking the cause of Palestinian nationalism to the idea of an "anti-imperialist front" tearing down the unjust structures of international society itself. Frustrated with the constraints of state-centric development and Cold War non-alignment, Third World leaders looked to revolutions in Cuba, Angola, and Vietnam as an emerging challenge to the entire "neoimperial order" of arbitrary geographic borders concealing the real power of finance capitalism. Coordination among revolutionary groups signaled "a new vision of global order and of a wider transnational political consciousness."[92] Their signature tactic of hostage-taking not only secured extensive and continuous media attention, but also validated their depiction of the status quo powers (especially the United States) as viewing human life in purely transactional terms. Hostage negotiations accorded legitimacy to terrorists simply by talking to them, and this interaction showed the world a medium of exchange that finally gave the have-nots a bargaining advantage over the haves.[93]

The PIRA's commitment to localism prevented it from fully taking advantage of the internationalist sentiment of the day, but they also recognized the value of attracting outside audiences to compensate for the limitations of the armed struggle. After drawing universal condemnation for its "Bloody Friday" attacks of July 21 1972, in which a series of car bombs killed nine people across Belfast (including five civilians), the PIRA recognized that the damage it could inflict on British forces was more than offset by the political backlash, including its own target audience.[94] Even though they had succeeded in prompting the British to abolish Stormont and impose direct rule, thereby allowing the PIRA to focus primarily on public opinion in London, but this did nothing to assuage their own vulnerabilities. So long as the boundary between Ulster and the Republic held firm, rampant escalation would spell disaster for Northern Catholics and spoil the PIRA's primary claim as protectors of Catholic neighborhoods against the retribution of the Ulster Volunteer Forces and other Protestant militias. After the British Army reintroduced a policy of mass internment of suspected republicans, the PIRA turned military weakness into political strength. According to Tom Hartley, who later became Chair of Sinn Féin and Lord Mayor of Belfast,

> "I would start with the statement by von Clausewitz: the strategy of one dictates the strategy of the other . . . the British are proceeding with their strategy of moving towards criminalization of the republican struggle via its prisoners; on the other hand they're engaging with republicans to bring them to a ceasefire situation. But the outcome of this is something that the British, I don't think, had foreseen and that what emerges is . . . a new leadership of the republican movement."

This new leadership that "wanted to move in a more emphatically political direction" could use the criminalization of republicanism as "the route by which such redirection could be pursued . . . a gelling of republican responses to two strands of British policy."[95] The result of this strategic shfift Dirty Protests and Blanketmen Protests within Northern Irish prisons over the question of political status for PIRA members, culminating in the 1980–1981 hunger strikes. While the prisoners fell short of their demands, the prison wars were critical for rebranding republicanism as a popular movement capable of drawing international sympathy, especially after PIRA prisoner Bobby Sands stood for and won a seat in Parliament before succumbing to the effects of his hunger strike.[96] Willful self-destruction was a hallmark tactic of the state-wrecker, but in this case it brought the PIRA and Sinn Féin closer than ever to political legitimacy.

Both the PLO and PIRA eventually substituted the threat of absolute war with a dual track strategy of armed struggle and political bargaining, which eventually forced them to make painful trade-offs between they contradictory priorities. As the PLO captured headlines around the world, it was losing on all fronts in its own neighborhood. After Israeli forces drove the PLO from Lebanon to Tunis in June 1982, splitting the organization among Yasser Arafat's loyalists, the Palestine National Alliance under the control of Syrian dictator Hafez al-Assad, and the Democratic Alliance under the thumb of Saddam Hussein.[97] The outbreak of the First *Intifada* ("shaking off") in 1987 promised a return to glory, as it demonstrated that the people of the West Bank and Gaza to claim the mantle of a resurgent Palestinian nationalism. However, it also prompted Arafat to expend that capital on a political solution before a more radical faction like Islamic Jihad or Hamas spoiled their homecoming.[98] A compromise solution, however imperfect, was preferable to an absolute war that would push them to the sidelines.

The PIRA similarly discovered that their attempted union of "the armalite and the ballot box" would in fact force an eventual choice between one or the other. British forces responded to the PIRA's "Long War" strategy with its own "dirty war" of covert networks conducting persistent surveillance and then engaging in extrajudicial killings or counter-ambushes that took an immense toll on numbers and morale.[99] As members of Sinn Féin undertook secret and preliminary negotiations with London and Dublin, the British were able to dangle the carrot of withdrawal and a new cross-confessional government in Stormont as a reward for diminished violence rather than a concession under pressure.[100] Faced with an exhausted public and diminishing odds of strategic success, the PIRA followed the PLO along a political path that did not so much secure their objectives as provide the opportunity to pursue those objectives within a consistent framework. In both cases, the popularity of their cause and sterling reputation as its preeminent champion eventually lent a trinitarian cast to the relationship among their cause, fighting forces, and target audience. Having achieved a degree of organizational solidity, they were able to trade an idealized objective for the push and pull of relative gains.

In the decades between the success of the anti-colonial movements and the compromise settlements in Ireland and Palestine, state-wreckers had played a predominantly subordinate role. Marxist groups like the West German *Rote Armee Fraktion* (RAF) struggled to balance their equally pressing need to rally public support for an idiosyncratic cause while attending to their own organizational integrity. Many young Germans, especially those with a similar background to RAF's mostly university-educated membership, either sympathized with their aims or at least looked fondly on their rebellion against the political and economic elites who had been complicit in the Nazi regime.[101] The RAF's choice of targets, especially U.S. military bases, struck a chord with a large audience given public opposition to the Vietnam War and Germany's role as a way station for American forces. Despite this wellspring of support and careful selection of targets, they could not raise their profile without exposing their small membership to police surveillance, especially when few Germans proved willing to express their ideological sympathy through active support.[102]

After a wave of arrests confined the majority of its leadership to Stammheim Prison in Stuttgart, the group advertised their incarceration to highlight "the perniciousness of the administered society, which made everyone an object of social control; and the alleged attempt at their destruction laid bare the fascistic nature of the Federal Republic."[103] The death of RAF members Holger Meins by hunger strike and Ulrike Meinhof by suicide "formed the experiential basis of the prisoners' denunciations of the Federal Republic as a terroristic state, determined to destroy them by means of torture."[104] In order to perpetuate the propaganda value of this narrative, they had to either break free of their confinement or issue steady reminders of the state's inveterate cruelty. After several failed attempts to negotiate their release, including the botched hijacking of a Lufthansa flight by the Popular Front for the Liberation of Palestine, the remaining leadership opted for mass suicide to reinvigorate its successors through a myth of martyrdom. Although this inspired many followers to continue their legacy, it also deprived the organization of what little direction it had and struck most observers as a concession of defeat.[105]

With state-makers forced to make painful compromises and state-wreckers routinely failing to mobilize a mass constituency, contemporary terrorism has exhibited even closer integration of the two models. Religion has provided the most effective bridge between them, permitting a wide range of convertibility between political activism and nihilistic violence. It gathers a network of local grievances under a vast ideological umbrella and infuses each of them with millenarian urgency. With a multitude of conflicts proving that the faith itself is under attack, violence is both necessary and desirable in and of itself. In situations such as the Lebanese Civil War or the ongoing occupation of the West Bank and Gaza, religion linked the character of the community with a fundamental critique of the sovereign state. Organizations such as the *Harakat al-Muqawama al-Islamiyya* ("Islamic Resistance Movement," commonly abbreviated to "Hamas") exemplifies the dual character of religious terrorism. Originating as a Palestinian arm of the Muslim Brotherhood, providing badly needed educational and charitable services for the people of the occupied territories, these *dawa* ("preaching") institutions provided a readymade source of funds and recruits. Hamas's reputation as fearless fighters of Israel, especially in stark contrast to PLO negotiations, further empowered the Hamas *dawa* which in turn advances its operational capabilities.[106]

While state-makers rally a mass audience to win acceptance into the prevailing order and state-wreckers gather a small vanguard to challenge it, religion provides a viable alternative form of political organization that can only achieve its complete fulfillment the total destruction of the prevailing order. Terrorist campaigns predicated on nationality or ethnicity has to fit itself around the contours of a cultural entity with a more or less distinct shape. By contrast, a religious organization can cull its membership from a large pool of potential recruits while restricting membership to its own social networks. Having formed a state within a state of its own particular design, the community of believers need not admit any commonality of interest between itself and its avowed enemy. In fact, it will likely draw mass support to the extent that the dynamics of its conflict take on the dimensions of a holy war, which blurs the difference between organizational objectives and religious imperatives binding on all adherents.

Suicide terrorism is the ultimate fusion of state-making and state-wrecking, and thus has proven critical for religious organizations as well as secular groups seeking to replicate their success. A suicide attack is both an act of self-sacrifice on behalf of one's own community and a declaration that life under the established order is entirely without meaning. The cult of martyrdom then serves as a focal point for the coalescence of communal identity. When multiple groups are competing for the same target audience, suicide attacks are a particularly useful means of "outbidding"[107] rivals, asserting ideological credibility and drawing the focus of both the state and external audiences. In adopting it, however, the group has all but foreclosed the possibility of a political resolution on terms other than an armed truce, both due to the visceral reaction it provoked among the targeted audience and the cultish devotion to armed struggle that it needed to develop in order to mobilize recruits.

Suicide terrorism exemplifies how contemporary terrorism has blurred the boundaries of state-making and state-wrecking. State-makers like Hamas, Hezbollah, and the Liberation Tigers of Tamil Eelam utilized suicide terrorism to demarcate the boundaries of their homeland along geographic and ideational lines. State-wreckers such as Al Qaeda advanced a narrative of an "army whose men love death,"[108] entirely free from the logistical and normative boundaries of the modern nation-state. State-makers may go long periods without suicide attacks, but they must maintain a credible threat to resume it. Indoctrinating followers in an ethos of self-sacrifice as a noble undertaking may make it difficult for the organization to halt and commence it in strict accordance with political necessity. Al Qaeda achieved its highest levels of recruits and influence within specific theaters in which it was able to set up parallel governing structures. Suicide terrorism pushes toward institutionalization and escalation at the same time, building a community that aspires toward political legitimacy but in the meantime is content to wage absolute war for its own sake.

NOTES

1. Gerard Chaliand and Arnaud Blin, "Zealots and Assassins," in Chaliand and Blin, eds., *The History of Terrorism*, 55–58.
2. Laqueur, *A History of Terrorism*, 8–9.
3. Chris Dishman, "Terrorism, Crime, and Transformation," *Studies in Conflict & Terrorism* 24 (2001): 43–58.
4. Ami Pedahzur and Arie Perliger, *Jewish Terrorism in Israel* (New York: Columbia University Press, 2011) 4–8.
5. David Rapoport, "Fear and Trembling: Terrorism in Three Religious Traditions," *The American Political Science Review* 78 (1984): 666–668.
6. Patricia Bibes, "Transnational Organized Crime and Terrorism: Colombia, A Case Study," *Journal of Contemporary Criminal Justice* 17 (2001): 243–258.
7. Philip Bobbitt, *Terror and Consent: The Wars for the Twenty First Century* (New York: Anchor Books, 2009), 26.
8. Max Boot, *Invisible Armies: An Epic History of Guerrilla Warfare from Ancient Times to the Present* (New York: W.W. Norton, 2013), 209.

9. John W. Meyer, et al., "World Society and the Nation-State," *American Journal of Sociology* 103 (1997): 158–159.

10. Manfred B. Steger, *The Rise of the Global Imaginary: Political Ideologies from the French Revolution to the Global War on Terror* (New York: Oxford University Press, 2008), 50–1.

11. Ernst B. Haas, *Nationalism, Liberalism, and Progress, Vol. I: The Rise and Decline of Nationalism* (Ithaca: Cornell University Press, 1997), 23.

12. Sidney Tarrow, "States and Opportunities: The Political Structuring of Social Movements," in *Comparative Perspectives on Social Movements: Political Opportunities, Mobilizing Structures, and Cultural Framings*, eds. Doug McAdam, et al. (New York: Cambridge University Press, 1996), 46.

13. Edward N. Muller and Karl-Dieter Opp, "Rational Choice and Rebellious Collective Action," *American Political Science Review* 80 (1986): 484.

14. Alexis de Tocqueville, trans. Harvey Mansfield and Delba Winthrop, *Democracy in America* (Chicago: University of Chicago Press, 2000), 608–609.

15. Martin Wight, *Power Politics* (New York: Penguin Books, 1986), 85.

16. Mark L. Haas, *The Ideological Origins of Great Power Politics, 1789–1989* (Ithaca: Cornell University Press, 2005), 74.

17. Astrid S. Tuminez, *Russian Nationalism Since 1856: Ideology and the Making of Foreign Policy* (Lanham: Rowman & Littlefield, 200), 67–69; Otto Pflanze, *Bismarck and the Development of German: The Period of Unification,1815–1871* (Princeton: Princeton University Press, 1973), 11.

18. J. Samuel Barkin and Bruce Cronin, "The State and the Nation: Changing Norms and the Rules of Sovereignty in International Relations," *International Organization* 48 (1994): 110–114.

19. Stephen D. Krasner, *Sovereignty: Organized Hypocrisy* (Princeton: Princeton University Press, 1999), 24–25.

20. John Schwartzmantel, *The Age of Ideology: Political Ideologies from the American Revolution to Postmodern Times* (New York: New York University Press, 1998), 43.

21. Anthony D. Smith, *Nationalism and Modernism* (New York: Routledge, 1998), 146.

22. Anthony W. Marx, *Faith in Nation: Exclusionary Origins of Nationalism* (New York: Oxford University Press, 2003).

23. Leonard Weinberg, "Turning to Terror: The Conditions under Which Political Parties Turn to Terrorist Activities," *Comparative Politics* 23 (1991): 424.

24. Friedrich Nietzsche, *The Will to Power* (London: Penguin UK Press, 2017), 5.

25. Ibid, 25.

26. Pankaj Mishra, *Age of Anger: A History of the Present* (New York: Farrar, Straus and Giroux, 2017), 29.

27. Paul Wilkinson, "Terrorism and the Media: A Reassessment," *Terrorism and Political Violence* 9 (1997): 51–64.

28. Frank L. Jones, "Toward a Strategic Theory of Terrorism: Defining Boundaries in the Ongoing Search for Security," in *U.S. Army War College Guide to National Security Issues, Vol. I—Theory of War and Strategy.* Edited by J. Boone Barthlomees, Jr., (Carlisle: Strategic Studies Institute, 2012), 100.

29. Martha Crenshaw, "The Causes of Terrorism," *Comparative Politics* 13 (1981): 384.

30. Audrey Kurth Cronin, *How Terrorism Ends: Understanding the Decline and Demise of Terrorist Campaigns* (Princeton: Princeton University Press, 2009), 210.

31. David Fromkin, "The Strategy of Terrorism," *Foreign Affairs* 53 (1975): 688.

32. Clausewitz, *On War*, 187.

33. Ibid., 178.

34. Ibid., 100.

35. Cronin, *How Terrorism Ends*, 110.

36. Clausewitz, *On War*, 178.

37. Ibid., 104.

38. Jerrold M. Post, "Terrorist Psycho-Logic: Terrorist Behavior as a Product of Psychological Forces," in *Origins of Terrorism: Psychologies, Ideologies, Theologies, States of Mind*, ed. Walter Reich (Washington, D.C.: Woodrow Wilson Center Press, 1998), 31.

39. Neil J. Smelser, *The Faces of Terrorism: Social and Psychological Dimensions* (Princeton: Princeton University Press, 2007), 100.

40. Louise Richardson, *What Terrorists Want: Understanding the Enemy, Containing the Threat* (New York: Random House, 2007), 81.

41. Max Abrahms and Philip B.K. Potter, "Explaining Terrorism: Leadership Deficits and Militant Group Tactics," *International Organization* 69 (2015): 315–317.

42. Jacob N. Shapiro, *The Terrorist's Dilemma: Managing Violent Covert Organizations* (Princeton: Princeton University Press, 2013), 28–29.

43. Max Abrahms, "What Terrorists Really Want: Terrorist Motives and Counterterrorism Strategy," *International Security* 32 (2008): 87–88.

44. Andrew H. Kydd and Barbara F. Walter, "The Strategies of Terrorism." *International Security* 31 (2006): 50.

45. Isabelle Duyvesteyn, "Paradoxes of the Strategy of Terrorism," in *Victory and Defeat in Contemporary Warfare*, eds. Jan Angstrom and Isabelle Duyvesteyn (New York: Routledge, 2007), 117.

46. Thomas Schelling, *Arms and Influence* (New Haven: Yale University Press, 2008). 2–3.

47. Ibid., 7.

48. Ibid., 16–17.

49. Ibid., 3–4.

50. Ibid., 71–74.

51. Albert Bandura, "Mechanisms of Moral Disengagement in Terrorism," in *Origins of Terrorism*, ed. Walter Reich, 162.

52. David B. Carter, "Provocation and the Study of Terrorist and Guerrilla Attacks," *International Organization* 70 (2016): 165.

53. Bruce Bueno de Mesquita, Ethan and Eric S. Dickson, "The Propaganda of the Deed: Terrorism, Counterterrorism, and Mobilization," *American Journal of Political Science* 51 (2007): 365.

54. Clark McCauley and Sophia Moskalenko, "Mechanisms of Political Radicalization: Pathways Toward Terrorism," *Terrorism and Political Violence* 20 (2008): 415–433.

55. Alex Wilner, *Deterring Rational Fanatics* (Philadelphia: University of Pennsylvania Press, 2015), 57.

56. Marc Sageman, *Turning to Political Violence: The Emergence of Terrorism* (Philadelphia: University of Pennsylvania Press, 2017), 17.

57. Paul K. Davis, et al. *Understanding and Influencing Public Support for Insurgency and Terrorism* (Santa Monica; RAND Corporation, 2012), 24.

58. Fred Charles Iklé, *Every War Must End* (New York: Columbia University Press, 2005), 20.

59. Karen Rasler and William R. Thompson, "Looking for Waves of Terrorism," in *Terrorism, Identity and Legitimacy: The Four Waves Theory and Political Violence*, ed. Jean E. Rosenfeld (New York: Routledge, 2011), 13–29.

60. David Rapoport, "The Four Waves of Modern Terrorism," in *Attacking Terrorism: Elements of a Grand Strategy*, eds. Audrey Kurth Cronin and James M. Ludes (Washington, D.C.: Georgetown University Press, 2004), 46–72.

61. Mark Sedgwick. "Inspiration and the Origins of Global Waves of Terrorism," *Studies in Conflict & Terrorism* 30 (2007): 97–112.

62. Tom Parker and Nick Sitter, "The Four Horsemen of Terrorism: It's Not Waves, It's Strains," *Terrorism and Political Violence* 28 (2016): 197–216.

63. Whitney Kassel, "Terrorism and the International Anarchist Movement of the Late Nineteenth and Early Twentieth Centuries," *Studies Conflict & Terrorism* 32 (2009): 239.

64. Quoted in Lindsay Clutterbuck, "The Progenitors of Terrorism: Russian Revolutionaries or Extreme Irish Republicans?" *Terrorism and Political Violence* 16 (2004): 162–163.

65. Ibid., 166.

66. Niall Whelehan, *The Dynamiters: Irish Nationalism and Political Violence in the Wider World* (New York: Cambridge University Press, 2012), 187.

67. Ibid., 296.

68. Richard Jensen, "Daggers, Rifles, and Dynamite: Anarchist Terrorism in Nineteenth Century Europe," *Terrorism and Political Violence* 16 (2004): 125.

69. Adam B. Ulam, *In the Name of the People: Prophets and Conspirators in Pre-Revolutionary Russia* (New York: Viking Press, 1977), 115.

70. Vera Figner, "Memoirs of a Revolutionist," in *Five Sisters: Women against the Tsar,* eds. Barbara Alpern Engel and Clifford N. Rosenthal (DeKalb, Northern Illinois University Press, 2013), 44.

71. Yves Ternon, "Russian Terrorism, 1878–1908," in *The History of Terrorism,* eds. Chaliand and Blin, 147.

72. Martin A Miller, *The Foundations of Modern Terrorism: State, Society, and the Dynamics of of Political Violence* (New York: Cambridge University Press, 2013), 82–83.

73. Sergey Nechaev, "The Catechism of the Revolutionist." In *Voices of Terror: Manifestos, Writings and Manuals of Al Qaeda, Hamas, and Other Terrorists from Around the World and Throughout the Ages,* ed. Walter Laqueur (New York: Reed Press, 2004), 71.

74. Samuel R. Williamson, Jr., "July 1914 Revisited and Revised," in *The Outbreak of the First World War: Structure, Politics, and Decision-Making,* eds. Jack S. Levy and John A. Vasquez (New York: Cambridge University Press, 2014), 42.

75. Sedgwick, "Inspiration ad Origins of Global Waves of Terrorism," 103.

76. Thomas R. Mockaitis, *The "New'"Terrorism: Myths and Reality* (Stanford: Stanford University Press, 2008), 23.

77. Rapoport, "The Four Waves of Modern Terrorism," 52–53.

78. Frantz Fanon, trans. Constance Farrington, *The Wretched of the Earth* (New York: Grove Weidenfeld, 1963), 192.

79. John Bowyer Bell, *Terror Out of Zion: The Fight for Israeli Independence* (New York: Routledge, 2017), 143.

80. Bruce Hoffman, *Anonymous Soldiers: The Struggle for Israel, 1917–1947* (New York: Vintage Books, 2016), 215–220.

81. Michael Burleigh, *Small Wars, Faraway Places: Global Insurrection and the Making of the Modern World, 1945–1965* (New York: Penguin, 2013), 324.

82. Pedahzur and Perliger, *Jewish Terrorism in Israel,* 23–24.

83. Alistair Horne, *A Savage War of Peace: Algeria, 1954–1962* (New York: Pan Macmillan, 2012), 230.

84. Irwin M. Wall, *France, the United States, and the Algerian War* (Berkeley: University of California Press, 2001), 67–70.

85. Burleigh, *Small Wars, Faraway Places,* 98.

86. Ariel Merari, "Terrorism as a Strategy of Insurgency," *Terrorism and Political Violence* 5 (1993): 213–251.

87. Martha Crenshaw Hutchinson, *Revolutionary Terrorism: The FLN in Algeria, 1954–1962* (Stanford: Hoover Institution Press, 1978), 48–52.

88. Benny Morris, *1948: A History of the First Arab-Israeli War* (New Haven: 2008), 398–399.

89. Ehud Sprinzak, "Right-Wing Terrorism in a Comparative Perspective: The Case of Split Delegitimization," *Terrorism and Political Violence* 7 (1995): 17–43.

90. Ed Moloney, *A Secret History of the IRA* (New York: W.W. Norton, 2002), 50–51.

91. Daniel Byman, *Deadly Connections: States That Sponsor Terrorism* (New York: Cambridge University Press, 2005), 125.

92. Paul Thomas Chamberlin, *The Global Offensive: The United States, the Palestine Liberation Organization, and the Making of the Post-Cold War Order* (New York: Oxford University Press, 2012), 21.

93. Walter Enders and Todd Sandler, *The Political Economy of Terrorism* (New York: Cambridge University Press, 2012) 162–164.

94. M.L.R. Smith, *Fighting for Ireland? The Military Strategy of the Irish Republican Movement* (New York: Routledge, 1995), 115–116.

95. Richard English, *Armed Struggle: The History of the IRA* (New York: Pan Macmillan, 2003), 187–188.

96. Ibid., 204–205.

97. Barry Rubin, *Revolution Until Victory: The Politics and History of the PLO* (Cambridge: Harvard University Press, 1994), 66.

98. Nigel Parsons, *The Politics of the Palestinian Authority: From Oslo to Al-Aqsa* (New York: Routledge, 2005), 32.

99. Rory Finegan, "Shadowboxing in the Dark: Intelligence and Counter-Terrorism in Northern Ireland," *Terrorism and Political Violence* 28 (2016): 511.

100. Roger Mac Ginty, "Irish Republicanism and the Peace Process: From Revolution to Reform," in *A Farewell to Arms? Beyond the Good Friday Agreement,* eds. Michael Cox, Adrian Guelke, and Fiona Stephen (New York: Manchester University Press, 2006), 135.

101. Konrad Kellen, "Ideology and Rebellion: Terrorism in West Germany," in *Origins of Terrorism,* ed. Walter Reich, 46–49.

102. Assaf Moghadam, "Failure and Disengagement in the Red Army Faction." *Studies in Conflict & Terrorism* 35 (2012): 156–181.

103. Jeremy Varon, *Bringing the War Home: The Weather Underground, the Red Army Faction, and Revolutionary Violence in the Sixties and Seventies* (Berkeley: University of California Press, 2004), 227.

104. Ibid., 223.

105. Stefan Aust, *Baader-Meinhof: The Inside Story of the R.A.F* (London: Random House, 2008), 432–433.

106. Matthew Levitt, *Hamas: Politics, Charity, and Terrorism in the Service of Jihad* (New Haven: Yale University Press, 2006), 61.

107. Mia Bloom, *Dying to Kill: The Allure of Suicide Terror* (New York: Columbia University Press, 2005), 94–95.

108. Jerry Long, "Delegitimizing Al-Qaida: Defeating 'An Army Whose Men Love Death," *International Security* 39 (2014): 128–129.

Chapter Five

The Absolute Engagement

Battle presents two major obstacles to a theoretical examination of terrorism as an approximation of absolute war. First, battle as a whole is resistant to theoretical analysis since the causes of victory and defeat lie much more with the facts of the individual case than general principles. Theory can only break down the components that make up the engagement, assess the operation of these components in reality, and postulate the aggregate effect of their interactions under a variety of circumstances. All engagements share the supreme objective of destroying enemy forces, with each side arranged in relative postures of attack and defense. The battle continues so long as both sides retain the capacity and, more importantly, the will to fight. Both sides also develop a "center of gravity" (*Schwerpunkt*), a "hub of all power and movement"[1] linking the operation of the parts with the purposes of the whole, and seek to identify and disrupt enemy centers of gravity. The ultimate decision is less a consequence of fighting than a confirmation of preexisting disparities between the combatants, which only become clear through the acid test of battle.

The second difficulty is that neither state-directed nor non-state terrorism fit neatly within the schema of a Clausewitzian engagement. A state terrorist campaign does not unfold as a series of battles but as a carefully crafted narrative of struggle and triumph against an enemy that is largely a projection of official propaganda. Whenever such a regime has to confront an actual enemy on the battlefield, it does so mainly through the prism of real war, although it may employ terrorist tactics to try and tilt the contest in its favor. While the contest between non-state terror and a state adversary resembles the basic parameters of the duel, part of the reason for adopting terrorism in the first place is the impossibility of destroying enemy forces through battle. Despite the apparent incongruity of terrorism and battle, a terrorist campaign constitutes what Clausewitz calls "the engagement in its absolute form,"[2] a self-contained battle in which both sides commit increasing portions of their strength until one of them loses the will to offer effective resistance. how terrorist campaigns are in fact a series of distinct engagements that each seek to approach a condition of absolute war, abruptly which terminate upon a loss of momentum, and then recommence in an entirely new form. This cycle of attack, disintegration, and reconstitution continues until it reaches the point of complete success or total exhaustion.

No theoretical account can compensate for the relentless evolution of the tactical environment and the consequent invalidation of existing lessons, and so the value of case studies are in many respects contingent upon their time and place. Saddam Hussein and Osama bin Laden have proven to be the most salient examples of state and non-state terrorism in the formulation of American counterterrorist policy in the last two decades, and thus both of these studies deserve careful examination. Both examples indicate that the real center of gravity for both types of terrorist campaigns is actually the negation of a fixed center of gravity in favor of complete tactical mutability. The extent to which it enjoys complete fluidity within engagement and between engagements determines its ability to fight in a manner completely beyond the enemy's powers of reciprocation. Although both men failed in their strategic objectives and suffered violent death at the hands of their American rivals, their successors have proven the extent to which they had established the foundation for a permanent war that was more than capable of outlasting their founder.

THE DUEL

Offense and Defense

The battle provides the clearest empirical evidence for absolute war as the purest expression of the logic of armed conflict. Direct contact between enemy forces strips away all the abstractions of politics and strategy, even when they are not actually engaged in combat. So long as the prospect is imminent, the participants can do no other than direct the whole of their reason and passion toward the other's destruction, taking their cues principally in response to one another's actions. The imminence of combat derives first from the permissive conditions of physical proximity and material capability of the opponents. Hobbes famously cited this as the defining feature of the international system, as "kings and persons of sovereign authority, because of their independency, are in continual jealousies and in the state and posture of gladiators." The active condition for combat emerges "in a tract of time, wherein the will to contend by battle is sufficiently known," and "during all the time there is no assurance to the contrary."[3] Likewise, Clausewitz defines the parameters of the engagement primarily in terms of the mutual willingness to fight, which needs no theoretical explanation or anterior cause. Just as the entire international system retains the capacity for war at all times, the will to fight is sufficient to generate the battle, which having commenced, "more than any other type of action . . . exists for its own sake alone."[4]

In the real world, the "mutual desire for victory assumes a minor role; rather, it ceases to be independent and has to be regarded as no more than the nerve which enables the higher political will to act."[5] The individual battle is inseparable from the preexisting conditions that generated the will to fight, the anticipated consequences of fighting at a particular place and time against a particular opponent, as well as countless factors of political and moral reasoning. The battle may take shape through a mutual willingness to fight, but the battle is also going to subject that willingness to tremendous stress, making it impossible to gauge until after one side or the other's has been irrevocably broken. In light of these vagaries, a theory of battle can only outline the ways in which the will to fight manifests itself, the means of harnessing one's own will and disrupting that of the enemy, and the process by which one side ultimately chooses to give up the field.

The essence of the battle is the dialectic of offense and defense. The mutual willingness to fight that commences the engagement can never be perfectly symmetrical for both combatants, since they undertake their specific objectives and positions relative to one another in real time and space. Even assuming that both have the ultimate intention of breaking the other's will, the actual moment of battle finds one side pursuing a positive objective against which the other offers resistance. Like all of Clausewitz's dialectics, the strict theoretical dichotomy serves mainly to provide a rational schema for evaluating concepts which will be far more ambiguous in reality. Combatants must be prepared to switch from a defensive to offensive position or vice versa to another as the situation evolves, and therefore retain elements of both postures at all times. The twin objectives of destroying enemy forces while keeping one's own forces intact makes it impossible to achieve victory through exclusively offensive or defensive means. Pure defense "goes against the essential nature of war, which certainly does not consist merely in enduring."[6] Effective resistance against an attacking force will sooner or later require some kind of positive action against at least part the attacking force, which of course will then put it on the defensive. As Clausewitz notes at the beginning of Book Six, titled "Defense," "if we are really waging war, we must return the enemy's blows."[7] The defensive form of warfare "should be used only so long as weakness compels, and be abandoned as soon as we are strong enough to pursue a positive object."[8]

Clausewitz's insistence that the "[defense] is simply a necessary evil, an impending burden created by the sheer weight of the mass"[9] stands uneasily alongside one of his most oft-repeated principles that "defense is a stronger form of fighting than attack."[10] He resolves this apparent contradiction by distinguishing the mutual desire for victory, which requires offensive action, from the policy that combat seeks to advance, which may be essentially negative. Raymond Aron explains that

> "at the most abstract level, defense and attack are defined by their end, their unchanging goal, to preserve on the one hand, to conquer or take on the other. Politically, the one who wants to keep what he has is on the defensive; the one who wants to take what the other possesses stages the offensive."[11]

A status quo is generally easier to maintain than to change, and the strategic defender enjoys a host of advantages including the selection of terrain, movement and communication along interior lines, proximity to fortifications and supply depots, and the presumed support of the local population.[12] By contrast, the attacker's primary advantage of initiative diminishes in the very act of conducting an offensive. For example, an invasion of enemy territory places attacking forces outside of familiar environs, pulls them further away from their communications, supply, and reinforcements, and subjects them to a hostile populace, all while drawing resources away to secure an ever-expanding rear.[13] Meanwhile, the defenders that limits themselves to "parrying to a greater or lesser extent beyond the preservation of tis territory, state and forces"[14] can enjoy all the tactical benefits of offense without having to take on a positive strategic objective.

Since the engagement represents only a fraction of the total experience of warfare, and since not all engagements even attempt the outright destruction of enemy forces, much less achieve it, the superiority of the defensive prevails mainly in the realm of policy and strategy, where "there is no such thing as victory," only the "exploitation of a victory won."[15] War places so many logistical and psychological restrictions on the will to fight that defense, despite lacking an independent capacity for positive action, encompasses the optimal preparation for the engagement and the preservation of its gains (or prevention of further loss) after the fact. The superiority of the defensive affirms that even in combat, where the urge to push toward the absolute is at its strongest, warfare remains subordinate to politics.

The Center of Gravity

In the moments leading up to an engagement, an armed force must find a way to maximize the strategic advantages of the defensive without compromising its ability to exploit an opportune moment to seize the initiative. The ability to harness tactical assets and then unleash them at exactly the right moment which Clausewitz refers to as the "center of gravity," a term that has received enormous scholarly attention and as such has become a subject of disagreement and distortion. As Antulio Echevarria points out, the U.S. military has generally understood the center of gravity as "critical vulnerabilities," "important sources of strength," or "principal sources of combat power,"[16] with specific definitions tailored to fit the operational prerogatives of a particular service branch. Clausewitz, in characteristic fashion, describes it differently at different points throughout the text, including the point "where the mass is concentrated most densely,"[17] the armies in a major battle,[18] as well as the battle itself.[19] Echevarria argues that any of these terms can accurately represent the center of gravity, which is not a concrete object but a "point of confluence where gravitational forces come together." The aforementioned examples refer "less to the concentrated forces than to the thing . . . that causes them to concentrate and gives them purpose and direction."[20] Just as boxers settle into a crouch from which to absorb punishment and generate leverage for their own punches, the center of gravity is the pivot from which a combatant moves from defense to offense and back to defense with a minimum expenditure of friction.

The center of gravity is an ideal type that will be present in greater or lesser degrees in actual examples. Within the strict logic of the engagement, the center of gravity "presents the most effective target for a blow,"[21] and thus "is the point against which all our energies should be directed."[22] In an actual campaign, this is an insufficient template for strategy for the same reason that a boxer cannot simply stand in the middle of the ring to try and deliver a knockout blow. Every engagement is a link in a sequential chain between the engagements that precede and follow it, and every war features a set of simultaneous engagements nestled within one another like a *matryoshka* doll. The battle is a "microcosm of war as a whole,"[23] the results of each prompting a realignment across the theater and up the chain of command. Furthermore, every armed force is an aggregation of independent wills, more likely to form a center of gravity around the lowest common denominator of collective action, rather than actually find an ideal point of concentration from which to attack and defend.

As a result, centers of gravity are unlikely to become sufficiently well-formed so as to render a force capable of wielding its full force or vulnerable to being knocked completely off balance. At the tactical level, the effects of battle are too mutually disruptive for either side to press its mass against the other without signifiant effects on its own cohesion. An exclusive focus on targeting an enemy's perceived center of gravity may encourage predictable tactical behaviors that render one's own side more vulnerable to disruption. At the level of strategy and policy, there are multiple centers of gravity that are as likely to interfere with one another as suffer from enemy action. Alan Beyerchen identifies the importance of nonlinearity in Clausewitz's conception of war, with cause and effect failing to follow a strictly logical sequence. For example, an enemy that succeeds on every military criteria can disrupt the "feedback loop" between military action and its political import, with "every building destroyed, every prisoner taken, every combatant killed, every civilian assaulted"[24] resetting the political calculus.

The myriad complexities of the engagement defy rational analysis, and yet Clausewitz argues that the outcome of the battle almost always "takes shape from the start" and "becomes more obvious"[25] as events reveal the relative strength of the combatants. Even more surprisingly, Clausewitz tends to downplay the direct role that combat plays in determining the results of the engagement. He dismisses casualty reports as "never accurate, seldom truthful, and in most cases deliberately falsified,"[26] and denies that there is an instructive correlation between the proportion of losses suffered in the engagement and the degree of strategic gain or loss reflected on the "final balance-sheet of the campaign."[27] The profits of a victorious battle are overwhelmingly accrued after its conclusion, when one side is able to capitalize on the other's temporary loss of resolve to harass an enemy in retreat and severely damage their capacity and willingness to resume the battle in the future.

Clausewitz's conclusion regarding the engagement is that they are not really won or lost through fighting. One takes place because both sides are sufficiently confident in their ability to register a material or psychological gain or at least forestall enemy gains. Combat then unfolds through a series of "subsidiary engagements that add up to the overall result," revealing the accuracy of their respective assessments "like the gradual sinking of a scale" until one side becomes sufficiently aware of its actual inferiority. The same principle holds for war as a whole, with each successive engagement providing the "crucial moments"[28] within a wider, continuous whole. At each stage of the engagement, the spilling of blood should be regarded as "killing of the enemy's spirit [rather] than of his men."[29] The difference is that soldiers are replaceable, while an army that loses its will in the field can at best conduct a fighting retreat and at worst is in danger of suffering a rout.[30] Military and political leaders are then in the position of the chess master who may choose to resign with the game still in progress to avoid an apparently inevitable checkmate. Since each component of the trinity has its own centers of gravity, the nexus of action binding them together is simply the will to fight. As soon as the people, armed forces, or government has its own will broken, the continued efforts of the others would only cross "the point beyond which persistence becomes desperate folly."[31] The battle that is actually fought for its own sake is not really battle at all but "mutual murder"[32] that does nothing other than validate a foregone conclusion.

Military Victory and Political Gains

Clausewitz's treatment of the engagement, which emphasizes that fighting is the "essential military activity" and that "direct annihilation of the enemy's forces must always be the dominant consideration," attempts to combine theoretical precision with practical utility. In addition to refuting the theorists who look for a "shortcut to victory" by developing a "particularly ingenious method of inflicting minor direct damage . . . by means of limited but skillfully applied blows," the commander should generally prefer "the simple and direct over the complex."At its heart, war retains the features of the absolute. Rooted in the "foundation-stones" of intelligence and courage, "the energetic conduct of war has always contributed most to glory and success," and "the destruction of enemy forces must be regarded as the main objective, not just in the war generally, but in each individual engagement."[33] However, that rule is subordinate to the supreme directive of using force as an extension of policy. In a system of symmetrically constituted political entities pursuing their interests directly at one another's expense, victory on the battlefield is the only surefire way to win obedience through a demonstration of superiority, against which there is no appeal other than a response in kind.

Unlike his treatment of absolute war, Clausewitz never explicitly qualifies his insistence that the aim of battle must ultimately be the destruction of enemy forces. Even so, the three hundred and fifty pages that he spends examining the minutiae of the battle implies that for all its theoretical elegance, combat is a remarkably inefficient method of advancing political interests. In terms of military victory, "only major engagements involving all forces lead to major success," and so "the more earnestly a war is waged, the more it is charged with hatred and animosity, and the more it becomes a struggle for mastery on both sides," one side is likely to achieve a "great and positive goal."[34] If two combatants were to put Clausewitz's advice into practice, the pursuit of victory would squander the opportunity to convert it into political gains.

As Clausewitz notes in his chapter, "Strategic Means of Exploiting Victory," "a prolonged struggle on the battlefield calls for exertions that complete" the normal exhaustion of the campaign, and so "the winning side is in almost as much disorder and confusion as the losers." While the expenditure of effort in pursuit of battlefield victory is necessary, "the victor may easily run the risk of losing his gains at any moment,"[35] especially if the loser only committed a portion of their total forces. In addition to diminishing its own effectiveness in the course of its utilization, combat also reveals the actual strength of the contending parties. Given the insufficiency of a single engagement for deciding a campaign, this creates a strong incentive on both sides to keep forces in reserve, both to preserve assets for future engagements and to deprive the enemy of critical information. A commander can only choose to seek or not to seek the destruction of enemy forces, and in principle the former is always preferable since neither victory nor lasting political gains are possible without it. Even so, across a sequence of engagements, each side's mutual pursuit of the decisive clash diminishes their physical capacity to wage it and improves their intellectual capacity to gauge its probable outcome, both of which should make its actual occurrence less likely. The dogged pursuit of victory in the face of the temporal and spatial friction inevitably turns tactical wisdom into strategic folly.

Non-State Terrorism and the Absolute Engagement

Clausewitz's account of the battle appears to place terrorism entirely outside the category of war. War "consists of a large number of engagements," in which "the object is the destruction or defeat of the enemy,"[36] while terrorism seeks an escape from the bounds of reciprocity, which necessarily precludes sustained contact with enemy forces. Non-state organizations frequently represent themselves as compelled to undertake desperate measures to offset their adversary's overwhelming conventional superiority, which justifies the employment of methods that have a much more direct and visceral impact on public opinion. The terrorist campaign never takes on anything resembling a distinction of offense or defense, and to adopt a discernible center of gravity would invite an intolerable risk of subversion or repression. A strict reading of Clausewitz would suggest that terrorism is a feeble imitation of war, incapable of matching its means and therefore highly unlikely to achieve its ends.

Although terrorism does not follow the standard logic of the engagement, its refusal to seek out a decisive battle ironically brings it closer to a condition of absolute war. For conventional forces, battle emerges from the presumption of reciprocity and distinct phases of activity and suspension. Opposing forces in continuous motion and therefore subject to the accumulating effects of friction can at best hope to inflict "a reduction of strength relatively larger than [their] own" and establish more favorable terms for subsequent engagements. Terrorism isolates the engagement from its temporal and spatial constraints, and thereby restores each engagement to its theoretical ideal as a self-contained whole. Rather than conduct a war through a series of engagements, a terrorist campaign is in fact a series of many campaigns, each of which consists of a single engagement. By conducting attacks that are immune to detection in advance and then disappearing before the enemy can directly retaliate, terrorism reduces the engagement to a single and self-contained moment of combat.

While a conventional force can erase a tactical setback by retaking lost ground or recommencing a stalled offensive, the outcome of a terrorist attack is irreversible. Just as punishing the perpetrator of a violent crime does little to alleviate the suffering of the victims, the immediate psychological effect of a terrorist attack is fixed regardless of what happens afterward. A successful terrorist attack fits Clausewitz's criteria of tactical success far more than is possible on the typical battlefield, even though in all likelihood it has a negligible effect on the enemy's military capabilities. Whether the attack inflicts physical damage or simply sends a fearsome message, the final "balance sheet"[37] will show the target as having suffered an unequivocal defeat, since it begins and ends with the unilateral infliction of psychological trauma.

A resounding tactical success does not automatically translate into strategic or political gains any more than in a conventional battle. A single attack may inspire some measure of sympathy and active support from target audiences, but many if not most potential supporters are likely to hold back until they can assess which side is better capable of protecting its supporters and punishing its enemies. No attack, no matter how devastating, is ever sufficient by itself to break the will of the enemy. A victim may not be able to undo the effects of the attack itself, but it can take measures to prevent its reoccurrence and thereby mitigate the impact of terrorism over time through any number of defensive or offensive measures. Even after suffering several attacks, the targeted state can draw motivation from a desire for retribution and learn to detect or preempt future attacks more effectively.

The insufficiency of the single attack appears to pose a more serious strategic dilemma for terrorists than for the conventional combatant given its presumption of both qualitative tactical superiority and overwhelming support among its target audience. Each time an attack fails to trigger communal self-consciousness and overcome resistance to its formation, this claim is proven false, and the perpetrators cannot remain in the field without suffering still greater setbacks. Consequently, the campaign draws to a close when the attack fails to generate its intended political result, after which the perpetrators go back to the drawing board until the next attack, which marks the commencement of an entirely new campaign. The collective identity of the attacker, target, and intended audience may be the same, as well as the cause which justifies the attack, but the attack itself represents an entirely new phase, both with respect to its tactical dimensions and the overall political conditions that infuse the attack with significance. With each iteration, the campaign must escalate its tactics and messaging in order to reproduce the same psychological effect as many times and as often as is necessary to turn the chaos and dread that follows their attacks into a permanent condition.

Terrorism attempts to reduce the battle entirely to its offensive dimensions, while shedding the disadvantages that inevitably slows its momentum over time and across space. Conducting war as a series of self-contained engagements, which are connected with one another only in the minds of participants and observers, isolates the act of fighting from the effects of reciprocity. A combatant that fights only at the point of maximum advantage and then dissolves immediately upon the expiration of its opportune moment is ideally positioned to impose the costs of combat unilaterally. However, the attacks themselves are unlikely to produce a decisive outcome, whether individually or in their aggregation, since the enemy enjoys the superiority of the defensive. The state is guarding its own civic order against revolutionary subversion, and merely improving its security measures can in many cases be sufficient to ease public anxiety and deter further terrorist action. The most effective way of overcoming this disadvantage is to engage in offensive action with a view to provoking a counteroffensive. A sequence of attacks can convince the state that a defensive posture is not sufficient to achieve security, and thereby compel it to seek a decisive engagement against an enemy that has in the meantime reverted from a position of pure offense to one of pure defense. Between attacks, terrorists can maximize the advantages of defensive warfares. Simply by avoiding the engagement until the mounting costs of the state's offensive action "diminish day by day"[38] its capabilities and political will.

Avoiding a sustained contact with the enemy does not exclude terrorists from the effects of attrition. Attacks can fail or entail unanticipated costs, and the state may prove adept at capturing or killing members, disrupting its logistical base, and discouraging the enlistment of new recruits. Alternating positions of pure offense and pure defense each place exceptionally high demands on different kinds of tactical skill, as well as the ability to shift from one phase of action to another. The chief advantage of terrorism relative to its enemies is its theoretically unlimited capacity for mutation and regeneration. As with any other combatant, the transition from offense to defense and back will generate centers of gravity around critical assets such as experienced operatives, sanctuary, and financial support, but the disruption of any or all of these assets need not cripple operational effectiveness. The ultimate center of gravity that guides the campaign through its phases of concentration and dispersion is the willingness and ability to pursue a fixed political objective and the ability to evade or bypass reciprocal contact with enemy forces.

Neither of these components are sufficient on their own. The mere willingness to fight would lead to a decisive and almost certainly losing battle, and either indefinite evasion or relentless attacks may sap morale if not calibrated to their audiences' relative eagerness or reluctance for battle and its attendant costs. Yet there is no inherent limit to the ways in which these components may reinforce one another or recombine in the wake of a setback. Terrorism attempts the complete mastery of the moral over the material. A conventional force invariably binds its morale to the viability of its concrete assets. A government, armed force, or people may have an exceptionally high tolerance for pain and privation, but its centers of gravity are based around concrete institutions, the long-term integrity of which takes precedence over the objectives of an ongoing engagement or campaign. Terrorists do not necessarily have to pursue any objective beyond the perpetuation of the struggle. The shared urge to create a new community expresses itself just as effectively through the willingness to fight on its behalf as any measurable advances toward a distinct political end state.

The conflation of the act of fighting and its political objectives permits terrorists a state of perpetual optimism irrespective of previous results. Typically, morale reflects and even magnifies battlefield outcomes. This is especially true for the loser, for whom defeat "gives rise to additional loss in material strength, which is echoed in loss of morale; [and then] the two become mutually interactive as each enhances and intensifies the other."[39] Terrorists are able to define victory entirely in moral terms, since their primary barometer of success is the willingness and capacity of its target audience to keep the fight going. In his vivid description of a defeated army, Clausewitz notes that there may be cases "in which the consequences of a victory may actually appear to be injurious because of the reaction aroused." He finds such an instance to be "very rare exceptions indeed," entirely "dependent on the character of the people or state defeated."[40]

Terrorism seeks to engender precisely this character by framing their campaign as a sequence entirely composed of unilateral victories followed by clumsy retaliations which prove the enemy's cruelty and reveal its tactical weaknesses. Both phases are equally useful in driving a relentless process of mobilization and innovation that, by virtue of its resolve and flexibility, can always hope to outthink and outfight an enemy for whom battle is a mere means to an end, and never an end unto itself.

State-Directed Terror and the Absolute Engagement

The success of state-directed terrorism requires that it operate entirely outside the logic of battle. Even as political life becomes consumed in the rhetoric of struggle, the enemy must remain inchoate, with its dimensions and ambitions entirely subject to the latest iterations of state propaganda. An enemy that is solid enough to engage in battle would provide a flashpoint around which opponents of the regime could organize and formulate a counter-narrative. Once it secures power and terminates its phase of terrorism, the regime generally prefers to operate within the parameters of real war rather than absolute war. Success establishes political institutions which then become synonymous with the advancement of the revolutionary cause. War threatens to exacerbate tensions between the military and political leadership, favoring limited campaigns that serve to validate the charisma of the political leadership in the minds of the people while reaffirming its reliance on military expertise. Aggressive acts will strike the status quo powers as indicative of sinister designs, but they are far more likely to reflect a severe version of an essentially trinitarian condition within the regime.

The exception to this general rule occurs when a conventional war reintroduces an existential threat to the regime, in which military force is a necessary but not a sufficient solution. A regime in this position must purge itself of internal threats hoping to take advantage of instability, without compromising the core institutions of the regime or its overall military effectiveness. Since internal threats and core institutions may be one in the same, the regime must be wary of forming concrete centers of gravity that could just as easily become the nucleus of opposition. Consequently, the regime must locate its center of gravity within the war itself. Combat becomes less a matter of achieving a distinct political end than a holding pattern by which the regime compels key audiences to invest in its survival until it can find a more secure political footing. The military objectives that originally prompted the war are likely to give way to ideological criteria. The results of the battlefield are not nearly as important as their impact on military cohesion, popular loyalty, and external political support, each of which could collapse at any moment. Alternations between offense and defense must serve a general policy of ensuring that the armed forces, people, governing elites, and relevant external actors are either emboldened with the prospect of victory or terrified by the threat of defeat.

Deliberately pushing a real war toward absolute war may very well prohibit the return to a Machiavellian system of relative gains and loses. The ideological premise of combat raises the political costs of an otherwise prudent negotiated settlement, and the war may unleash social forces far worse and difficult to manage than those that the war was originally meant to contain. Not even the most totalitarian regime can perpetually drive its population to the fullest extent without eventually collapsing. However, a regime that boxes itself into the corner of indefinite warfare is not necessarily doomed to defeat. So long as the likely conditions of peace present a greater risk than the trial of arms, the regime can whittle itself down to its ideal dimensions of willingness and capability. The experience of warfare may perpetually reinforce a community's resolve and hone its skills until the boundaries of its trinity are all but erased, leaving only a primitive urge to fight carried out through increasingly sophisticated means. The state will most closely approximate a condition of absolute war precisely when combat continues apace toward no discernible purpose other than to fight another day.

STATE TERRORISM AND WAR: SADDAM HUSSEIN'S IRAQ, 1979–2003

Saddam the Terrorist

Few world leaders have terrorized the United States as much as Saddam Hussein. The Iraqi invasion of Kuwait in August 1990 fixed an indelible image in the public consciousness of a monstrous dictator bent on destruction for its own sake. This perception derived at least in part from Saddam's brash attempts at deterring an American response, especially his outsized rhetoric promising a "mother of all battles" and a clumsy television appearance with Western hostages.[41] Another major contribution was the U.S. government's insistence that Saddam fused the malevolence of a Hitler with chemical, biological, and nuclear capabilities. President George H.W. Bush commented that "I see many similarities by the way the Iraqi forces behaved in Kuwait and the Death's Head regiments behaved in Poland," and that only American firmness would avert another Munich. While Bush was able to limit the objectives of the war, he declared afterward the mere existence of Saddam as an interference with the self-determination of the Iraqi people.[42]

The crippling of Saddam's military machine following the Gulf War did little to assuage policymakers regarding the Iraqi threat. His very ability to stay in power under the crushing weight of sanctions, a no-fly zone over Iraqi Kurdistan, and relentless policing of his WMD programs seemed to give evidence of a sinister design. President Clinton repeatedly struck Iraq without UN or Congressional authorization, but with overwhelming bipartisan support nonetheless, and made it the policy of the United States to seek regime change. His failure to deliver on this promise by the conclusion of his second term made it an imperative for the many officials of the incoming George W. Bush administration who had been part of the elder Bush's team and sorely regretted the decision not to topple him after the Gulf War.[43] As Condoleeza Rice argued during the 2000 election, "Saddam Hussein's regime is isolated . . . his people live in poverty and terror, he has no useful place in international politics. He is therefore determined to develop WMD. Nothing will change until Saddam is gone."[44] The September 11th attacks metastasized the threat of Saddam still further, as the nightmare scenario of nuclear terrorism dovetailed with the preexisting conviction that Saddam's acquisition of WMD would be tantamount to their imminent use. The absence of an immediate threat was itself a cause for immediate action, lest failure to remove Saddam at his moment of vulnerability emboldened him and other evil actors who had no purpose other than inflicting as much damage on America as possible.[45]

Assuming that terrorism is a fixed and determinative trait of a leader's personality was the fountainhead from which the countless errors and miscalculations of the Iraq War flowed. With the United States, Iraq, and the region likely to spend decades managing the fallout, it is critical to look back at the decision-making within the Ba'athist regime and its patterns of conflict with the United States in order to arrive at a more profound understanding of state terrorism in the post–Cold War Middle East. Most of the soul-searching following the Iraq War has focused on the dangers of American hubris, and this is a theme well worth exploring, but a more moderate disposition is insufficient for understanding the dynamics of conflict with terror-based regimes. Tracing the process by which limited wars escalate toward the absolute, and absolute wars become more limited is critical at a time when the region as a whole appears to be on the brink a war of all against all.

Terrorism and War in the Baathist Regime

The designation of Saddam as a terrorist, while profoundly misleading in its intent, was not itself inaccurate. The Ba'ath ("Renaissance") Party declared itself to be "the vanguard of the Arab revolution,"[46] aiming toward a pan-Arab state free from the taint of Western colonialism, although the specific dimensions of that state remained open to a wide range of interpretations. By the time Saddam assumed the presidency in 1979, terror had for decades been the primary instrument of keeping power in a state riven with ethnic and confessional divisions and enfolded within the dynamics of the Arab-Israeli conflict and the Cold War. After having gained and then promptly lost power in 1963, it had returned in 1968 and held on through a policy of *al-tarhib wal-targhib* ("intimidation and attraction"). Equipped with an infinitely flexible ideology and enormous cash reserves following the 1973 oil crisis, the Sunni-dominated regime elevated Shia to its leadership positions, enacted land reform for Shia peasants and negotiated provisional autonomy for the Kurds. These positive incentives to adopt an Iraqi national identity, all of which favored the centralization of state authority, went hand in glove with the relentless suppression of ethnic, clerical, and tribal networks that offered the mere possibility of an alternative source of political loyalty.[47]

Following in the footsteps of his idol Stalin, Saddam secured personal dictatorship by employing the Party's own tactics against it, convening a special assembly and declaring a "painful and atrocious plot"[48] within the Ba'ath elite to overthrow Saddam and facilitate a Syrian takeover, and that the guilty parties were all present. While Saddam sat and smoked a cigar, the commander of the Party militia read the names of sixty-six individuals who were immediately dragged out of the room and all executed within weeks. This stunning and widely publicized purge permanently tarnished the Party institutions as subject to foreign penetration, leaving Saddam as the leader of the state, the Ba'ath Party, and by extension the Arab cause.

A cult of personality emerged that lauded Saddam as the indispensable guardian of the Arab people against "the evil forces of imperialism and Zionism."[49] Such a claim needed an enemy against which to demonstrate prowess, and Israel was of course the most likely candidate, but by the time Saddam assumed the presidency in July 1979, Iraq was ill-equipped to take a starring role in efforts to liberate Palestine. The Camp David Accords deprived Syria of its second front against Israel, prompting Syrian president Hafez al-Assad to to reach out to his fellow Ba'aathist state and "seek attainment of the closest kind of unionist ties between the two regions."[50] Eager to flaunt his Arab credentials but wary of an alliance that could encourage a pro-Syrian faction within the army and Revolutionary Command Council (RCC), Saddam identified the new Islamist regime in Iran as the preeminent threat to the Arab nation, with Iraq serving as the first line of defense.[51]

Saddam's initial decision for war with Iran was a textbook example of *realpolitik*.[52] As an advisor told Saddam in the week prior to the start of the invasion, the chaotic aftermath of the Islamic Revolution afforded a "historical chance" to "move Iraq into a big and dangerously effective position . . . there are benefits for building a revolutionary, ideological army . . . [and] the international circumstances and the Arab circumstances are the best they have ever been at this time." Saddam centered his conflict with Khomeinism on the disputed Shatt-al-Arab waterway, aiming to secure a maritime route for oil exports while selling a narrative of "extorted land . . . [that] takes you to another level of ability and to another psychological effect on the Arab people and [pan-Arab] public opinion."[53] A quick and decisive victory, which appeared likely given Iraq's technological advantages and the dissolution of the Iranian officer corps following the revolution, would establish Saddam as a twentieth-century Saladin that restored pride to Arab arms after decades of humiliation at the hands of Israel and the West.

The Iran-Iraq War defied these optimistic expectations and degenerated into an eight-year slugging match featuring the mutual use of chemical weapons, indiscriminate missile attacks on cities, and human wave assaults consisting of thousands of teenagers and young boys. However, direct combat between the two states stopped short of the absolute as each learned to countermand the other's advantages. Neither side was ever able to overcome the superiority of the defensive for long, especially since Saddam and the Ayatollahs were equally loath to permit senior commanders to operate beyond strict political controls.[54] The periodic exchange of missiles known as the "war of the cities" started and stopped intermittently over a period of several years, with one side (usually Iraq) looking to relieve pressure on the battlefield with attacks on civilians and then halting in the face of retaliation in kind.[55] Most significantly, the war ended with the complete opposite of a decisive victory, with a restoration of the *status quo ante bellum* and a relapse into armed observation that persisted until the fall of Saddam's regime in 2003.

With respect to battlefield strategy, Saddam's decision-making was profoundly flawed and at times disastrous, but it fell clearly within the bounds of real war. Saddam and his generals struggled throughout to increase military effectiveness while keeping the officer corps under close political scrutiny, which paid dividends in the successful Iraqi offensives of 1987–1988.[56] Yet the failure of the initial offensives had introduced a political problem for which there was no clear military solution. Iran's unexpected tenacity confronted Saddam with the same prospect that he had tried to impose upon the

Ayatollahs, namely an invasion that threatened to expose the hollowness of popular loyalty to a new, unsettled regime and spur its dissidents into open revolt. The collapse of the front would obviously be the most likely cause of wider instability, but once the opportunity for a lightning victory had passed, there were also dangers in pressing the Iranians too hard. Saddam himself confessed to advisors that "we do not want a full-scale war. We do not want the destruction of oil [fields], and we do not want raids on the cities." In addition to the risks of sinking public opinion, there was a likelihood that other Arab states were "either spectators, rejoicing over the misfortune, or they are paid conspirators"[57] eager to take advantage of Iraqi vulnerability.

Fear of defeat but also unwilling to take the risks necessary for victory, Saddam made the war an end unto itself until the regional politics permitted its termination on more favorable terms. As Kanan Makiya comments, the war became "the first truly 'great war' of the 'Third' World,"[58] the vehicle by which both states would force their societies into the modern age. Like the First World War, the Iran-Iraq war perfected the development of a military and bureaucratic apparatus which completed the triumph of the bureaucratic state over its tribal and confessional rivals. But unlike its European analogue, the war did not actually engender a sense of Iraqi patriotism, nor was it intended to. With respect to official propaganda, the branding of the war as "Saddam's Crusade" (*Qadissiyyat Saddam*), named after the 636 A.D. battle in which Arab Muslims conquered Mesopotamia from the Zoroastrian Persians, framed the conflict as the latest chapter of the historic struggle against the barbaric *majus* ("fire-worshipper"). In practice, Iraqis did not so much rally around the flag as find themselves isolated and forced to link their own personal survival to that of the regime. Battlefield commanders were prohibited from acting without higher authorization, were routinely rotated in and out of different theaters, and were systematically deprived of intelligence. At the same time, failure to stand their ground would spell disaster regardless of the ultimate results. Deserters would of course be exposed to the regime's wrath should it halt the Iranian offensive and stabilize the front. If the front collapsed then the regime would surely fall with it, which would unleash the "hidden potential for even more violence inside Iraq"[59] as each marginalized group struggled against one another to claim a share of the spoils. This left Iraqi commanders and soldiers with nothing to aspire toward other than living another day, whether against the Iranian troops to their front or the regime at their back.

Sustaining the war indefinitely required a concerted effort to minimize the effect of war on civilians and to reward military personnel who proved most capable of fighting the war on Saddam's terms. The families of veterans were rewarded with cars, homes, and other luxuries. In 1982, imports rose by $5 billion while the budget for domestic development projects increased by 12 percent.[60] This guns-and-butter strategy was in large part possible due to a "broad and deep-pocketed" set of foreign creditors, especially the Gulf monarchies whose mixed assessment of Saddam paled before the threat of an Iranian foothold on their borders.[61] Even as the war reached horrific costs with no end in sight, the regime "prevented food riots, kept the soldiers in the trenches, and secured the loyalty of the army's officer corps."[62] The very unlikelihood of a resolution created a vested interest in its perpetuation, ranging from the Republican Guardsmen who saw combat as an avenue of social mobility to the outside powers hoping to prevent one side from gaining an advantage or reap the windfall of arms sales.

The critical weakness of Saddam's strategy was that a shift in calculation among any of his audiences could wreck the delicate network of common interest in keeping the regime afloat. The military apparatus of Republican Guard that Saddam had cultivated under his personal direction grew frustrated with the restraints on their ability to take the offensive, especially after the Iranians seized the al-Faw Peninsula in February 1986. They proved to be the one cadre that could both credibly threaten a coup and yet remain safe from repression, as they were the linchpin of Saddam's control over the army at large.[63] Saddam's attempts to break Iran's will to fight through missile attacks and the targeting of Iranian oil tankers led to increased international pressure to end the war. In the meantime, retaliatory Iranian missile attacks on Baghdad that specifically targeted neighborhoods of Ba'ath loyalists threatened to puncture the "fiction that Iraqi society was insulated"[64] from the war's escalation.

For several years, Saddam sought in vain for a breakthrough that would force Iran to the table, only to have the Iran refuse to negotiate unless Saddam was removed from power. Saddam could either escalate still further and risk a rupture with his domestic base, or deescalate and lose his bargaining power over Tehran, which could then encourage a faction of military leaders to pursue negotiations on the Ayatollahs' stated terms.[65] Fortunately for Saddam, improvements in Iraqi military doctrine coincided with favorable developments in the broader political environment, tipping the scales far enough in Iraq's favor to expedite a face-saving resolution that kept his domestic coalition intact. In March 1988, Iraqi forces halted an Iranian offensive into Iraqi Kurdistan, including a gruesome chemical attack on the village of Halabja. Although this incident later formed the basis of Saddam's trial and execution, the CIA and Western media initially reported the attack as an Iranian operation. Iraq feinted a counterattack in Kurdistan while directing its forces toward the reconquest of the al-Faw peninsula, isolating Iranian forces in Kurdistan and leaving Khuzestan vulnerable to a renewed Iraqi offensive.[66] In the meantime, the United States had taken an increasingly active role in suppressing the Iranian threat to maritime traffic in the Gulf, and the Soviet Union agreed to pressure Iran to accept a ceasefire in exchange for American assistance in facilitating its simultaneous withdrawal from Af-

ghanistan.[67] Although the end of the war left Iraqi forces precisely where
they had begun, the experience of repelling Iranian forces from Iraq and
coercing the ailing Khomeini to accept the UN-mediated ceasefire gave Saddam sufficient cover to declare that "what was accomplished was the highest
of my hopes."[68]

Winning by Losing

The conclusion of the *Qadissiyyat Saddam* placed the regime back in the
world of conventional power politics before it was able to transition itself out
of absolute war. The regime owed $80 billion in outstanding loans to its Arab
neighbors, and the weakness of the civilian economy meant that its massive
army "remained by and large mobilized, costing the destitute Iraqi treasury a
fortune."[69] Kuwait had eagerly supported Saddam during the war, but "no
sooner was the danger of an immediate Iranian threat no longer looming on
the horizon, than Kuwait resumed its traditional Gulf policy of the balance of
power by playing the northern and eastern neighbors against one another."[70]
Saddam was floating proposals to the RCC for economic and even political
liberalization, but as the crumbling of the Soviet empire attested, such measures could not come from a position of weakness. Kuwait's friendly ties with
Iran, its overproduction of oil, alleged "slant drilling" in Iraqi territory, and
refusal to forgive wartime loans trapped Iraq between its short-term needs
and long-term plans, prompting a dramatic attempt to place the former at the
service of the latter.

A week after the start of Operation Desert Storm, Saddam and his minis-
ters met to prepare a public justification for their refusal to evacuate Kuwait
after having invaded and annexed it in August 1990. Deputy Prime Minister
Taha Yasin Ramadan offered the following:

> "how were we going to maintain the loyalty of the people and their support for
> the leader if they saw the inability of the leadership to provide a minimal
> standard of living in this rich country? In this situation, could lead the army
> and the people in any battle, no matter what its level and under any banner? I
> think not."[71]

The conquest of Kuwait doubled Iraq's GDP overnight, wiped out $10 bil-
lion in debt, and gave Iraq 120 miles of Gulf coastline, but this time Saddam
could not satisfy his domestic constituency without alienating his neighbors
and the Great Powers. Furthermore, each diplomatic step he made to resolve
the crisis made his military position increasingly precarious. Saddam first
sought to assuage Arab protests by denouncing the "Zionist and foreign
schemes"[72] of Kuwait's al-Sabah dynasty. Saddam's avowed mission to restore the Arab nation from the bitter legacy of colonialism played well in the
Arab street, and precisely for this reason prompted King Fahd, King Hussein,

Hafez al-Assad, and Hosni Mubarak to throw in their lot with the U.S.-led coalition.[73]

Once he attempted to "Zionize" the Kuwait crisis, calling the annexation the first step toward "the liberation of Jerusalem,"[74] Saddam could not back down to the fountainhead of Western imperialism, and instead hoped to draw them into a bloody stalemate. Just as they did with Iran, Iraqi forces would dig into their fortifications, withstand punishment, and then strike back with overwhelming firepower once the enemy became exhausted. As Kenneth Pollack argues, "this approach was not just Iraq's best strategy, *it was their only possible strategy*" [emphasis in original]. Any other approach would have called upon a level of initiative and tactical sophistication of which they were purposefully rendered incapable.[75] This turned Iraqi units into easy target practice for Coalition airpower, sending most of the army into full retreat by the start of the ground campaign six weeks later. With Iran, Saddam was blessed with an enemy whose commitment to the war was similar to his own. Both of them could place their own societies into a permanent war footing based on a stable mutual expectation of their enemy doing the same and the predictable reactions of outside powers. The dynamics of the international system created the space for a total war between the two states and an approximation of the absolute within them. The Coalition lined overwhelming military superiority to a clearly defined and limited set of political ends that accommodated the immediate interest of regional players. Unless they all suddenly and inexplicably dropped *realpolitik* and adopted pan-Arab ideology for its own sake, the outcome of the war was practically a foregone conclusion.

Despite the magnitude of the military setback in Kuwait, Saddam's claim to victory was not entirely an empty boast. Laurence Freedman and Efraim Karsh argue that such a one-sided defeat "in an ironic way helped Saddam . . . overnight he was reduced from being the 'most dangerous man in the world' to a pathetic figure, a typical brutal Third World dictator struggling for his personal survival."[76] Convinced that his downfall was inevitable, the Coalition stood by as the Republican Guard suppressed a Shi'a uprising in the south and attacked the cities of Iraqi Kurdistan before withdrawing later in the year. From that point forward, Saddam concentrated almost entirely on regime survival. To deter another attack by outside powers, Saddam thumbed his nose at international inspectors and sowed the seeds of doubt regarding his alleged WMD stockpiles. Should the Iranians or Americans call his bluff, Iraqi strategy followed two parallel tracks. First, border guards and the regular army would trade space for time while the Republican Guard would hold the interior, although only a select few were even given maps of Baghdad, much less permitted to operate there.[77] Second, to protect against an internal uprising, "each village, town, and city would become a small semi-independent citadel,"[78] with units of lightly armed Fedayeen containing the insurgency until regular forces arrived.

Only the first of these strategies was apparent to American planners, which reinforced their hypothesis that Baghdad was the regime's center of gravity and that seizing it in a rapid campaign would render them incapable of effective resistance.[79] The initial phase of Operation Iraqi Freedom in March–April 2003 once again revealed the incredible disparity in conventional strength, which Saddam's strict political controls on military doctrine rendering his inferior forces even less effective. However, the post-invasion environment quickly revealed that the United States and its allies had made the inverse mistake which Saddam had made in the First Gulf War. In the earlier case, Saddam attempted to bypass his relative weakness through a qualitative escalation that only expedited the conventional war he had no chance of winning. In 2003, the sheer speed and decisiveness through which Coalition forces seized Baghdad exposed them to precisely the kind of war that Saddam had hoped for in 1991.

If the Ba'athist regime had simply been a conventional actor, the end of Saddam and his coterie would have ended the war, but Saddam clung to power as long as he did because even those who hated and feared him knew that his ouster could erupt in an absolute war among the fragments of a shattered state, with individuals trained to regard its neighbor as no less threatening than the *Mukhabarat*. The end of Saddam simply drove his vast network of officers, collaborators, and beneficiaries underground, with no motive to cooperate with a Shi'a-dominant government eager to take revenge for decades of repression. They would simply fight to survive and adopt whichever political program offered the most promising center of gravity. To attract foreign sponsors and fighters, and overcome tribal rivalry, the servants of a formerly secular regime would eagerly take to jihadism in order to rescue Sunni identity from the wreckage of the Ba'athist state.[80] When Operation Iraqi Freedom formally ended in December 2011, the premise of Saddam's ties to terrorism which justified the invasion had finally come to pass, as the Islamic State of Iraq had effected an alliance between foreign jihadists, disaffected Iraqi Sunnis, and former Ba'athist officers. Having each lost the capacity to fight a real war, they would reconstitute a new identity as the breakdown of the Iraqi and Syrian states gave ample opportunities for the recommencement of absolute war.

NON-STATE TERRORISM AT WAR: AL QAEDA, 1996–2018

Bin Ladenism without Bin Laden

More than two decades after its initial declaration of *jihad* on the United States, Al Qaeda has enjoyed few strategic victories and suffered a number of tactical setbacks. As of 2018, the threat of an Al Qaeda attack on the West, and the United States in particular, is practically nil. It has lost much of its leadership and operational sanctuary to U.S. drone strikes and raids, suffered a series of internal ruptures between its central leadership and regional affiliates, and thus far failed to rally a mass constituency to its banner.[81] Even after the Arab Spring fulfilled Al Qaeda's dream of tossing secular Arab rulers from power and posing severe challenges to others, the organization is no closer to its avowed goal of replacing them with Islamic states. In the Syrian Civil War, it watched its greatest strategic opportunity to to seize power instead turn to catastrophe as the Islamic State declared its independence from Al Qaeda and proceeded to win the lion's share of fighters, funding, and international notoriety By July 2016, Al Qaeda had no official presence in the central theater of international jihadism, with its Syrian affiliate *Jubhat al-Nusra* disavowing its ties to Al Qaeda of loyalty to Al Qaeda emir Ayman al-Zawahiri in favor of closer collaboration with local resistance groups.

Despite all of these failures, Al Qaeda is by no means on the brink of defeat. While Zawahiri's tenure has lacked the charismatic leadership or high drama for which Osama bin Laden was legendary, his more modest approach may prove to be more effective in linking Al Qaeda's structure to its objectives. Bruce Hoffman argues that Zawahiri's commitment to decentralization and collaboration with local actors has made the organization "truly 'glocal,' having effectively incorporated local grievances and concerns into a global narrative that forms the foundation of an all-encompassing grand strategy."[82] Dozens of Al Qaeda affiliates ranging from Bangladesh to the Maghreb boast fighting forces numbering in the tens of thousands, compared to the four hundred or so it had at its disposal on 9/11.[83] The death of bin Laden has ironically encouraged the diffusion of bin Ladenism, with these sharing expertise with one another and bolstering the value of their shared brand without having to coordinate their respective operations.[84] As a globally recognized symbol rather than a cohesive organization, Al Qaeda does not necessarily have to reap the concrete political rewards of the campaign in order to be successful. Fanning the flames of militancy is sufficient to validate its narrative of the Islamic *umma* throwing off the yoke of infidels and apostates. However fanciful its ultimate objectives may be, it has thus far succeeded in framing a vast array of conflicts within a framework of an absolute war that will either end with victory or will not end at all.

The Foundation

At the time of its founding in 1988, Al Qaeda was an organization without a clearly defined purpose. Bin Laden and his Palestinian mentor Abdullah Azzam looked to the example of their *Maktab al-Khidamat* ("Afghan Services Bureau"), which facilitated the recruitment of Arab *mujahideen* to fight the Soviet Union in Afghanistan, and sought to replicate it on a broader scale. Bin Laden's wealth, political connections to Gulf elites, and independence from powerful factions such as the Muslim Brotherhood or Egyptian Islamic Jihad made him a suitable candidate for managing a cohort of "Arab Afghans" who would elevate the jihadist cause above the fray of organizational rivalry.[85] This objective met its first setback within Afghanistan itself, where the Soviet withdrawal gave way to a bitter feud among Afghan warlords that shattered the unity of the anti-communist *jihad.* A disappointed bin Laden returned to his native Saudi Arabia and offered his fighters for a guerrilla campaign against the Marxist republic of South Yemen, only to have the House of Saud confiscate his passport.[86]

Expelled from Saudi Arabia after denouncing the introduction of American forces in 1990, bin Laden found sanctuary in Sudan after its military government established the National Islamic Front as the sole legitimate political party, thereby making it the only Sunni Islamist state in the world. Bin Laden became a "quartermaster of jihad,"[87] serving as a central node of finance, training, and ideological inspiration for campaigns including Algeria, Egypt, Somalia, the Balkans, Chechnya, and his ancestral home of Yemen. In 1996 the Sudanese government caved to international pressure and forced bin Laden into exile once again, returning to Afghanistan just as the Taliban was imposing its brutal form of Deobandism on Kabul. This period marks the beginning of Al Qaeda as an actual terrorist campaign rather than a facilitator of terrorism elsewhere. The local campaigns which bin Laden had supported were either collapsing under the weight of repression, negotiated settlements, or internal divisions, and there was a risk that the Saudi government would use its influence as Taliban financier and diplomatic sponsor to expel or even extradite bin Laden.[88] Rebranding Al Qaeda as the vanguard of a "World Islamic Front for Combat against Jews and Crusaders" would transform bin Laden from shadowy bankroller into a militant celebrity with a global following. Provocative attacks against the United States would likely fray his already testy relationship with Taliban emir Muhammad Omar, who was loath to draw international attention, but then a man who had labeled himself *Amir al-Mu'minin* ("Commander of the Faithful") would be forced to back bin Laden in a confrontation with a non-Muslim superpower.[89]

Bin Laden's first *fatwa* against the United States in August 1996 reflects this balancing act between a desire for maximum publicity with a recognition of tactical limits. In a long document rife with references to the Quran, Islamic history and classical scholarship, bin Laden identifies a sinister "Zionist-Crusader alliance," of which the United States was the most serious offender, plotting to reduce the Islamic world to servitude. The actual jihad, however, extends only to American military personnel stationed in Saudi Arabia, "the land of the two holy places." The brazen act of declaring war, along wit along with the media blitz that followed, gave bin Laden a platform from which to disseminate different messages to different audiences. Western news outlets were eager to seek out an explanation, which bin Laden was happy to provide, representing his jihad as an eminently reasonable and comparatively restrained response to unbearable Western aggression. To prospective followers, bin Laden was establishing his credentials and using his prestige to reframe the jihadist movement as a collective struggle against the United States rather than an aggregation of local struggles.[90]

In order to rally the mass movement necessary to challenge American hegemony, bin Laden would have to move beyond esoteric musings and an exclusive focus on Saudi Arabia. His second fatwa, issued in February 1998, marks a decisive shift from justification to mobilization, a brief call to arms calling upon every Muslim on Earth to "kill the American and their allies-civilians and military . . . in any country in which it is possible to do it" until they are "defeated and unable to threaten any Muslim." Co-signed by the leaders of jihadist movements in Egypt, Pakistan, and Bangladesh, the second fatwa implied that the Islamic world had become sufficiently aware of the necessity for absolute war against the U.S. and was now ready to make it a reality.[91]

The August 1998 attacks on U.S. embassies in Kenya and Tanzania were a fitting commencement to this campaign precisely because it principally targeted non-American civilians in two Christian-majority states. A mere symbol of American power anywhere in the world constituted a valid target, and the pool of potential combatants theoretically exceeded a billion people. With practically no restrictions on theater or target selection, the *umma* would prove itself to be the actual beneficiary of the global communications networks that the West had hoped would refashion the entire world in its image. Each attack everywhere would expand the outer limits of that community and expose the United States to reveal its true face as a paper tiger or a cruel oppressor of Muslims worldwide.[92] Either outcome would prove that the American empire would break down as soon as it absorbed the kind of punishment it was accustomed to inflicting on others.

9/11 and the Absolute Battle

Al Qaeda's self-representation as the vanguard of a global resistance made it impossible to articulate or pursue a clear strategy or political end-state. The ideal of purging the Islamic world of Western influence and restoring a caliphate proved more useful as a rallying cry than an actual model of political organization. Its open-ended mandate made its Afghan headquarters a beacon for a diverse range of combatants, but this meant that its priorities would take shape in strict accordance with the resources at its disposal. Maintaining its haven of training and propaganda meant that bin Laden was essentially licensing his brand of jihad to a network of semi-independent franchises. As Assaf Moghadam points out,

> "when Al Qaeda linked up with individuals or groups for a joint terrorist project, it tended to be approached more by the other party than vice versa. The militant groups that sent members to be trained in the camps, or who sought bin Laden's financial assistance, and various reasons to seek Al Qaeda's support, which were sometimes purely local." [93]

Such an arrangement was mutually beneficial insofar as it produced more operatives in more places with better capabilities, all of which would burnish the myth of Al Qaeda and draw still more recruits and refining its methods of training and indoctrination. Those directly under bin Laden's control operated entirely independently of one another, each maintaining contact with the leadership through a chain of handlers stretching from the target area to safe havens in Afghanistan or Pakistan. [94] Each cell would conduct its planned attack and promptly dissolve, its members either martyred or relocated to a new cell, providing every other cell with an inspirational and tactical model to which they could add their own innovations.

The September 11th attacks demonstrated the extent to which Al Qaeda's model of isolated cells under central direction could combine tactical genius with systemic impact. At the cost of nineteen operatives and approximately four hundred thousand dollars, [95] bin Laden performed the most costly and strategically significant act in the history of non-state terrorism, and compelled the United States to mirror his own narrative of civilization locked in an existential struggle with barbarism. However, the very success of the operation compared with its aftermath revealed the limits of an exclusive reliance on combat as an instrument of political change. Operating on the principle of "centralization of decision and decentralization of execution," [96] the transition from general directive to operation entailed the creation of an entirely new cell designed entirely for the purpose of carrying it out. Once in motion, the plot became an end unto itself, removed from the political calculation that generated it. Since there was no option other than to terminate the plot or see it through to completion, tactical logic would gain in importance as the moment of decision approached, even as it diverged from the interests of the organization as a whole.

All terrorist campaigns struggle to reconcile political considerations with tactical realities, but the structure of Al Qaeda as well as the grandeur of its ambition shows the dilemma at its most profound. Bin Laden's decision to strike the U.S. homeland had to be sufficiently provocative to elicit the desired American response but not so brutal as to tilt public sympathy toward the victims. Whereas conventional armies, and most terrorist groups, would have to square this basic imperative with its available resources, Al Qaeda was uniquely empowered to subcontract the operation to whomever it deemed most fit for the task among its wide range of affiliates and clients. While this power of choice was ideal for optimizing tactical effectiveness, it permitted outsiders like Khalid Sheikh Muhammad to market their own ideas and win the sponsorship of the organization for what was essentially a single transaction.

As a result of this arrangement, bin Laden's abstract desire to attack America crystallized through KSM's long-cherished idea of using planes as guided missiles and desire to destroy the Twin Towers, and thereby succeeding where his nephew Ramzi Yousef had failed in February 1993. Every Al Qaeda plot, from the October 2000 bombing of the USS *Cole* in Aden harbor to the "Millennium plots" of December 1999 were trial balloons toward the common goal of provoking an American response. This was tactically wise insofar as multiple plots were necessary to guard against failure (in the case of the Millennium plots) or a success that did not generate the desired response (as in the *Cole* bombing), but each would have a unique impact regardless of its result. Since each operation was independent of the others, there was no way for the organization to anticipate their aggregate impact and coordinate the appropriate response.

The special status of the 9/11 plot exacerbated this tension. Since the success of the "Planes Operation" depended upon its total secrecy, even within Al Qaeda ranks, the organization was incapable of exploiting any tactical gains even when the plan proved to be a complete success. Capturing the world's attention was meaningless if Al Qaeda could not continue to shape the desired reactions among its diverse audiences, which the sheer scale of the attack prohibited. Bringing down symbols of American financial and military power was meant to signal a decisive turn in the struggle between the West and Islam, but the attack struck most observers as the commencement of a new and profoundly uncertain conflict rather than the climax of an ongoing one. Al Qaeda was in effect demanding that its vast target audience proclaim their allegiance without their having any knowledge of how the organization would fare in the war it had just initiated. To make matters worse, this call to arms came after Al Qaeda had shot its bolt and could do nothing further to incite its audience other than issue threats and exhortations via taped message. Al Qaeda could do other than hope that the attacks and the imminent American retaliation would be sufficient to trigger a universal sense of Islamic self-consciousness and militant fervor.

The searing psychological impact of the attacks temporarily concealed the limits of Al Qaeda's operational reach, giving it an appearance of immense power by virtue of the governments and publics the world over that now had to take them into account. Yet now that Al Qaeda successfully drew the United States into war, it would have to demonstrate that it could replicate the effect of 9/11 on an actual battlefield. As the long-expected conflict actually approached, the organization could boast many advantages. Bin Laden and his coterie were a prohibitive underdog in a direct conflict with American forces, but there was no better location in the world for humbling a superior military power than Afghanistan. Even if it lost its sanctuary, its diffuse structure rendered it practically invulnerable to outright defeat, and it would retain a credible threat of organizing or inspiring an attack practically anywhere in the world. Its chief weakness lay within the period between engagements, where the pace and complexity of politics overwhelmed its simplistic narrative and modest influence. Al Qaeda would never be able to carry out a sequence of events that conditioned the expectations of its audiences enough to make them behave in accordance with its ideological template.

Many critics of American power, Muslim and non-Muslim alike, may have watched the Towers fall with some measure of satisfaction and deplored the invasion of Afghanistan, but despite the widespread appeal of Al Qaeda's global brand, it was ill-suited for mass recruitment. As Jessica Stern points out, bin Laden's savvy use of mass media succeeding in ways contrary to its actual purpose, making jihad a "global fad . . . a cool way to express dissatisfaction with a power elite whether that elite is real or imagined."[97] Western-style media platforms filtered jihadist material through its own prevailing assumptions, namely that all content is a commodity which the consumer tailors to their personal preferences. The overwhelming majority of Al Qaeda sympathizers, which themselves were a tiny fraction of Muslims, were content to live vicariously through television and the internet. Distance from the conflict made it easier for the individual to isolate their sympathies from any sense of obligation upon their own conduct, especially if the obstacles to participation were high and the likelihood of reward was low.[98] The thousands of Arabs who flocked to Afghanistan in the 1980s did so with ample Saudi, Pakistani, and American encouragement, and were able to embed themselves within Peshawar, fighting as much or as little as they pleased, as a small contingent within a wider war.[99] That was a far different matter than traveling with a high risk of capture to take one's place in a front that was rapidly collapsing under the weight of American air power and Northern Alliance ground assaults.

After losing its Afghan sanctuary, Al Qaeda immediately began urging its affiliates and sympathizers to bring the war home, leading to attacks in Tunisia, Kenya and Bali in 2002, Saudi Arabia (twice), Morocco, Turkey, and Jakarta in 2003, Spain in 2004, as well as the United Kingdom and Bali again in 2005. Every attack boasted of Al Qaeda's resilience in the face of major setbacks, but they spoke more to the durability of its Pakistan-based network than an increase in popular support. Even "homegrown" attacks such as the Madrid train bombings in March 2004 or the London 7/7 attacks resulted from collaboration between local groups and Al Qaeda, the latter case including training in Pakistan.[100] Although the Madrid attacks scored a political victory with the withdrawal of Spanish forces from Iraq a month later, it also resulted in the termination of the Al Qaeda cell in Spain and massive denunciations among Spanish Muslims, including leading clerics. These attacks represent Al Qaeda's most pressing dilemma under bin Laden's leadership. On one hand, such attacks kept them in the headlines and forced governments to expend resources indefinitely to minimize the risk of more attacks. On the other hand, every attack proved that Al Qaeda could only recruit among a minuscule fringe whose actions drew the full-throated opprobrium of their community, giving governments a free hand to contain terrorism without alienating their Muslim populations. Tactical gains could not be accrued without incurring strategic losses.

The battlefields of Afghanistan and Iraq offered a more promising opportunity to "drag the masses into battle," compelling their target audience "to fight in the ranks of the people of truth in order to die well."[101] The invasion of Iraq in particular ceded a range of tactical advantages to Al Qaeda. The collapse of the Ba'athist state and the embitterment of a once-dominant Sunni minority provided the ideal setting for Al Qaeda to metastasize. Iraq's central location and porous borders made it an easy destination for weapons and foreign fighters, especially with Syria eager to undermine the American presence on its border. Many Muslims with no affinity for bin Laden nonetheless regarded the insurgency as a clear-cut example of "defensive jihad"[102] against a foreign aggressor. In Iraq, Al Qaeda could at last assemble a sequence of engagements within a coherent ideological package. Enjoying a firm base of operations in a target-rich environment, Al Qaeda had countless opportunities to exhibit its leading role in the fight against a hated occupier, draw more recruits and resources, and thereby become make itself even deadlier.[103]

President George W. Bush repeatedly described the Iraq War as the "central front in the War on Terror," an unintentionally accurate way of stating that it had come to serve as Al Qaeda's center of gravity. Iraq was the central node connecting the leadership in Pakistan with its far-flung affiliates, providing a chief theme of propaganda, a proving ground for recruits (especially suicide bombers), and inspiration for attacks elsewhere. Al Qaeda was within reach of a decisive military defeat against Coalition forces, the destruction of the nascent Iraqi government, and its replacement with an Islamic state. Yet as victory became an actual prospect, fault lines emerged between Al Qaeda's dual status as transnational terrorist campaign and leading player in the Iraqi insurgency.

The Sunni tribesmen and Ba'athist holdouts who constituted the original insurgency initially embraced Al Qaeda sponsorship as a means of making the whole greater than the sum of its parts. Its vast resources and religious proved especially appealing to weaker tribes without the wealth or influence to compete on their own.[104] Bin Laden and Zawahiri anticipated that its affiliate would manage a broad-based coalition of guerrilla fighters who would attrit American forces to the point of withdrawal. Yet the man whom they designated as the emir of their Iraqi affiliate, the Jordanian Abu Musab al-Zarqawi, was unwilling to expel the Americans with a conventional force only to confront a Shi'a majority with unlimited Iranian backing. In order to survive the wider war, Al Qaeda in Iraq (AQI) would have to rouse the entire Sunni population into militancy through the imminent prospect of absolute war. As he wrote to bin Laden,

"the solution that we see . . . is for us to drag the Shi'a into the battle because this is the only way to prolong the fighting between us and the infidels . . . someone might say that in this matter, we are being hasty and rash and leading the [Islamic] nation into a battle for which it is not ready, a battle that will be revolting and in which blood will be spilled. This is exactly what we want."[105]

Despite bin Laden and Zawahiri's fierce objections to this approach, they had no choice but to justify Zarqawi's rampant targeting of Muslims in public or else lose what little influence they had over their wayward affiliate. The split within the insurgency between the proponents of real war against the Americans and absolute war against the Shi'a provided the opening through which U.S. forces could co-opt the support of tribal elites in Anbar province. In exchange for money, protection, and military advising, the tribes would reassert control over villages, cities, and highways, marrying local intelligence with American firepower.[106] AQI had the manpower, motivation, and battlefield skill to wage a bitter and bloody struggle against the *Sahawa al-Anbar* ("Anbar Awakening"), but their response to tactical setbacks weakened their position still further. Unable to negotiate with the tribes without undermining their propulsive march toward absolute war, AQI doubled down on brutality with attacks on civilians affiliated with hostile tribal leaders, suicide bombings against Iraqi Shi'a, and an increased reliance on foreign fighters.[107]

AQI's shocking tactics further turned the jihadist movement against itself, with the remnants of Zarqawi's network rebranding themselves as the Islamic State of Iraq and demanding the loyalty of Iraqi Sunnis through the brutal enforcement of *hudud* (punishments rooted in Sharia law). The popular backlash broke the back of AQI in their urban centers of gravity, after which it lived on as a dangerous insurgency but was patently unable to validate its claim to statehood until the degeneration of Syria into civil war granted it an opportunity for renewal. The temporary defeat of Al Qaeda in Iraq exhibited its principal strengths and weaknesses as a direct combatant. Within the theater of battle, Al Qaeda has been without peer in its ability to foment escalation and sustain a fight under enormous pressure. Despite their lack of direct operational control, bin Laden and Zawahiri could still drive a bidding war between local fighters in which each demonstrated their prowess so as to merit the coveted Al Qaeda brand, with all its rewards and notoriety. The central leadership expected obedience in exchange for its sponsorship, which included curtailing escalation when it harmed the organization's overall brand, such as the rampant killing of Muslims. However, escalation was the key to survival for the local affiliate, as any slackening in the pace would introduce the possibility of a political solution that would necessarily sideline Al Qaeda affiliates in favor of local actors.[108] This left the central leadership with the choice of either disavowing their wayward subordinate and dealing themselves out of the theater or affirming their support, which would discredit the overall cause.[109]

So long as Osama bin Laden was alive, his reputation as the emir of Al Qaeda ensured direct competition between the center and the periphery. His death, and the succession of the much less charismatic Zawahiri, has turned each affiliate into the principal within their own theater of operations. Its defeat in Iraq has generated two sets of lessons, with each Al Qaeda offshoot free to choose between them. The first is to refashion Al Qaeda into an ideological brand rather than a direct participant in hostilities, lending legitimacy to guerrilla struggles around the Islamic world while deferring to local political realities. Organizations like Jubhat al-Nusra in Syria try to have their cake and eat it too, alternately flaunting and disavowing its ties to Al Qaeda based on the audience.[110] The remnants of its Iraqi affiliate drew the opposite lesson, seeking to obliterate the distinction between local conflicts and the overarching mission through furious escalation, which necessitated a complete break with the Al Qaeda brand. It is doubtful that Al Qaeda will achieve a decisive victory against the "near enemy" (apostate Islamic regimes) or the "far enemy" (the U.S.), but it was never designed for the purpose of fighting and winning wars. Its cellular structure and vague ideology, which speaks far more to a general longing for restored Islamic honor rather than a coherent political program, generates new combatants and brings them into battle with optimal efficiency. Even if it never establishes anything resembling a viable caliphate, Al Qaeda has successfully created a template for capitalizing on a set of grievances and recurring social conditions, fashioning an image of a worldwide community defined entirely by its willingness to fight.

NOTES

1. Clausewitz, *On War,* 595–596.
2. Ibid., 236.
3. Thomas Hobbes, *Leviathan* (London: Oxford University Press, 1965), 96–98.
4. Clausewitz, *On War,* 248.
5. Ibid., 245.

6. Ibid., 370.

7. Ibid., 357.

8. Ibid., 358.

9. Ibid., 524.

10. Ibid., 84.

11. Raymond Aron, *Clausewitz: Philosopher of War*, trans. Christine Booker and Norman Stone (New York: Touchstone, 1983), 169.

12. Clausewitz, *On War*, 364–366.

13. Ibid., 527.

14. Aron, *Clausewitz*, 167.

15. Clausewitz, *On War*, 363.

16. Antulio J. Echevarria II, "Clausewitz's Center of Gravity: It's Not What We Thought," *Naval War College Review* 56 (2003):108–109.

17. Clausewitz, *On War*, 485.

18. Ibid., 258 .

19. Ibid., 248.

20. Echevarria, "Clausewitz's Center of Gravity," 112–113.

21. Clausewitz, *On War*, 486.

22. Ibid., 596.

23. Ibid., 236.

24. Beyerchen, "Clausewitz, Nonlinearity, and the Unpredictability of War," 89.

25. Clausewitz, *On War*, 249.

26. Ibid., 234.

27. Ibid., 230.

28. Ibid., 240.

29. bid., 259.

30. Ibid., 271.

31. Ibid., 251.

32. Ibid., 259.

33. Ibid., 227–229.

34. Ibid., 258–259.

35. Ibid., 263.

36. Ibid., 227.

37. Ibid., 230.

38. Ibid., 528.

39. Ibid., 253.

40. Ibid., 257.

41. John E. Mueller, *Policy and Opinion in the Gulf War.* Chicago (University of Chicago Press, 1994), 41.

42. Quoted in Rachel Martin Harlow, "Agency and Agent in George Bush's Gulf War Rhetoric," in *The Rhetorical Presidency of George H.W. Bush,* ed. Martin J. Medhurst (College Station: Texas A&M University Press, 2006). 66–75.

43. George Packer, *The Assassin's Gate: America in Iraq* (New York: Farrar, Straus, and Giroux, 2005), 27–28.

44. Alex Roberto Hybel and Justin Matthew Kaufman, *The Bush Administrations and Saddam Hussein: Deciding on Conflict* (New York: Palgrave Macmillan, 2006), 83.

45. Joseph M. Siracusa and Aiden Warren, *Presidential Doctrines: U.S. National Security From George Washington to Barack Obama* (Lanham: Rowman & Littlefield, 2016), 181–182.

46. Joseph Sassoon, *Saddam Hussein's Ba'ath Party: Inside an Authoritarian Regime* (New York: Cambridge University Press, 2012), 19.

47. Amatzia Baram, *Culture, History and Ideology in the Formation of Ba'athist Iraq, 1968–89* (New York: Palgrave Macmillan, 1991), 19–20.

48. Aaron M. Faust, *The Ba'athification of Iraq: Saddam Hussein's Totalitarianism* (Austin: University of Texas Press, 2015), 40–41.

49. Efrain Karsh and Inari Rautsi, *Saddam Hussein: A Political Biography* (New York: Grove Press, 2002), 117.

50. Malik Mufti, *Sovereign Creations: Pan-Arabism and Political Order in Syria and Iraq* (Ithaca: Cornell University Press, 1996). 210.

51. Williamson Murray and Kevin M. Woods, *The Iran-Iraq War: A Military and Strategic History* (New York: Cambridge University Press, 2014), 94.

52. Walt, *Revolution and War*, 241–242.

53. Kevin Woods, et al., *The Saddam Tapes: The Inner Workings of a Tyrant's Regime, 1978–2001* (New York: Cambridge University Press, 2011), 133–135.

54. Kevin Woods, et al., *Saddam's War: An Iraqi Military Perspective of the Iran-Iraq War* (Washington, D.C.: Institute for National Strategic Studies, 2009), 5.

55. Thomas L. McNaugher, "Ballistic Missiles and Chemical Weapons: The Legacy of the Iran-Iraq War," *International Security* 15 (1990): 5–34.

56. Caitlin Talmadge, *The Dictator's Army: Battlefield Effectiveness in Authoritarian Regimes* (Ithaca: Cornell University Press, 2015), 160–162.

57. Woods et al., *The Saddam Tapes*, 135.

58. Kanan Makiya, *Republic of Fear: The Politics of Modern Iraq* (Berkeley: University of California Press, 1998) 261.

59. Ibid., 276.

60. Dilip Hiro, *The Longest War: The Iran-Iraq Military Conflict* (New York: Routledge, 1991), 58.

61. Glen Rangwala, "The Finances of War: Iraq, Credit and Conflict, September 1980 to August 1990," in *The Iran-Iraq War: New International Perspectives,* eds. Nigel John Ashton and Bryan R. Gibson (New York: Routledge, 2013), 96.

62. Amatzia Baram, *Building Toward Crisis: Saddam Husayn's Strategy for Survival* (Washington, D.C.: Washington Institute for Near East Policy, 1998), 3.

63. Talmadge, *The Dictator's Army,* 154.

64. Daniel Byman, et al., "Coercing Saddam Hussein: Lessons from the Past," *Survival* 40 (1998): 131.

65. Murray and Woods, 290.

66. Pierre Razoux, trans. Nicholas Elliott, *The Iran-Iraq War* (Cambridge: Harvard University Press, 2015), 439–442.

67. Ibid., 451.

68. Woods, et al., *The Saddam Tapes*, 162.

69. Lawrence Freedman and Ephraim Karsh, *The Gulf Conflict, 1990–1991: Diplomacy and War in the New World Order* (Princeton: Princeton University Press, 1993), 30.

70. Majid Khadduri and Edmund Ghareeb, *War in the Gulf, 1990–1991: The Iraq-Kuwait Conflict and Its Implications* (New York: Oxford University Press, 1997), 82.

71. Quoted in F. Gregory Gause III, "Iraq's Decision to Go to War, 1980 and 1990." *The Middle East Journal* 56 (2002): 59.

72. Quoted in Karsh and Rautsi, *Saddam Hussein*, 217.

73. Ken Matthews, *The Gulf Conflict and International Relations* (New York: Routledge, 1993), 66.

74. Rory Miller, *Desert Kingdoms to Global Powers: The Rise of the Arab Gulf* (New Haven: Yale University Press, 2016), 95.

75. Kenneth M. Pollack, *Arabs at War: Military Effectiveness, 1948–1991* (Lincoln: University of Nebraska Press, 2002), 261.

76. Freedman and Karsh, *The Gulf Conflict*, 418.

77. Kevin Woods, et al., *Iraqi Perspectives Project: A View of Operation Iraqi Freedom from Saddam's Senior Leadership* (Norfolk: Joint Center for Operational Analysis, 2006), 27.

78. Michael R. Gordon and Bernard E. Trainor, *Cobra II: The Inside Story of the Invasion and Occupation of Iraq* (New York: Vintage Books, 2007), 71.

79. Ibid., 91.

80. Bryan Glyn Williams, *Counter Jihad: America's Military Experience in Afghanistan, Iraq, and Syria* (Philadelphia: University of Pennsylvania Press, 2017), 190–191.

81. Fawaz A. Gerges, *The Rise and Fall of Al-Qaeda* (New York: Oxford University Press, 2011), 93.

82. Bruce Hoffman, "Al-Qaeda's Resurrection," Council on Foreign Relations, March 6 2018. https://www.cfr.org/expert-brief/al-qaedas-resurrection

83. Ali Soufan, *Anatomy of Terror: From the Death of Bin Laden to the Rise of the Islamic State* (New York: W.W. Norton, 2017), xvi.

84. Daniel Byman, "Buddies or Burdens? Understanding the Al Qaeda Relationship with Its Affiliate Organizations," *Security Studies* 23 (2014): 440–441.

85. Mustafa Hamid and Leah Farrall, *The Arabs at War in Afghanistan* (New York: Oxford University Press, 2015), 106–119.

86. Bruce Riedel, *The Search for Al Qaeda: Its Leadership, Ideology, and Future* (Washington, D.C.: Brookings Institution Press, 2008), 47–49.

87. Daniel Benjamin and Steven Simon, *The Age of Sacred Terror: Radical Islam's War Against America* (New York: Random House, 2003), 113.

88. Alex Strick van Linschoten and Felix Kuehn, *An Enemy We Created: The Myth of the Taliban-Al Qaeda Merger in Afghanistan* (New York: Oxford University Press, 2012), 128.

89. Lawrence Wright, *The Looming Tower: Al-Qaeda and the Road to 9/11* (New York: Vintage Books, 2006), 326.

90. Osama bin Laden, "Declaration of Jihad Against the Americans Occupying the Land of the Two Holiest Sites," *Al Quds Al Arabi*, August 23 1996. https://is.muni.cz/el/1423/jaro2010/MVZ448/OBL___AQ__Fatwa_1996.pdf

91. Osama bin Laden, et al., "Jihad Against Jews and Crusaders," *Al Quds Al Arabi* February 23 1998.https://fas.org/irp/world/para/docs/980223-fatwa.htm

92. Peter L. Bergen, *The Longest War: The Enduring Conflict between America and Al-Qaeda* (New York: Free Press, 2011), 6.

93. Assaf Moghadham, *The Globalization of Martyrdom: Al Qaeda, Salafi Jihad, and the Diffusion of Suicide Attacks* (Baltimore: The Johns Hopkins University Press, 2008), 133.

94. Rohan Gunaratna, *Inside Al Qaeda: Global Network of Terror* (New York: Columbia University Press, 2002), 97.

95. Thomas Kean, et al., *The 9/11 Commission Report: Final Report of the National Commission on Terrorist Attacks upon the United States* (Washington, D.C.: Government Printing Office, 2004), 499.

96. Mark Stout, et al. *The Terrorist Perspectives Project: Strategic and Operational Views of Al Qaida and Associate Movements* (Annapolis: United States Naval Institute Press, 2008), 37.

97. Jessica Stern, "A Radical Idea," *Hoover Digest*, January 23 2012. https://www.hoover.org/research/radical-idea .

98. Charles Kurzman, *The Missing Martyrs: Why There Are So Few Muslim Terrorists* (New York: Oxford University Press, 2011), 30–31.

99. Steve Coll, *Ghost Wars: The Secret History of the CIA, Afghanistan, and bin Laden, From the Soviet Invasion to September 10, 2001* (New York: Penguin, 2005), 144–146.

100. Seth G. Jones, *Hunting in the Shadows: The Pursuit of Al Qa'ida Since 9/11* (New York: W.W. Norton, 2012) 176–177.

101. Quoted in Matthew W.S. Ryan, *Decoding Al-Qaeda's Strategy: The Deep Battle Against America* (New York: Columbia University Press, 2013), 77.

102. Bergen, *The Longest War,* 171.

103. Michael R. Gordon and Bernard E. Trainor, *Endgame: The Inside Story of the Struggle for Iraq, From George W. Bush to Barack Obama* (New York: Vintage, 2012), 191–2.

104. Carter Malkasian, *Illusions of Victory: The Anbar Awakening and the Rise of the Islamic State* (New York: Oxford University Press, 2017), 64–66.

105. Joby Warrick, *Black Flags: The Rise of ISIS* (New York: Anchor Books, 2016), 128.

106. Gordon and Trainor, *Endgame,* 251.

107. Malkasian, *Illusions of Victory,* 151–152.

108. Barak Mendelsohn, *The Al-Qaeda Franchise: The Expansion of Al-Qaeda and Its Consequences* (New York: Oxford University Press, 2015), 80–81.

109. Michael Scheuer, *Osama Bin Laden* (New York: Oxford University Press, 2011), 143–144.

110. Charles R. Lister, *The Syrian Jihad: Al-Qaeda, the Islamic State and the Evolution of an Insurgency* (New York: Oxford University Press, 2015), 65.

Chapter Six

The Nature of Battle Today

Contemporary examples of terrorist campaigns do not fit as neatly into the categories of state-directed, non-state, state-maker, or-state wrecker. At the same time, the breakdown of these conceptual boundaries has moved the practice of terrorism closer than ever to the theoretical ideal of absolute war. Modern-day terrorists are no more likely than their historical antecedents to inflict a decisive defeat against their enemies, but they are better able to form a community of combatants and perpetuate the struggle regardless of the prospects for outright victory. The categories which traditionally defined the objectives and parameters of a terrorist campaign are now more likely to serve as a menu of options, with combatants jumping from one phase of action to another to capitalize on new opportunities or recover momentum after a setback. This development brings terrorism further beyond traditional models of warfare, coercive diplomacy, and counterterrorism, and calls for a revised set of guiding principles and assumptions for interpreting and responding to contemporary terrorism.

There is a dire need for greater theoretical discipline with respect to questions of terrorism and counterterrorism. Public and political discourse regarding terrorism, especially in the United States, tends to assume a problem calling for a solution, with debates centering around the proper balance of diplomacy, community outreach, law enforcement, economic development, and military force.[1] The search for a solution has spawned a counterterrorism industry composed of thousands of government agencies and private organizations analyzing every conceivable aspect of terrorist recruitment, finance, and operations.[2] As terrorists kill more people and cause more damage than at any time in history,[3] the budgets and mandates of these agencies expand still further, until their sheer size and complexity renders them invulnerable to political oversight, public accountability, or questioning of why all their spilled ink has failed to reduce the spilling of blood.

A Clausewitzian perspective is necessary to arrest this cycle and reframe the public debate within the realm of political possibility rather than fear and bureaucratic inertia. Colin Wight identifies three factors which are crucial to the development of a theory of terrorism:

> "an integration of theories of the state and its development into the field; the adoption of a structural approach over the more psychological approaches that currently dominate; and a more historically grounded understanding of terrorism as opposed to the presentism that dominates post-9/11."[4]

Terrorism, like war, is an inevitable byproduct of the international system, resulting from the paradox of the nation-state as a universally valid model for particular peoples to determine their own political destiny. When political reality appears to have completely diverged from the ideal in the eyes of a people (or a vanguard claiming to represent them), terrorism supplies the methodology and rationale for achieving a more authentic expression of the free and independent community. One cannot root out terrorism without also eliminating the belief that guiding principles and rational design can shape and continuously improve political institutions, a belief which underpins the legitimacy of the modern state.

The increasing prevalence of terrorism and the blurring of its state-directed and non-state variants indicates growing dissatisfaction with the nation-state, especially as the liberal international order suffers from a variety of external pressures and internal maladies. The weakening or outright breakdown of that order in several regions has prompted a wider variety of actors to experiment with alternative methods of power projection and communal formation.[5] The prevailing methods of inductive, "actor-specific"[6] studies of terrorism are patently insufficient for keeping pace with the proliferation of these examples. A deductive theory of terrorism rooted in the concept of absolute war locates the vast range of examples along the spectrum between the extremes of state-making and state-wrecking. Contemporary examples will not fit neatly into one category or another, but the many nuanced ways in which they integrate the two has only confirmed the integrity of the theoretical model and made it better able to explain reality. This is cold comfort for the analysts and policymakers who have to reconcile the public's demand for solutions against a phenomenon that has become increasingly embedded within the international system. Even so, a proper theoretical baseline is necessary for crafting and implementing strategies that enfold terrorism within the logic of reciprocity rather than pursue a decisive victory, only to tear down barriers to escalation and enter a condition of absolute war which they are ill-equipped to fight.

THE SPIRIT OF THE AGE

War by Other Means

Clausewitz's insistence on war as an extension of policy by other means speaks to the tension between theory and practice at the heart of his work. Logically, war cannot be anything other than a political instrument since politics alone dictates its commencement, continuation, and termination. Throughout most of the history of warfare prior to the writing of *On War*, this observation would be so obviously true as to be uninteresting, and so most military writings confined the theory of warfare to the latest lessons drawn from the battlefield. Clausewitz's axiom only became a classic statement of military wisdom when social and technological developments made it a contestable proposition. As the raw power of peoples burst through traditional political constraints, warfare "took on an entirely different character, or rather closely approached its true character."[7] For many of Clausewitz's contemporaries, Napoleon revealed that war had become the canvas of "the supreme commander . . . who by sheer intellect and will dominated the men who served him and used them to defeat his enemies."[8] Clausewitz countered this assertion with the counterintuitive claim that the expanding scale and violence of warfare made its rational essence all the more apparent. The actual approximation of decisive warfare revealed the trinity in its fullest dimensions and defined the outer limits of what war could achieve.

The abolition of traditional limits was regrettable insofar as technological and customary restrictions on warfare would never again be sufficient to halt escalation toward its theoretical perfection. The additional weight given each component of the trinity and the broader range of potential outcomes would leave policymakers with no easy answers for how to keep war limited while reserving the capacity to fight should those efforts fail. In these treacherous waters, the principal of warfare as an extension of policy by other means served as a compass to focus the soldier and statesman on the one permanently operating truth that persists amid a general condition of radical uncertainty. The prospect of total war turns Clausewitz's famous phrase into a piece of practical advice as well as a theoretical postulate. Even the most total instances of warfare generated formal and informal political structures which preserved and restored the logic of reciprocity after an outburst of elemental violence smashed the existing constraints. Napoleon, Ludendorff, and Hitler had each "fallen in love with war," believing that the certainties of combat would overwhelm the subtle political calculations of the Coalitions aligned against them. Yet each succumbed to enemies who discovered a more complete truth of warfare through "the simultaneous comprehension of contradictions"[9] of theory, training, policy, and countless other factors that prohibit the race from simply going to the swift.

Terrorism emerged from the same set of forces that subjected the international system to a permanent risk of total war. The capabilities and ideologies that enabled states to mobilize an unprecedented share of their population also enabled states to mobilize against its people or for people to mobilize against their states in larger numbers and with increasingly innovative tactics. Throughout most of the history of terrorism, it occupied a place within the international system comparable to the warfare of *l'ancien regime*, in that technological advancements did not make it more threatening to the system since the overall correlation of forces favored the status quo. For example, Peter Neumann distinguishes "new" terrorism from the "old" as the transition from hierarchical to network-based structures, the avowal of religious ideologies, and greater reliance on indiscriminate violence.[10] Terrorist organizations would continually be a source of instability as they evolved in their ability to strike targets, communicate with a mass audience, and evade state surveillance. But so long as states drew the proper lessons from these innovations, counterterrorist forces would be able to keep the threat within manageable dimensions.[11]

Similar logic applied to instances of state-directed terrorism. During the Cold War, most instances of state-directed terrorism either failed to distract the Great Powers from their rivalry or were too enfolded within that rivalry to permit a reaction. When the collapse of the Soviet Union loosened the restrictions on the exercise of American power, the power to calibrate precise degrees of military and diplomatic power appeared to grant policymakers the freedom to tailor their strategies in accordance with the particular character of a rogue state. The most noxious actors, such as Saddam Hussein, called for a policy of active rollback with the ultimate goal of regime change. Others, such as North Korea or Iran, would call for the classic containment model of sustained diplomatic and economic isolation combined with deterrent military capabilities to maximize the stress on the regime's internal weaknesses. Any regime that expresses a desire for *rapprochement* would merit a policy of "conditional containment" with a restoration to the good graces of international society hinging on continued demonstrations of good behavior.[12] Disagreements over the relative merits of engaging or pressuring a particular regime took place under the common assumption that the liberal international order was basically stable and that there was a fully formed strategy around which the interests of major players could converge.[13]

Absolute War and Endless War

The impact of the September 11th attacks on prevailing notions of terrorism was comparable to Goethe's reaction to the Battle of Valmy in September 1792. Serving alongside Clausewitz in the Prussian army, which suffered a shocking defeat at the hands of the French Revolutionary Army, the future luminary of German literature commented that "from this place and from this day forth commences a new era in the world's history and you can all say that you were present at its birth."[14] Likewise, it has become commonplace to divide the "pre-9/11 world" from everything that has occurred since. The attacks "caused an abrupt shift in national assumptions about terrorism," which "began to be spoken of an as an existential threat to the United States."[15] Terrorism itself seemed to have morphed from a political nuisance to a pure expression of fury for its own sake. As Louis Richardson describes it,

> "first was the sense that the organization was driven by irrational religious fanatics, so their behavior was likely to be both unpredictable and unconstrained . . . second was the belief that al-Qaeda wanted to kill as many Americans as it could; if it would destroy the World Trade Center, al-Qaeda would not hesitate to use weapons of mass destruction against the United States."[16]

Such conclusions were not the exclusive province of a fearful and ignorant public. Even Bruce Hoffman, a major figure in the field of terrorism studies, argued that

> "terrorism motivated either in whole or in part by a religious imperative, where violence is regarded by its practitioners as a divine duty or sacramental act, embraces markedly different man of legitimation and justification that that committed by secular terrorists, and these distinguishing features lead, in turn, to yet greater bloodshed and destruction."[17]

The claim that everything changed after 9/11 was ironic in that its most fervent proponents relied on familiar patterns of thought to market their favored policies. American politicians cited an unprecedented threat from terrorism to advance an interventionist grand strategy which had been waiting in the wings since the collapse of the Soviet Union.[18] Scholars proclaiming the arrival of Huntington's "clash of civilizations" fell back on a centuries-old "constructed image of Islamic civilization" as mystical and backward compared with a rational and progressive West.[19] The new terrorism called for a new response, most notably an ongoing Global War on Terror without clear spatial, temporal, or political limits, but this assumption simply reconstructed the pre-9/11 logic of counterterrorism on a broader scale. Still, an alternating reliance on regime change, counterinsurgency, targeted killing, public diplomacy, and state-building have all been revolutionary attempts to maintain a system-wide status quo in which states (preferably democracies) dictate and enforce the terms of political competition.

From the perspective of the modern advanced democracies, terrorism is a Hydra-headed and permanently dangerous nemesis, against which victory is practically assured given sufficient vigilance, resolve, and tactical imagination.[20] The common assumption linking these seemingly contradictory claims is that terrorism exists entirely outside the boundaries of international order. So long as counterterrorism methods are successful in keeping it to the margins, even an indefinite campaign will still have minimal impact on overall health of the system. Ian Shapiro advocates for a strategy of containment, which "flows naturally out of the democratic understanding of non-domination," rooted in the collective security within the liberal order and patient support for democratization and development outside of it."[21] Michael Rubin offers a more hawkish alternative, albeit one rooted in a similarly binary interpretation of international politics. Democracies may safely engage "rivals" who share a basic commitment to international laws and norms, but with "rogue" dictators and terrorist organizations, dialogue will only "convince [them] that bad behavior pays."[22] A policy of relentless confrontation may be no more tenable than appeasement, but the integrity of the liberal order depends on its ability to face down and gradually phase out the last vestiges of opposition.

Even in the complete absence of agreement on the laws of war or the appropriate character of the peace, the mere ability to engage terrorism implies a symmetrical relationship and the possibility of reciprocal action. Furthermore, a prolonged experience of war or security competition invariably gives way to a process of tactical mirroring between the adversaries even as the experience of combat hardens their respective hostility. This is more obvious with respect to interstate competition, no matter the internal differences or divergent interests between them. During the Cold War, for example, the United States learned to adjust its typical suspicion of centralized authority with the patent necessity of maintaining a state of permanent readiness for total war.[23] The symmetrical foundations of interstate rivalry made it easier for the U.S. and U.S.S.R. to tweak their grand strategy with an eye toward external necessity as well as domestic institutions and values. American liberalism and Soviet communism offered parallel visions of international order, each with sufficient institutional coherence to set the parameters of a fierce yet relative competition over allies, growth rates, first-strike capability, and Olympic gold medals.

Rogue states and terrorist organizations appear to have placed themselves beyond the pale of comparison, and "from an ontological perspective, terrorist organizations pose a more significant danger to political communities than conventional state enemies" since they reject the legitimacy of the system itself. Yet this fundamental dispute over modes of legitimacy springs from terrorists having thoroughly appropriated the logic of the modern state as a means of challenging its dominant modes and orders. State-makers "evoke territoriality and claim legitimation in ways reminiscent of the nation-state principle,"[24] while state-wreckers look beyond the physical dimensions of statehood to the guiding ideals of self-determination and egalitarianism. State-directed terror of course takes on the concrete form of the modern state, and also claims a more straightforward approximation of its underlying character. A state-directed terrorist campaign flouts all the rules which the status quo powers have imposed from a position of relative comfort, and in doing so more fully approaches the Hobbesian ideal of the "mortal God"[25] whose word is no less binding than its cosmic model.

With the September 11th attacks, Al Qaeda precisely targeted the dual conception of the modern state as exclusive guardian of national security and facilitator of globalization. The destruction of the World Trade Center and the Pentagon were designed to prove the impossibility of a superpower taking on both roles, forcing a painful trade-off between freedom and security compared to Al Qaeda's adept navigation of transnational networks and courageous defense of the *umma*.[26] In response, the United States sought to guarantee its own domestic security by isolating terrorists from global systems of travel, finance, and media and then destroying them piecemeal. However, the declaration of a War on Terror combined with a rejection of any commonality between the two sides has in fact accelerated the mimetic tendencies of combat, a trend which terrorism is already designed to magnify.

While proclaiming a complete moral difference between itself and its opponent, the United States accepted Al Qaeda's ideological interpretation of a clash between the West and Islam, albeit reframed as the affirmation of modernity over barbarism.[27] In doing so, it adopted the premise that combat is a positive good for communal formation, both in terms of keeping the knife of American power sharp and ushering the Islamic world into their liberal future. For example, in 2006 then-Secretary of State Condoleezza Rice referred to the Israeli war with Hezbollah as "the birth pangs of a new Middle East . . . we have to be certain that we're pushing forward to the new Middle East, not going back to the old one."[28] Subsequent U.S. administrations have toned down the rhetoric of transformation, while still defending indefinite military action as the necessary precondition of good governance in Afghanistan, Iraq, Syria, Yemen, and Somalia, along with a pseudo-secret campaign in Pakistan.[29] The American insistence on unequivocal military victory in each theater has in turn prompted its adversaries to make similarly hardline demands against U.S.-backed regimes and proxies. Now that the U.S. is delegating the burdens of fighting to those local allies without compromising its basic objectives, each of these states is trapped in a war in which both sides have made utterly irreconcilable and unalterable demands that neither side can reasonably hope to achieve.

Each side's demand for total victory combined with the practical impossibility of decisive results has compelled them to shed political restraints and instead progress toward a purely competitive logic, with the enemy serving as the primary frame of reference. ISIS recruits who claim to despise all "innovation" since the Prophetic generation take to Facebook and Twitter to espouse a "selfie individualism"[30] while undertaking a thoroughly modern effort in state-building and social engineering. Every U.S. presidential administration since 9/11 has in one way or another argued that the effective targeting of terrorists requires enormous latitude with regard to the laws of war (if not their explicit rejection) on issues such as indefinite detention, enhanced interrogation, or standard definitions of what constitutes a legitimate combatant.[31] This has placed the state in what Stanley Hoffman calls a "perfectly paradoxical situation," in which it is:

> "open to all forms of insecurity coming from the outside, and its attempts to overcome these, by controlling access or by extensive surveillance of potential suspects, risk delivering it to various policies and to professional anti-liberals, as well as creating citizens with limited rights and immigrants under suspicion, without, however, ever reaching the famous 'homeland security' about which so much is said."[32]

The elusiveness of perfect domestic security permits the continued use of American military power abroad, which with ample practice has honed the projection of power at multi-continental distances. Refinements in the art of surveillance and targeted killing in particular have enabled the armed services and intelligence agencies to adopt the advantages traditionally associated with the other, at vanishing risks to themselves.[33] Yet this has lowered the costs of the enemy in unanticipated ways. The grinding down of tribal society in Yemen and Pakistan under sustained drone warfare has produced a steady trickle of displaced persons into the cities. This makes terrorist recruitment considerably easier in these areas, has driven peoples on the social periphery with little refuge, making him easy prey to recruitment, which in turn creates a determined and wide-ranging network out of individuals with no other prospects for an honorable existence.[34]

War usually entails a symmetrical measurement of gains and loss. This campaign permits both sides to perceive themselves as winning and losing at the same time, giving rise to a mixture of optimism and despair that perpetuates the mutual will to fight indefinitely.[35] Open-ended warfare intended to secure the dominance of the sovereign state has instead led to "the fragmentation and increasing impotence of territorial sovereign states in both governing the political process and controlling violence." The breakdown of traditional institutions results in "the escalation of unchecked competition amongst political subjects-turned individual sovereigns,"[36] who are both atomized and enjoy instant access to others sharing their grievances. The War on Terror has succeeded in its stated goal of tearing down the obstacles to individual freedom, only to weaken the power of states vis-à-vis motivated individuals with the urge and capacity to leverage that freedom against the state and one another.

The New Spectrum of Terrorism

Clausewitz's career as an officer and scholar centered on a similar intermingling of ostensible ideological opposites. The spread of Napoleon's empire promised the universalization of *liberté*, *égalité*, *et fraternité*, only to exhibit the same habits of feudal nepotism as the Hapsburg dynasty into which he had married. Monarchies such as Prussia had learned at great cost that their military effectiveness depended upon their adopting the Napoleonic model of a highly motivated mass army, even as they desperately looked for ways to avoid imbibing the egalitarian politics that typically came with it.[37] The advanced Western democracies have reacted to terrorism as the monarchs of the Holy Alliance reacted to liberal democracy, operating on the assumption that the preservation of the system principally entails the complete destruction of the enemy. Just as the monarchic counterrevolution had the unintended consequence of making nationalism compatible with authoritarianism, the worldwide campaign against terrorism has brought terrorist tactics and state institutions into closer alignment than ever.

The Islamic world has of course borne the brunt of these convulsions. The collapse of the Iraqi state in 2003 and its descent into sectarian infighting enabled Iran to put its longstanding ties to foreign militias, terrorist organizations, and Shi'a political parties to good use and dial the degree of instability up and down as its interests required.[38] After the Arab Spring spread the prospect of subversion to the entire region, Saudi Arabia has since done its best to copy the Iranian playbook, locking the region into a sectarian conflagration that neither of its principals can control.[39] The Syrian Civil War epitomizes the nature and consequences of this conceptual breakdown. The Assad regime is engaged in a full-scale campaign of state terrorism, with the full and active support of a Great Power, forming a new community of the faithful from the wreckage of the old state. This campaign has in turn spawned numerous dyads between states and non-state organizations, creating a fiendishly complex patchwork of terrorism and power politics.[40]

The fracturing of the Syrian state has breathed new life into the nationalist ambitions of the Kurdistan Workers' Party (PKK), which has earned American sponsorship and armaments despite its remaining on the State Department's list of foreign terrorist organizations and the fierce opposition of NATO ally Turkey.[41] Hezbollah had already made a success transition from its terrorist campaign of the 1980s to the most dominant political party in Lebanon, a state within the state, and a occasional champion of nationalism in a divided country.[42] Breaking from its traditional focus on Lebanon, Hezbollah forces have deployed alongside their Syrian allies and taken part in major combat operations, while an escalating cycle of bombings and assassinations with Sunni militias and Israel has brought the war home to Hezbollah's core audience.[43] Iran, Turkey, Russia, and the U.S. are all direct participants, seeking to keep the others in check by extending deterrence to favored militias and terrorist organizations. Due to the secrecy surrounding these ties and their asymmetry of objectives, it is even more difficult than usual for states to issue clear warnings, guarantee that a certain enemy action against the proxy will merit a specific result, and coordinate the behavior of their proxy accordingly.[44] As a result, the traditional traditional risk of inter-state confrontation and unintended escalation into major war caps off this quintessentially modern conflict.

There is no blueprint or set of core principles for resolving any of these crises, but the beginning of effective diplomacy and strategy is the establish-ment of a proper theoretical basis through which to interpret each case as part of a broader whole. Terrorism has always sought out an approximation of absolute war, forming a community composed entirely of combatants whose passion and skills would steadily increase in a continuous effort to break the enemy's will, with the creation of that community serving as the real moment of decision. Of course, this ideal is no more achievable than a decisive victory in real war, for the simple fact that terrorists occupy the same physi-cal and psychological reality as conventional combatants, and are thus simi-larly liable to friction and political calculation.

Historically, two principal methods emerged for circumventing these lim-its as much as possible. The first was to utilize the full power of the modern state to obliterate the premodern society over which it ruled, at which point it can reenter a conventional, Machiavellian system with a qualitative advan-tage over its rivals. The second was to rally a popular constituency against the state until the experience of warfare achieved the decisive result of ele-vating the people to a *de facto* condition of statehood or dragging the state into the muck of revolutionary upheaval. Their strategic was fundamentally similar insofar as they employed systematic violence and propaganda to mobilize compliance among an audience beyond their direct victims.[45] Re-gimes that secured power through terrorism usually lasted long enough to transition into conventional politics (such as the Soviet Union and China) or were overthrown, whereupon they either collapsed or reverted to guerrilla warfare against the new regime (such as the Suharto regime in Indonesia or Khmer Rouge in Cambodia, respectively).

Similarly, many non-state campaigns lasted long enough to become thoroughly conventional political actors, and some contemporary examples still follow this model. The most recent example is Colombia's *Fuerzas Armadas Revolucionarias de Colombia-Ejército del Pueblo* (FARC-EP), the world's longest-lasting insurgency, which agreed to a cease-fire following promises of agrarian reform, widespread amnesty, broader avenues for multi-party competition in exchange for an end to militancy and cooperation in suppressing the drug trade.[46] Other campaigns become fixed in a militant posture that cedes the political ground to governments who may then use that power to lay the foundation for severe repression. Sri Lanka's Liberation Tigers of Tamil Eelam (LTTE) had a well-deserved reputation as a force to be reckoned with, which ultimately spurred similar efforts of national mobilization among the Sinhalese majority. As the government of Mahinda Rajapaksa stepped up efforts to cleanse the Tigers from their avowed homeland, India was no longer willing to intervene on behalf of a group that had long disavowed a compromise solution, and only the faintest complaints of human rights abuses interfered with the consensus of a stunning victory against a fearsome organization.[47]

Contemporary terrorists have proven themselves to be far more capable of integrating politics and militancy into a continuous, mutable campaign that can run the full gamut between the institutionalized repression of a state bureaucracy to the self-motivated violence of a lone individual. This tactical fluidity enables them to approximate more closely the ideal of absolute war. This does not automatically mean that terrorists today are more passionate, more skilled, or more likely to succeed relative to their predecessors. Rather, they are able to form communities of fighters with greater efficiency and make tactical adjustments that make them better able to persist or restart the struggle in the wake of resistance or setbacks. They still fall short of the pure ideal of absolute war in that their patterns of escalation can be uneven and the progress of their campaign does not bend unerringly toward a decisive result. Even so, they approach that ideal by making politics coextensive with warfare, rendering all tactical setbacks and momentary compromises subordinate to the indefinite pursuit of the decision, in the meantime drawing sustenance from the conflict itself.

The tactical fluidity of contemporary terrorism has not displaced the categories of state-making and state-wrecking. To the contrary, it has allowed campaigns to adopt either of the two extremes, as well as everything in between, as circumstances dictate. The Taliban represent one side of the spectrum, in which a practitioner of state-directed terrorism-turned-insurgency has gradually incorporated the features of non-state terrorism. Prior to September 11th, the Taliban was on the verge of completing a successful campaign of state terrorism that began with its sudden emergence as a conventional army and governing body in Kandahar in 1994. Its task of reconstituting the Afghan state in line with its harsh form of Deobandism was made easier by the absence of strong institutions after years of civil war, divisions among its enemies, and the extensive support of the Pakistani Inter-Services Intelligence (ISI).[48] Its toleration of Al Qaeda and other foreign militants reflected a prudent, if ultimately faulty, calculation that the benefits of its training fighters for campaigns against the Northern Alliance and India would outweigh the costs of international censure.[49]

Al Qaeda's unilateral attack on the United States upset this delicate calculation and then forced Mullah Omar to defend his disobedient guests against

American demands to hand them over or face invasion. Ever since, the dominant inclination of America policy has been to regard the Taliban as practically synonymous with Al Qaeda, with their complete disarmament being a prerequisite for victory.[50] This conflation of the two entities has in many respects become a self-fulfilling prophecy, as their shared exile in Pakistan's Federally Administered Tribal Areas turned what had been a frosty coexistence into an active partnership to undermine the Afghan government.[51] The magnitude of its defeat in late 2001 permitted a structural overhaul into a network of cells on either side of the Durand Line, new tactics use of suicide bombings, and the birth of a Pakistani affiliate, the *Tehrik-i-Taliban Pakistan*, that has carried out brazen attacks against its erstwhile sponsors.[52] At the same time, the Taliban enjoys enough sanctuary, funding, and support among its core Pashtun constituency to operate simultaneously as a shadow government that collects taxes, regulates the opium trade and administers justices in the vast swaths of countryside where the power of Kabul and its local allies is weak or nonexistent.[53]

The Taliban's resurgence thwarted efforts to hand off Afghan security to Karzai's government, and by the time the Obama administration undertook a concerted response, it faced public fatigue with a nearly decade-long war with no clear payoff. Instead of shifting its strategic priorities, the Obama administration undertook a simultaneous pursuit of battlefield victory, good Afghan governance, and mollification of public opinion. A December 2010 internal review proposed efforts to:

> "continue to degrade the Taliban military and build Afghan capacity to fight the war . . . execute a transition to place Afghan forces in the lead combat role . . . negotiate a long-term strategic and security agreement with Afghanistan . . . stabilize Afghanistan through regional diplomacy . . . [and] pursue reconciliation with the Taliban, through direct talks."[54]

This Rubik's cube of conflicting priorities, to be solved within a maximum timetable of four years, called for a blitz against Taliban forces to bring its leadership to the table while offering a massive aid package through which the Afghan government could draw its rank-and-file into civil society. This strategy collapsed on itself through the "targeting and killing several of the more politically minded leaders . . . in their place, a younger, more radical generation filled the ranks."[55] The U.S. has since settled into a permanent war at minimum cost, as opinion polls show low tolerance for the war itself and overwhelming support for the assassination of perceived terrorists.[56] Expectations that the Taliban will eventually tire are belied by evidence of their increased tactical effectiveness, launching assaults on urban targets and occupying provinces outside of their traditional base of operations in the Pashtun-dominant south.[57] Even if the United States continually provides enough support to the Afghans for as long as it takes to deprive the Taliban of a victory, or the Taliban proves unable to restore the entire country to their rule, they appear better equipped to design their institutions and ideology around the reality of endless war.

At the other end of the spectrum is the self-proclaimed Islamic State (commonly referred to as ISIS), which began as a non-state terrorist campaign and then incorporated the features of state-directed terrorism as it grew in power. Many non-state terrorist campaigns have attempted the transition to statehood, and some have succeeded, but typically on the premise that institutional stability would reduce the need for terroristic violence. ISIS broke from this model and drew on the fruits of its military success to ramp up its efforts at revolutionary agitation beyond the borders of its declared caliphate.[58] ISIS turned Randolph Bourne's axiom that "war is the health of the state" into a literal policy. Having drawn tens of thousands of foreign fighters to supplement its already substantial contingent of Iraqi and Syrian Sunnis, ISIS carved out an empire which at its peak in 2014 and 2015 ruled half the territory of Syria and Iraq, a territory approximately the size of the United Kingdom, with an estimated eight million people under its control.[59] Recent reviews of documents retrieved from its extraordinarily complex bureaucracy describe entire agencies devoted to expropriating the property of religious minorities and allocating them to those for whom the mere joy of serving the caliphate may not have been sufficient motivation.[60] As its conquests and attendant atrocities prompted the formation of a U.S.-led coalition, terrorist attacks on coalition members such as the November 2015 Paris massacre would deter intervention, earn ample rewards for the families of its executors, and reify its motto of "endure and expand" on a global scale.[61] In the meantime, it maintained popular support through the maintenance of a civil society at least as effective as that provided by the Iraqi government, if not more so. In addition to soliciting fighters, ISIS leadership also made explicit appeals to "scholars . . . preachers, especially the judges, as well as people with administrative, military, and service expertise, and medical doctors and engineers of all different specializations and fields,"[62] whose contributions would in turn make the state an increasingly attractive destination for increased migration.

In each of its iterations, ISIS has made a cruel mockery of American objectives in Iraq and the region at large. As Al Qaeda in Iraq from 2004 to 2006, it reassembled the shattered remnants of the Ba'athist state and enfolded it within a multinational jihadist network, a "coalition of the willing" capable of balancing against the U.S. and its allies. As the Islamic State of Iraq from 2006 to 2013, it undermined the project of sectarian integration by exploiting the precise points where Sunni grievance outstripped governmental authority. U.S. forces were able to link up with the Iraqi Security Force and local Sunni tribes to expel them from their sanctuaries in Anbar, Diyala, or Salah-al-Din provinces. Despite these successes, the Shi'a-dominated government in Baghdad began to balk at the prospect of raising paramilitary forces across the entirety of Sunni Iraq, beginning a campaign of persecution that ruined its alliance with the tribes just as American forces were departing.[63] The Islamic State of Iraq and al-Sham (2013 onward) subverted Western optimism regarding the Arab Spring by leveraging discontent with established regional rulers into a full-scale assault on the states themselves. Armed with their own set of universal principles with which to engineer an ideological transformation of the Middle East, they proved no less capable of drawing an overwhelmingly young and social media-savvy audience to embrace their conception of a "just and inclusive order."[64]

As of August 2018, ISIS has lost nearly all of the territory it once occupied, including every city, and mostly earns its headlines through self-motivated individuals around the world who pledge allegiance to it moments before committing terrorist attacks, in many cases with no actual direct connection between them. Yet ISIS still claims dozens of *wilayat* ("provinces") in Nigeria, Libya, Sinai, Uzbekistan, Bangladesh, Afghanistan, the Philippines, among many others, any of which are capable of disrupting local government or provoking an American response to boost their profile. Despite their apparently failed attempt to build an actual state, they have successfully established a parallel model of the state as an invisible linkage of like-minded and motivated individuals, capable of transcending cultural and geographical barriers on behalf of a unifying principle. Within the erstwhile caliphate, the enormous costs of the campaign to reclaim occupied territory have inhibited a reconciliation between its former subjects, even its most unwilling ones, and the Iraqi government. The substantial role of Iranian-backed "Popular Mobilization Forces" in the retaking of Sunni-majority cities such as Mosul and Ramadi all but guarantees an undercurrent of sectarian tension, if not a renewed bout of fighting.[65] ISIS may be confined to the underground fringe of Sunni discontent, but they have also displayed the capacity to ensure that no higher form of government can function when that discontent is activated, and that the world as a whole can never have the luxury of forgetting it.

CONCLUSION: COUNTERTERRORISM AND LIMITED WAR

Appeals to the wisdom of Clausewitz have become so common in the literature of military theory and strategy that his most famous precepts are at risk of becoming clichés. This book has shown how Clausewitz's method can improve the study of terrorism, even if his strategic precepts do not quite apply. Returning to Clausewitz is an especially worthwhile endeavor at this point because the current state of terrorism indicates a political environment similar to that which prompted the writing of *On War*. Terrorists can erect new communities through violence and propaganda in an instant, which like total war before the age of Napoleon had always been possible but was rare due to technological and political limits. Clausewitz sought to reconcile the desirability for political control over warfare with the objective reality of its potential escalation. His formulation of war as an extension of policy by other means contains a dual meaning as either "policy" or "politics" (a distinction more clearly encapsulated within the original German word *politik*).[66] As an extension of policy, the military instrument must remain subordinate to political ends. As an extension of politics, the character of warfare will result from the aggregation of systemic developments which then countermand the preferences of any particular state.[67] Clausewitz argues that a frank recognition of the potential for total war should generally favor habits of relative restraint, whether out of fear of reciprocity or an affirmation of common norms believed to be vital for systemic maintenance. Such constraints are never guaranteed to hold, but even a relapse into total war will eventually produce a new balance of power and a revised set of conventions for the restoration of normality.

The current campaign against terrorism has combined the means of limited war with the ends of decisive warfare. It acknowledges that the threat is far from existential while refusing to grant it a place within the international system other than that of a cancer to be excised. As many commentators have pointed out, the notion of decisive victory is flatly incompatible with such an imprecise collection of individuals, groups, and ideas.[68] Recent efforts to establish a warlike binary by popularizing a common label of "radical Islamic terrorism" is a gross oversimplification of reality that mirrors and reinforces the premises of terrorist propaganda.[69] The expectation of decisive victory finds its only satisfaction in tactical achievements, upon which a sense of restored security inhibits the political will to invest in the post-conflict environment to a degree commensurate with the scale of the damage. Such a strategy is rational with reference to a policy of killing terrorists and defending the homeland at minimum cost, but the policy fails to account for the broader political consequences. A conception of warfare that begins and ends with the engagement has proven acceptable to public opinion, while ceding the battlefield in the period between engagements to whomever is most capable of exploiting the resultant instability.

A revised understanding of war and terrorism begins with the acknowledgement that states and terrorists, like combatants in a conventional war, have a fundamental point of symmetry. Whereas war typically involves a contest over territory, resources, prestige, or other contestable assets, states and terrorists are engaged in a tug-of-war between two competing ideals of the relationship between war and politics. The state is the embodiment of the Clausewitzian ideal of war as an extension of *politik,* while the architects of a terrorist campaign regard escalation for its own sake as both a political necessity and moral good. Like a conventional war, combat between a state and terrorist campaign does not definitively settle the dispute, but rather nudges it in one direction or another in relative degrees. These adjustments are only loosely connected with military measures of success and failure. A state can smash a cadre of terrorists, only to secure the results of its victory through indefinite repression over their prospective supporters. Alternately, a terrorist campaign can achieve startling military successes only to have its enemies summon the resolve that deprives those successes of any political value.

In light of this likely disparity between military victory and political gains, engagements with terrorist campaigns render the subordination of warfare to politics even more evident and necessary than in conventional warfare. It is tempting for a state to bow to the logic of reciprocal escalation, especially without a reasonable expectation that the enemy will not respect any act of voluntary restraint. However, the pursuit of tactical advantages presumes that one side will reach an intolerable threshold of pain, with the expectation that such pain will lessen or cease in response to a set of desired actions. Wars break out and persist when force is necessary to bring the enemy closer to one's own understanding of an acceptable settlement, but they will only end when both sides are confident that the termination of hostilities will in fact give way to a mutually agreeable form of political interaction. Even with a wide margin of victory, both sides must in some way be able to impose their will upon the enemy and allow it to be imposed in turn. If any kind of settlement short of total victory and defeat is off the table, then the will to fight and endure pain increases in importance as escalation continues.

In sum, the principle objective in an engagement with a terrorist campaign is to bring it from the pursuit of absolute war to within the dimensions of trinitarian calculation. Military force, negotiation, and public engagement must have the common goal of exposing and exploiting the disagreements, trade-offs, and errors that distinguish the realities of war from the ideal of its absolute condition. Before a state can hope to achieve victory, it must first establish the parameters in which the character of its victory is even conceivable. Just as reconnaissance and skirmishing precedes a battle, the initial purpose of engagements should be to develop the fullest possible picture of the enemy's military assets, popular appeal, and political objectives. No less important is the task of determining the likely systemic impact of military action. Judgments will be no less subject to informational gaps and mistaken assumptions than in war, but conventional forces cannot make effective use of their superior firepower without a thorough assessment of how the enemy escalates and how best to arrest that process. Some groups will collapse when a critical mass of its membership dies, goes to prison, or gives up; others may break with a target audience willing to accept political compromises in exchange for a renunciation of violence; others still will focus on holding onto what they has already gained. The particulars of course depend upon the nature of the case, but absolute war will define its basic parameters in the immediate attempt to achieve it, the prospect of introducing it in retaliation for conditions unmet, or giving up on it and transitioning to alternative modes of political action.

Battles reveal the true disparity between opponents, and engagement with terrorist campaigns should likewise serve as a revelatory exercise. In many cases, the experience of combat will reveal a terrorist campaign to be despicable fanatics with no viable basis of popular support, in which case the state can resort to methods more akin to law enforcement than warfare. With respect to terrorists who prove incapable of responding to political incentives and are bent on escalation at all costs, a demonstrated capacity for superior governance is the primary element in weaning a target audience away from the terrorists and their claim that absolute war is the necessary precondition of their ultimate security. Yet there will also be cases in which combat reveals the inability of states to pry a campaign from its audience, at least short of measures whose political effects far outweigh any military benefits. While states need never acknowledge the actions of terrorism as legitimate, they cannot banish it from international politics any more than they can abolish war. States must be in principle willing to accept losses, just as they would accept an unfavorable result to a war as opposed to scorching the earth simply to preserve one's reputation. It is no more dishonorable to cede a marginal interest to a terrorist than a state when the cure of combat is worse than the disease of humiliation, especially given the heterogeneous competition for popular loyalty that characterizes international politics in the twenty-first century. The future is sure to feature near-constant combat with terrorists, but in doing so states must prioritize the avoidance of absolute war over the unconditional defeat of those who threaten it. The international system, rooted as it is in a Machiavellian conception of principled rivalry, can best limit the threat of terrorism by reaffirming the supremacy of political wisdom over moral outrage, and refusing to mirror its enemy's attempted conflation of warfare and politics.

NOTES

1. Seth G. Jones and Martin C. Libicki, *How Terrorist Groups End: Lessons for Countering Al Qa'ida* (Santa Monica: RAND Corporation, 2008), 121–140.

2. Dana Priest and William M. Arkin, *Top Secret America: The Rise of the New American Security State* (New York: Little, Brown & Company, 2011), 85–87.

3. Institute for Economics and Peace, "Global Terrorism Index 2017: Measuring and Understanding the Impact of Terrorism." http://visionofhumanity.org/app/uploads/2017/11/Global-Terrorism-Index-2017.pdf

4. Colin Wight, "Theorising Terrorism: The State, Structure, and History" *International Relations* 23 (2009): 100.

5. Vanda Felbab-Brown, Harold Trinkunas, and Shadi Hamid. *Militants, Criminals, and Warlords: The Challenge of Local Governance in an Age of Disorder* (Washington, D.C.: Brookings Institution Press, 2017), 15.

6. Alexander L. George, "The Need for Influence Theory and Actor-Specific Behavioral Models of Adversaries," *Comparative Strategy* 22 (2003): 463–487.

7. Clausewitz, *On War*, 593.

8. John Shy, "Jomini," in *Makers of Modern Strategy*, ed. Peter Paret, 157.

9. John Lewis Gaddis, *On Grand Strategy* (New York: Penguin Press, 2018), 215.

10. Peter R. Neumann, *Old and New Terrorism: Late Modernity, Globalization and the Transformation of Political Violence* (Cambridge: Polity Press, 2009), 16.

11. Robert J. Art and Louise Richardson, "Democracy and Counterterrorism: Lessons From the Past," in *Democracy and Counterterrorism: Lessons from the Past*, eds. Robert J. Art and Louise Richardson (Washington, D.C.: United States Institute of Peace Press, 2007), 1–24.

12. Robert S. Litwak, *Rogue States and U.S. Foreign Policy: Containment after the Cold War* (Baltimore: The Johns Hopkins University Press, 2000), 103.

13. Thomas J. Wright, *All Measures Short of War: The Contest for the Twenty-First Century and the Future of American Power* (New Haven: Yale University Press, 2017), 10–11.

14. Quoted in Michael A. Bonura, *Under the Shadow of Napoleon: French Influence on the American Way of Warfare from the War of 1812 to the Outbreak of WWII* (New York: New York University Press, 2012), 11.

15. Brian Jackson, ""Don't Let Short-Term Urgency Undermine a Long-Term Security Strategy," in *The Long Shadow of 9/11: America's Response to Terrorism,* eds. Brian Michael Jenkins and John Godges (Santa Monica: RAND Corporation, 2011), 134.

16. Richardson, *What Terrorists Want*, 148.

17. Hoffman, *Inside Terrorism*, 83.

18. Gary Dorrien, *Imperial Designs: Neoconservatism and the New Pax Americana* (New York: Routledge, 2004), 35–37.

19. Khaled Abdul El Fatl, "9/11 and the Muslim Transformation," in *September 11 in History: A Watershed Moment?*, ed. Mary L. Dudziak (Durham: Duke University Press, 2003), 82.

20. Barak Mendelsohn, "Sovereignty Under Attack: International Society Meets the Al Qaeda Network," *Review of International Studies* 31 (2005): 45–68.

21. Ian Shapiro, *Containment: Rebuilding a Strategy Against Global Terror* (Princeton: Princeton University Press, 2009), 102.

22. Michael Rubin, *Dancing With the Devil: The Perils of Engaging Rogue Regimes* (New York: Encounter Books, 2014), 322.

23. Aaron L. Friedberg, *In the Shadow of the Garrison State: America's Anti-Statism and Its Cold War Grand Strategy* (Princeton: Princeton University Press, 2012), 62.

24. Ayse Zarakol, "What Makes Terrorism Modern?" Terrorism, Legitimacy, and the International System," *Review of International Studies* 37 (2011): 2311–2336.

25. Hobbes, *Leviathan*, 132.

26. Mark Juergensmeyer, *Global Rebellion: Religious Challenges to the Secular State, From Christian Militias to Al Qaeda* (Berkeley: University of California Press, 2008), 205–206.

27. Christopher McIntosh, "Counterterrorism as War: Identifying the Dangers, Risks, and Opportunity Costs of U.S. Strategy toward al Qaeda and Its Affiliates," *Studies in Conflict & Terrorism* 38 (2015): 23–24.

28. Quoted in Thanassis Cambanis, *A Privilege to Die: Hezbollah's Legions and Their Endless War against Israel* (New York: Simon & Schuster, 2010), 118

29. Ronan Farrow, *War on Peace: The End of Diplomacy and the Decline of American Influence* (New York: W.W. Norton, 2018), 155.

30. Mishra, *Age of Anger*, 294.

31. Jason Ralph, *America's War on Terror: The State of the 9/11 Exception from Bush to Obama* (New York: Oxford University Press, 2013), 114.

32. Stanley Hoffman, *Chaos and Violence: What Globalization, Failed States, and Terrorism Mean for U.S. Foreign Policy* (Lanham: Rowman & Littlefield, 2006), 23.

33. Mark Mazzetti, *The Way of the Knife: The CIA, A Secret Army and a War at the Ends of the Earth* (New York: Penguin, 2013), xxx.

34. Akbar Ahmed, *The Thistle and the Drone: How America's War on Terror Became a Global War on Tribal Islam* (Washington, D.C.: Brookings Institution Press, 2013), 334–335.

35. Audrey Kurth Cronin, "What Is Really Changing? Change and Continuity in Global Terrorism," in *The Changing Character of War*, eds. Hew Strachan and Sibylle Scheiper (New York: Oxford University Press, 2011), 141–142.

36. Elisabetta Brighi, "The Mimetic Politics of Lone-Wolf Terrorism," *Journal of International Political Theory* 11 (2015): 10.

37. John Hutchinson, *Nationalism and War* (New York: Oxford University Press, 2017), 39.

38. Kenneth Katzman, *Iran's Activities and Influence in Iraq* (Washington, D.C.: Congressional Research Institute, 2009), 1–9.

39. F. Gregory Gause III, *Saudi Arabia in the New Middle East* (New York: Council on Foreign Relations, 2011), 17–20.

40. Raymond Hinnebusch, "From Westphalian Failure to Heterarchic Governance in MENA: The Case of Syria," *Small Wars & Insurgencies* 29 (2018): 391–413.

41. Adam Baczko, Gilles Dorronsoro, and Arthur Quesnay, *Civil War in Syria: Mobilization and Competing Social Orders* (New York: Cambridge University Press, 2017), 176.

42. Eitan Azani, "The Hybrid Terrorist Organization: Hezbollah as a Case Study," *Studies in Conflict & Terrorism* 36 (2013): 899–916.

43. Augustus Richard Norton, *Hezbollah: A Short History* (Princeton: Princeton University Press, 2014), 192–198.

44. Alex Wilner, "The Dark Side of Extended Deterrence: Thinking Through the State Sponsorship of Terrorism," *Journal of Strategic Studies* 40 (2017): 5–11.

45. David Claridge, "State Terrorism? Applying a Definitional Model," *Terrorism and Political Violence* 8 (1996): 50.

46. Carlos Nasi, "The Peace Process with the FARCP-EP," in *Truth Justice, and Reconciliation in Colombia: Transitioning from Violence*, ed. Fabio Andres Diaz Pabon (New York: Routledge, 2018), 34–49.

47. Ahmed S. Hashim, *When Counterinsurgency Wins: Sri Lanka's Defeat of the Tamil Tigers* (Philadelphia: University of Pennsylvania Press, 2013), 183–185.

48. Larry P. Goodson, *Afghanistan's Endless War: State Failure, Regional Politics, and the Rise of the Taliban* (Seattle: University of Washington Press, 2001), 114.

49. Anne Stenerson, *Al-Qaida in Afghanistan* (New York: Cambridge University Press, 2017), 131.

50. Van Linschoten and Kuehn, *An Enemy We Created*, 326.

51. Jones, *In the Graveyard of Empires*, 279–295.

52. Hassan Abbas, *The Taliban Revival: Violence and Extremism on the Pakistan-Afghanistan Frontier* (New Haven: Yale University Press, 2014), 151.

53. Rajiv Chandrasakeran,. *Little America: The War within the War for Afghanistan* (New York: Alfred A. Knopf, 2012), 45.

54. Steve Coll, *Directorate S: The C.I.A. and America's Secret Wars in Afghanistan and Pakistan* (New York: Penguin Press, 2018), 511.

55. Jack Fairweather, *The Good War: Why We Couldn't Win the War or the Peace in Afghanistan* (New York: Basic Books, 2014), 311–312.

56. Ibid., 331.

57. Stephen M. Walt, "ISIS as Revolutionary State." *Foreign Affairs* 94 (2015): 42–51.

58. David Kilcullen, *Blood Year: The Unraveling of Western Counterterrorism* (New York: Oxford University Press, 2016), 180–181.

59. Ibid., 151–152.

60. Rukmini Callimachi, "The ISIS Files," *The New York Times*, April 4 2018.

61. William McCants, *The ISIS Apocalypse: The History, Strategy, and Doomsday Vision of the Islamic State* (New York: St. Martin's Press, 2015), 145–146.

62. Mia Bloom, "Constructing Expertise: Terrorist Recruitment and 'Talent Spotting' in the PIRA, Al Qaeda, and ISIS," *Studies in Conflict & Terrorism* 40 (2017): 616.

63. Patrick B. Johnson, et al. *Foundations of the Islamic State: Management, Money, and Terror in Iraq, 2005–2010* (Santa Monica: RAND Corporation, 2016), 46–47.

64. Fawaz A. Gerges, *ISIS: A History* (Princeton: Princeton University Press, 2016), 46.

65. Renad Mansour and Faleh A. Jabar, *The Popular Mobilization Forces and Iraq's Future* (Washington, D.C.: Carnegie Endowment for International Peace, 2017), 23–24.

66. Hugh Smith, *On Clausewitz: A Study of Military and Political Ideas* (New York: Palsgrave Macmillan, 2004), 98–99.

67. Bassford, *Clausewitz in English*, 22.

68. Ian S. Lustick, *Trapped in the War on Terror* (Philadelphia: University of Pennsylvania Press, 2006), 68.

69. David L. Altheide, *Terrorism and the Politics of Fear* (Lanham: Rowman & Littlefield, 2017), 205.

Bibliography

Abbas, Hassan. *The Taliban Revival: Violence and Extremism on the Pakistan-Afghanistan Frontier*. New Haven: Yale University Press, 2014.

Abrahms, Max. "What Terrorists Really Want: Terrorist Motives and Counterterrorism Strategy." *International Security* 32 (2008): 78–105.

Abrahms, Max and Philip B.K. Potter. "Explaining Terrorism: Leadership Deficits and Militant Group Tactics." *International Organization* 69 (2015): 311–342.

Aftalion, Florin. *The French Revolution: An Economic Interpretation*. New York: Cambridge University Press, 1990.

Ahmed, Akbar. *The Thistle and the Drone: How America's War on Terror Became a War on Tribal Islam*. Washington, D.C.: Brookings Institution Press, 2013.

Altheide, David L. *Terrorism and the Politics of Fear*. Lanham: Rowman & Littlefield, 2017.

Anderson, Benedict. *Imagined Communities: Reflections on the Origin and Spread of Nationalism*. New York: Verso, 2006.

Applebaum, Anne. *Gulag: A History*. New York: Anchor Books, 2003.

———. *Iron Curtain: The Crushing of Eastern Europe, 1944–1956*. New York: Anchor Books, 2013.

Ardito, Alissa M. *Machiavelli and the Modern State: The Prince, The Discourses on Livy, and the Extended Territorial Republic*. New York: Cambridge University Press, 2015.

Arendt, Hannah. *The Origins of Totalitarianism* (New York: Houghton Mifflin Harcourt, 1994.

Aron, Raymond. *The Century of Total War*. Boston: Beacon Press, 1954.

———. *Clausewitz: Philosopher of War*. New York: Touchstone, 1983.

———. *Peace & War: A Theory of International Relations*. New Brunswick: Transaction Publishers, 2003.

Art, Robert J. and Louise Richardson. "Democracy and Counterterrorism: Lessons from the Past." In *Democracy and Counterterrorism: Lessons From the Past*. Edited by Robert J. Art and Louise Richardson, 1–24. Washington, D.C.: United States Institute of Peace Press, 2007.

Aust, Stefan. *Baader-Meinhof: The Inside Story of the R.A.F.* London: Random House, 2008.

Azani, Eitan. "The Hybrid Terrorist Organization: Hezbollah as a Case Study." *Studies in Conflict & Terrorism* 36 (2013): 899–916.

Baczko, Adam, Gilles Dorronsoro, and Arthur Quesnay. *Civil War in Syria: Mobilization and Competing Social Orders*. New York: Cambridge University Press, 2017.

Bandura, Albert. "Mechanisms of Moral Disengagement in Terrorism." In *Origins of Terrorism: Psychologies, Ideologies, Theologies, States of Mind*. Edited by Walter Reich, 161–191. New York: Cambridge University Press, 1990.

Amatzia Baram, *Building toward Crisis: Saddam Husayn's Strategy for Survival.* Washington, D.C.: Washington Institute for Near East Policy, 1998.

——. *Culture, History and Ideology in the Formation of Ba'athist Iraq, 1968–89.* New York: Palgrave Macmillan, 1991.

Barkin, J. Samuel and Bruce Cronin. "The State and the Nation: Changing Norms and Rules of Sovereignty in International Relations." *International Organization* 48 (1994): 107–30.

Bassford, Christopher. *Clausewitz in English: The Reception of Clausewitz in Britain and America.* New York: Oxford University Press, 1994.

——. "The Primacy of Policy and the 'Trinity' in Clausewitz's Mature Thought." In *Clausewitz in the Twenty-First Century*, edited by Hew Strachan and Andreas Herberg-Rothe, 74–90. New York: Oxford University Press, 2007.

Bell, John Bowyer. *Terror out of Zion: The Fight for Israeli Independence.* New York: Routledge, 2017.

Bendix, Reinhard. *Nation-Building & Citizenship: Studies of Our Changing Social Order.* New Brunswick: Transaction Publishers, 1996.

Bergen, Peter L. *The Longest War: The Enduring Conflict between America and Al-Qaeda.* New York: Free Press, 2011.

Beyerchen, Alan. "Clausewitz, Nonlinearity, and the Unpredictability of War." *International Security* 17 (1992–3): 59–90.

Bibes, Patricia. "Transnational Organized Crime and Terrorism: Colombia, A Case Study." *Journal of Contemporary Criminal Justice* 17 (2001): 243–258.

Bin Laden, Osama. "Declaration of Jihad against the Americans Occupying the Land of the Two Holiest Sites," *Al Quds Al Arabi*, August 23 1996.https://is.muni.cz/el/1423/jaro2010/MVZ448/OBL___AQ__Fatwa_1996.pdf

Bin Laden, Osama, Ayman al-Zawahiri, Abu-Yasir Rifa'i Ahmad Taha, Mir Hamzah, and Fazlur Rahman. "Jihad Against Jews and Crusaders." *Al Quds Al Arabi*, February 23 1993. https://fas.org/irp/world/para/docs/980223-fatwa.htm

Black, Jeremy. *Insurgency and Counterinsurgency: A Global History.* Lanham: Rowman & Littlefield, 2016.

Blainey, Geoffrey. *The Causes of War.* New York: Free Press, 1988.

Blakeley, Ruth."State Terrorism in the Social Sciences: Theories, Methods, and Concepts." In *Contemporary State Terrorism: Theory and Practice.* Edited by Richard Jackson, Eamon Murphy, and Scott Poynting, 12–27. New York: Routledge, 2010.

Bloom, Mia. "Constructing Expertise: Terrorist Recruitment and 'Talent Spotting' in the PIRA, Al Qaeda, and ISIS. *Studies in Conflict & Terrorism* 40 (2017): 603–623.

——. *Dying to Kill: The Allure of Suicide Terror.* New York: Columbia University Press, 2005.

Bobbitt, Philip. *The Shield of Achilles: War, Peace, and the Course of History.* New York: Anchor Books, 2002.

——. *Terror and Consent: The Wars for the Twenty-First Century.* New York: Anchor Books, 2009.

Boeke, Sergei and Bart Schuurman. "Operation 'Serval': A Strategy Assessment of the French Intervention in Mali, 2013–2014." *The Journal of Strategic Studies* 38 (2015): 801–825.

Boix, Carles and Milan W. Slovik. "The Foundations of Limited Authoritarian Government: Institutions, Commitment, and Power-Sharing in Dictatorships." *The Journal of Politics* 75 (2013): 300–316.

Bolloten, Burnett. *The Spanish Civil War: Revolution and Counterrevolution.* Chapel Hill: University of North Carolina Press, 1991.

Bonura, Michael A. *Under the Shadow of Napoleon: French Influence on the American Way of Warfare from the War of 1812 to the Outbreak of WWII.* New York: New York University Press, 2012.

Boot, Max. *Invisible Armies: An Epic History of Guerrilla Warfare from Ancient Times to the Present.* New York: W.W. Norton, 2013.

Brodie, Bernard. *Strategy in the Missile Age.* Princeton: Princeton University Press, 1965.

Boudon, Raymond. *The Analysis of Ideology.* Chicago: University of Chicago Press, 1989.

Boyle, Michael J. "The Costs and Consequences of Drone Warfare," *International Affairs* 89 (2013): 1–29.

Bueno de Mesquita, Ethan and Eric S. Dickson. "The Propaganda of the Deed: Terrorism, Counterterrorism, and Mobilization." *American Journal of Political Science* 51 (2007): 364–381.

Bukovansky, Mlada. *Legitimacy and Power Politics: The American and French Revolutions in International Political Culture.* Princeton: Princeton University Press, 2002.

Bull, Hedley. *The Anarchical Society: A Study of Order in World Politics.* New York:Cambridge University Press, 2002.

Burleigh, Michael. *Small Wars, Faraway Places: Global Insurrection and the Making of the Modern World, 1945–1965.* New York: Penguin, 2013.

Bush, George W. "Commencement Address at the United States Military Academy. Speech, West Point, NY, 1 June 2002. White House Archives. https://georgewbush-whitehouse. archives.gov/news/releases/2002/06/20020601-3.html

——. "The National Security Strategy of the United States of America." Executive Office of the President. Washington, D.C., 2002.

Byman, Daniel. "Buddies or Burdens? Understanding the Al Qaeda Relationship with Its Affiliate Organizations." *Security Studies* 23 (2014): 431–470.

——. *Deadly Connections: States That Sponsor Terrorism.* New York: Cambridge University Press, 2005.

——. "Friends Like These: Counterinsurgency and the War on Terrorism." *International Security* 31 (2006): 79–115.

Byman, Daniel Kenneth Pollack, and Matthew Waxman. "Coercing Saddam Hussein: Lessons from the Past." *Survival*, Vol. 40, No. 3 (Autumn, 1998) 127–51.

Callaway, Rhonda and Julie Harrelson-Stephens. "Toward a Theory of Terrorism: Human Security as a Determinant of Terrorism." *Studies in Conflict & Terrorism* 29 (2005): 679–702.

Callimachi, Rukmini. "The ISIS Files." *The New York Times,* April 4 2018.

Cambanis, Thanassis. *A Privilege to Die: Hezbollah's Legions and Their Endless War against Israel.* New York: Simon & Schuster, 2010.

Carter, David B. "Provocation and the Study of Terrorist and Guerrilla Attacks." *International Organization* 70 (2016): 133–173.

Chaliand, Gerard and Arnaud Blin. "The Invention of Modern Terror." In *The History of Terrorism: From Antiquity to ISIS.* Edited by Gerard Chaliand, 95–112. Oakland: University of California Press, 2016.

Chamberlin, Paul Thomas. *The Global Offensive: The United States, the Palestine Liberation Organization, and the Making of the Post-Cold War Order.* New York: Oxford University Press, 2012.

Chandrasakeran, Rajiv. *Little America: The War within the War for Afghanistan.* New York: Alfred A. Knopf, 2012.

Cimbala, Stephen J. *Clausewitz and Escalation: Classical Perspectives on Nuclear Strategy.* New York: Frank Cass, 1991.

——. *The Politics of Warfare: The Great Powers in the Twentieth Century.* Philadelphia: Penn State University Press, 2010.

Claridge, David. "State Terrorism? Applying a Definitional Model." *Terrorism and Political Violence* 8 (1993): 47–63.

Clausewitz, Carl von. *Historical and Political Writings.* Edited and Translated by Peter Paret and Daniel Moran. Princeton: Princeton University Press, 1992.

——. *On War.* Edited and Translated by Peter Paret and Michael Howard. Princeton: Princeton University Press, 1984.

Clutterbuck, Lindsay. "Law Enforcement." In *Attacking Terrorism: Elements of a Grand Strategy.* Edited by Audrey Kurth Cronin and James M. Ludes, 140–161. Washington, D.C.: Georgetown University Press, 2004.

——. "The Progenitors of Terrorism: Russian Revolutionaries or Extreme Irish Republicans?" *Terrorism and Political Violence* 16 (2004): 154–181.

Cohen, Eliot A. *Supreme Command: Soldiers, Statesmen, and Leadership in Wartime*. New York: Simon & Schuster, 2002.

Coll, Steve. *Directorate S: The CIA and America's Secret Wars in Afghanistan and Pakistan*. New York: Penguin, 2018.

——. *Ghost Wars: The Secret History of the CIA, Afghanistan, and Bin Laden, from the Soviet Invasion to September 10, 2001*. New York: Penguin, 2005.

Connelly, Owen. *The Wars of the French Revolution and Napoleon, 1792–1815*. New York: Routledge, 2006.

Conquest, Robert. *The Great Terror: A Reassessment*. New York: Oxford University Press, 2008.

Cormier, Youri. *War as Paradox: Clausewitz and Hegel on Fighting Doctrines and Ethics*. Montreal: McGill-Queen's University Press, 2016.

Crenshaw, Martha. "The Causes of Terrorism." *Comparative Politics* 13 (1981): 379–399.

——. *Revolutionary Terrorism: The FLN in Algeria, 1954–1962*. Stanford: Hoover Institution Press, 1978.

Crenshaw, Martha and Gary LaFree. *Countering Terrorism: No Simple Solutions*. Washington, D.C.: Brookings Institution Press, 2017.

Cronin, Audrey Kurth. *How Terrorism Ends: Understanding the Decline and Demise of Terrorist Campaigns*. Princeton: Princeton University Press, 2009.

——. "ISIS Is Not a Terrorist Group: Why Counterterrorism Won't Stop the Latest Jihadist Threat," *Foreign Affairs* 94 (2015): 87–98.

——. "What is Really Changing? Change and Continuity in Global Terrorism." In *The Changing Character of War*. Edited by Hew Strachan and Sibylle Scheipers, 134–150. New York: Oxford University Press, 2011.

Daase, Christopher. "Clausewitz and Small Wars." In *Clausewitz in the Twenty-First Century*, edited by Strachan and Herberg-Rothe, 182–195.

Davis, Donald E. and Walter S.G. Kohn. "Lenin's 'Notebook on Clausewitz." In *Soviet Armed Forces Review Annual, Vol. I*. Edited by David R. Jones, 188–229. Gulf Breeze: Academic International Press, 1977.

Davis. Paul K, Eric V. Larson, Zachary Halderman, Mustafa Oguz, Yashodhara Rana. *Understanding and Influencing Public Support for Insurgency and Terrorism*. Santa Monica: RAND Corporation, 2012.

DeVotta, Neil. "The Liberation Tigers of Tamil Eelam and the Lost Quest For Separatism in Sri Lanka." *Asian Survey* 49 (2009): 1021–1051.

Dishman, Chris. "Terrorism, Crime, and Transformation." *Studies in Conflict & Terrorism* 24 (2001): 43–58.

Dorrien, Gary. *Imperial Designs: Neoconservatism and the New Pax Americana*. New York: Routledge, 2004.

Dueck, Colin. *The Obama Doctrine: American Grand Strategy Today*. New York: Oxford University Press, 2015.

Duelfer, Charles and Stephen Benedict Dyson. "Chronic Misperception and International Conflict: The U.S.-Iraq Experience." *International Security* 36 (2011): 73–100.

Duyvesteyn, Isabelle. *Clausewitz and African War: Politics and Strategy in Liberia and Somalia*. New York: Routledge, 2005.

"Paradoxes of the Strategy of Terrorism," in *Victory and Defeat in Contemporary Warfare*. Edited by Jan Angstrom and Isabelle Duyvesteyn, 117–141. New York: Routledge, 2007.

——. "Rethinking the Nature of War: Some Conclusions." In *Rethinking the Nature of War*. Edited by Jan Angstrom and Isabelle Duyvesteyn, 225–241. New York: Routledge, 2005.

Eatwell, Roger. "The Concept and Theory of Charismatic Leadership," *Totalitarian Movements and Political Religions* 7 (2006): 141–156.

Echevarria II., Antulio J. "Clausewitz's Center of Gravity: It's Not What We Thought." *Naval War College Review* 56 (2003): 108–123.

——. *Clausewitz and Contemporary War*. New York: Oxford University Press, 2007.

——. "Clausewitz and the Nature of the War on Terror." In *Clausewitz in the Twenty-First Century*, edited by Strachan and Herberg-Rothe, 196–218.

Edelstein, Dan. *The Terror of Natural Right: Republicanism, The Cult of Nature and the French Revolution*. Chicago: University of Chicago Press, 2009.

El Fatl, Khaled Abdul. "9/11 and the Muslim Transformation." In *September 11 in History: A Watershed Moment?* Edited by Mary L. Dudziak, 70–111. Durham: Duke University Press, 2003.

Enders, Walter and Todd Sandler, *The Political Economy of Terrorism*. New York: Cambridge University Press, 2012.

English, Richard. *Armed Struggle: The History of the IRA*. New York: Pan Macmillan, 2003.

——. *Does Terrorism Work? A History*. New York: Oxford University Press, 2016.

Eubank, William L. and Leonard Weinberg. "Does Democracy Encourage Terrorism?" *Terrorism and Political Violence* 6 (1994): 417–435.

Fairweather, Jack. *The Good War: Why We Couldn't Win the War or the Peace in Afghanistan*. New York: Basic Books, 2014.

Fanon, Frantz. *The Wretched of the Earth*. New York: Grove Weidenfeld, 1963.

Farrell, Theo and Antonio Giustozzi. "The Taliban at War: Inside the Helmand Insurgency, 2004–2012." *International Affairs* 89 (2013): 845–871.

Farrow, Ronan. *War on Peace: The End of Diplomacy and the Decline of American Influence*. New York: W.W. Norton, 2018.

Figner, Vera. "Memoirs of a Revolutionist." In *Five Sisters: Women against the Tsar*. Edited by Barbara Alpern Engel and Clifford N. Rosenthal, 1–58. DeKalb, Northern Illinois University Press, 2013.

Finegan, Rory. "Shadowboxing in the Dark: Intelligence and Counter-Terrorism in Northern Ireland." *Terrorism and Political Violence* 28 (2016): 497–519.

Fitzpatrick, Sheila. "Signals from Below: Soviet Letters of Denunciation of the 1930s." *The Journal of Modern History* 68 (1996): 831–866.

Fleming, Colin M. *Clausewitz's Timeliness Trinity: A Framework For Modern War*. Burlington: Ashgate, 2013.

Forrest, Alan. *Conscripts and Deserters: The Army and French Society during the Revolution*. New York: Oxford University Press, 1989.

——. "*La Patrie en Danger:* The French Revolution and the First *Levee en Masse*." In *The People in Arms: Military Myth and National Mobilization since the French Revolution*. Edited by Daniel Moran and Arthur Waldron, 8–32. New York: Cambridge University Press, 2003.

Franks, Jason. *Rethinking the Roots of Terrorism*. New York: Palgrave Macmillan, 2006.

Freedman, Lawrence. *The Evolution of Nuclear Strategy*. New York: Palgrave Macmillan, 2003.

——. *Strategy: A History*. New York: Oxford University Press, 2013.

Freedman, Lawrence and Ephraim Karsh. *The Gulf Conflict, 1990–1991: Diplomacy and War in the New World Order*. Princeton: Princeton University Press, 1993.

Friedberg, Aaron L. *In the Shadow of the Garrison State: America's Anti-Statism and Its Cold War Grand Strategy*. Princeton: Princeton University Press, 2012.

Fromkin, David. "The Strategy of Terrorism." *Foreign Affairs* 53 (1975): 683–698.

Frum, David and Richard Perle, *An End to Evil: How to Win the War on Terror*. New York: Random House, 2004.

Furet, Francois. *Interpreting the French Revolution* (New York: Cambridge University Press, 1981.

——. "Rousseau and the French Revolution." In *The Legacy of Rousseau*. Edited by Clifford Orwin and Nathan Tarcov, 169–183. Chicago: University of Chicago Press, 1997.

Gaddis, John Lewis. *On Grand Strategy*. New York: Penguin Press, 2018.

Gallie, W.B. *Philosophers of Peace and War: Kant, Clausewitz, Marx, Engels, and Tolstoy*. New York: Columbia University Press, 1978.

Galula, David. *Counter Insurgency Warfare: Theory and Practice*. New York: Frederick A. Praeger, 1971.

Gat, Azar. *A History of Military Thought: From the Enlightenment to the Cold War*. New York: Oxford University Press, 2001.

——. "Clausewitz and the Marxists: Yet Another Look." *Journal of Contemporary History* 27 (1992): 363–382.

Gause, F. Gregory III. "Iraq's Decision to Go to War, 1980 and 1990." *The Middle East Journal* 56 (2002): 47–70.

——. *Saudi Arabia in the New Middle East*. New York: Council on Foreign Relations, 2011.

Gellner, Ernest. *Nations and Nationalism*. Ithaca: Cornell University Press, 2006.

George, Alexander. *Forceful Persuasion: Coercive Diplomacy as an Alternative to War*. Washington, D.C.: U.S. Institute of Peace Press, 1991.

George, Alexander L. "The Need for Influence Theory and Actor-Specific Behavioral Models of Adversaries." *Comparative Strategy* 22 (2003): 463–487.

Gerges, Fawaz A. *ISIS: A History*. Princeton: Princeton University Press, 2016.

——. *The Rise and Fall of al Qaeda*. New York: Oxford University Press, 2011.

Getty, J. Arch. *Origins of the Great Purges: The Soviet Communist Party Reconsidered, 1933–1938*. New York: Cambridge University Press, 1987.

Goldman, Wendy Z. *Inventing the Enemy: Denunciation and Terror in Stalin's Russia*. New York: Cambridge University Press, 2011.

Goodson, Larry P. *Afghanistan's Endless War: State Failure, Regional Politics, and the Rise of the Taliban*. Seattle: University of Washington Press, 2001.

Gordon, Michael R. and Bernard E. Trainor. *Cobra II: The Inside Story of the Invasion and Occupation of Iraq*. New York: Vintage Books, 2007.

——. *Endgame: The Inside Story of the Struggle for Iraq, from George W. Bush to Barack Obama*. New York: Vintage Books, 2012.

Gorodetsky, Gabriel. *Grand Delusion: Stalin and the German Invasion of Russia*. New Haven: Yale University Press, 1999.

Gray, Colin. *Modern Strategy*. New York: Oxford University Press, 1999.

Gregory, Paul R. *Terror by Quota: State Security from Lenin to Stalin (An Archival Study)*. New Haven: Yale University Press, 2009.

Giustozzi, Antonio. "Novelty is in the Eye of the Beholder: Understanding the Taliban in Afghanistan." In *The Character of War in the 21st Century*. Edited by Caroline Holmqvist-Jonsäter and Christopher Coker, 57–71. New York: Routledge, 2010.

Gunaratna, Rohan. *Inside Al Qaeda: Global Network of Terror*. New York: Columbia University Press, 2002.

Gunning, Jeroen and Richard Jackson. "What's So Religious about 'Religious Terrorism?'" *Critical Studies on Terrorism* 4 (2011): 369–388.

Haas, Ernst. *Nationalism, Liberalism, and Progress, Vol. I: The Rise and Decline of Nationalism*. Ithaca: Cornell University Press, 1997.

Haas, Mark L. *The Ideological Origins of Great Power Politics, 1789–1989*. Ithaca: Cornell University Press, 2005.

Hagermann, Karen. *Revisiting Prussia's Wars against Napoleon: History, Culture, and Memory*. New York: Cambridge University Press, 2015.

Hamid, Mustafa and Leah Farrall. *The Arabs at War in Afghanistan*. New York: Oxford University Press, 2015.

Handel, Michael I. *Clausewitz and Modern Strategy*. Abingdon: Frank Cass, 2004.

——. *Masters of War: Classical Strategic Thought*. New York: Routledge, 2001.

Harlow, Rachel Martin. "Agency and Agent in George Bush's Gulf War Rhetoric." In *The Rhetorical Presidency of George H.W. Bush*. Edited by Martin J. Medhurst, 56–80. College Station: Texas A&M University Press, 2006.

Harris, James. *The Great Fear: Stalin's Terror of the 1930s*. New York: Oxford University Press, 2016.

Hashim, Ahmed S. *When Counterinsurgency Wins: Sri Lanka's Defeat of the Tamil Tigers*. Philadelphia: University of Pennsylvania Press, 2013.

Haslam, S. Alexander, Stephen D. Reicher, and Michael J. Platow. *The New Psychology of Leadership: Identity, Influence, and Power*. New York: Psychology Press, 2011.

Herberg-Rothe, Andreas. *Clausewitz's Puzzle: The Political Theory of War*. New York: Oxford University Press, 2007.

Heuser, Beatrice. *Reading Clausewitz*. London: Pimlico, 2002.

Hillgruber, Andreas. Translated by William C. Kirby. *Germany and the Two World Wars*. Cambridge: Harvard University Press, 1981.

Hinnebusch, Raymond. "From Westphalian Failure to Heterarchic Governance in MENA: The Case of Syria." *Small Wars & Insurgencies* 29 (2018): 391–413.

Hiro, Dilip. *The Longest War: The Iran-Iraq Military Conflict*. New York: Routledge, 1991.

Hobbes, Thomas. *Leviathan*. London: Oxford University Press, 1965.

Hoffman, Bruce. "Al-Qaeda's Resurrection," Council on Foreign Relations, March 6 2018. https://www.cfr.org/expert-brief/al-qaedas-resurrection

———. *Anonymous Soldiers: The Struggle for Israel, 1917–1947*. New York: Vintage Books, 2016.

———. *Inside Terrorism*. New York: Columbia University Press, 2006.

Hoffman, David Lloyd. *Stalinist Values: The Cultural Norms of Soviet Modernity, 1917–1941*. Ithaca: Cornell University Press, 2003.

Hoffman, Stanley. *Chaos and Violence: What Globalization, Failed States, and Terrorism Mean for U.S. Foreign Policy*. Lanham: Rowman & Littlefield, 2006.

Holmes, Terence M. "The Clausewitzian Fallacy of Absolute War." *Journal of Strategic Studies* 40 (2017): 1–20.

Horne, Alistair. *A Savage War of Peace: Algeria, 1954–1962*. New York: Pan Macmillan, 2012.

Hosti, Kalevi J. *The State, War, and the State of War*. New York: Columbia University Press, 1996.

Honig, Jan Willem. "Clausewitz's *On War:* Problems of Text and Translation." In *Clausewitz in the Twenty-First Century*, edited by Strachan and Herberg-Rothe, 57–73.

Howard, Michael. *Clausewitz: A Very Short Introduction*. New York: Oxford University Press, 2002.

———. *War in European History*. New York: Oxford University Press, 2009.

Huntington, Samuel. *The Clash of Civilizations and the Remaking of World Order*. New York: Penguin, 1996.

———. *The Soldier and the State: The Theory and Politics of Civil-Military Relations*. Cambridge: Harvard University Press, 1985.

Hutchinson, John. *Nationalism and War*. New York: Oxford University Press, 2017.

Hybel, Alex Roberto and Justin Matthew Kaufman. *The Bush Administrations and Saddam Hussein: Deciding on Conflict*. New York: Palgrave Macmillan, 2006.

Iklé, Fred Charles. *Every War Must End*. New York: Columbia University Press, 2005.

Institute for Economics and Peace. "Global Terrorism Index 2017: Measuring and Understanding the Impact of Terrorism." http://visionofhumanity.org/app/uploads/2017/11/Global-Terrorism-Index-2017.pdf

Jackson, Brian."Don't Let Short-Term Urgency Undermine a Long-Term Security Strategy." In *The Long Shadow of 9/11: America's Response to Terrorism*. Edited by Brian Michael Jenkins and John Godges, 133–146. Santa Monica: RAND Corporation, 2011.

Jacobson, Jon. *When the Soviet Union Entered World Politics*. Berkeley: University of California Press, 1994.

Jensen, Richard Bach. "Daggers, Rifles, and Dynamite: Anarchist Terrorism in Nineteenth Century Europe." *Terrorism and Political Violence* 16 (2004): 116–153.

Jervis, Robert. "Understanding the Bush Doctrine." *Political Science Quarterly* 118 (2003): 365–388.

Johnston, Patrick B., Jacob N. Shapiro, Howard J. Shatz, Benjamin Bahney, Danielle F. Jung, Patrick K. Ryan, and Jonathan Wallace. *Foundations of the Islamic State: Management, Money, and Terror in Iraq, 2005–2010*. Santa Monica: RAND Corporation, 2016.

Jones, Frank L. "Toward a Strategic Theory of Terrorism: Defining Boundaries in the Ongoing Search for Security." In *U.S. Army War College Guide to National Security Issues, Vol. I—Theory of War and Strategy*. Edited by J. Boone Barthlomees, Jr., 95–106. Carlisle: Strategic Studies Institute, 2012.

Jones, Seth G. *Hunting in the Shadows: The Pursuit of Al Qa'ida Since 9/11*. New York: W.W. Norton, 2012.

——. *In the Graveyard of Empires: America's War in Afghanistan.* New York: W.W. Norton, 2010.

Jones, Seth G. and Martin C. Libicki, *How Terrorist Groups End: Lessons for Countering Al Qa'ida.* Santa Monica: RAND Corporation, 2008.

Juergensmeyer, Mark. *Global Rebellion: Religious Challenges to the Secular State, From Christian Militias to Al Qaeda.* Berkeley: University of California Press, 2008.

——. *Terror in the Mind of God: The Global Rise of Religious Violence.* Berkeley: University of California Press, 2017.

Kahn, Herman. *On Thermonuclear War.* New Brunswick: Transaction Publishers, 2010.

Kaldor, Mary. "Inconclusive Wars: Is Clausewitz Still Relevant in These Global Times?" *Global Policy* 1 (2010): 271–281.

——. "In Defense of New Wars." *Stability: International Journal of Security and Development* 2 (2013): 1–16.

——. *New & Old Wars: Organized Violence in a Global Era.* Malden: Polity, 2012.

Karsh, Efrain and Inari Rautsi. *Saddam Hussein: A Political Biography.* New York: Grove Press, 2002.

Kassel, Whitney. "Terrorism and the International Anarchist Movement of the Late Nineteenth and Early Twentieth Centuries." *Studies Conflict & Terrorism* 32 (2009): 237–252.

Katzman, Kenneth. *Iran's Activities and Influence in Iraq.* Washington, D.C.: Congressional Research Institute, 2009.

Keegan, John. *A History of Warfare.* New York: Vintage Books, 1994.

Kellen, Konrad. "Ideology and Rebellion: Terrorism in West Germany," in *Origins of Terrorism,* edited by Walter Reich, 43–58.

Kersten, Krystyna. *The Establishment of Communist Rule in Poland, 1943–1943.* Berkeley: University of California Press, 1991.

Khadduri, Majid and Edmund Ghareeb. *War in the Gulf, 1990–1991: The Iraq-Kuwait Conflict and its Implications.* New York: Oxford University Press, 1997.

Kilcullen, David. *Blood Year: The Unraveling of Western Counterterrorism.* New York: Oxford University Press, 2016.

Kipp, Jacob W. "Lenin and Clausewitz: The Militarization of Marxism, 1914–1921." *Military Affairs* 49 (1985): 184–191.

Kissinger, Henry. *A World Restored: Metternich, Castlereagh, and the Problems of Peace, 1812–1822.* Boston: Houghton Mifflin, 1973.

Kitson, Frank. *Low Intensity Operations: Subversion, Insurgency, Peacekeeping.* Harrisburg: Stackpole Books, 1971.

Klein, Bradley S. *Strategic Studies and World Order: The Global Politics of Deterrence.* New York: Cambridge University Press, 1994.

Kotkin, Stephen. *Stalin, Volume I: Paradoxes of Power, 1878–1928.* New York: Penguin Books, 2014.

——. *Stalin, Volume II: Waiting for Hitler, 1929–1941.* New York: Penguin Books, 2017.

Krasner, Stephen D. *Sovereignty: Organized Hypcrisy.* Princeton: Princeton University Press, 1999.

Krieg, Andreas. "Externalizing the Burden of War: The Obama Doctrine and U.S. Foreign Policy in the Middle East." *International Affairs* 92 (2016): 97–113.

Kuromiya, Hiroaki. *Stalin's Industrial Revolution: Politics and Workers, 1928–1931.* New York: Cambridge University Press, 1988.

Kydd, Andrew H. and Barbara F. Walter. "The Strategies of Terrorism." *International Security* 31 (2006): 49–80.

Laqueur, Walter. *A History of Terrorism.* New Brunswick: Transaction Publishers, 2012.

Lebow, Richard Ned. "Clausewitz and Nuclear Crisis Stability." *Political Science Quarterly* 103 (1988): 81–110.

Lefebvre, Georges. *The French Revolution, Volume II: From 1793 to 1799.* New York: Columbia University Press, 1964.

Leffler, Melvyn. "9/11 and the Past and Future of American Foreign Policy." *International Affairs* 79 (2003): 1045–1063.

Levitt, Matthew. *Hamas: Politics, Charity, and Terrorism in the Service of Jihad.* New Haven: Yale University Press, 2006.

———. *Hezbollah: The Global Footprint of Lebanon's Party of God.* Washington, D.C.: Georgetown University Press, 2013.

Lewis, Jeffrey William. *The Business of Martyrdom: A History of Suicide Bombing.* Annapolis: Naval Institute Press, 2012.

Li, Quan. "Does Democracy Promote or Reduce Transnational Terrorism?" *Journal of Conflict Resolution* 49 (2005): 278–297.

Liff, Adam P. "Cyberwar: A New 'Absolute Weapon'? The Proliferation of Cyberwarfare Capabilities and Interstate War." *Journal of Strategic Studies* 35 (2012): 401–428.

Linton, Marisa. *Choosing Terror: Virtue, Friendship, and Authenticity in the French Revolution.* New York: Oxford University Press, 2013.

Linz, Juan J. *Totalitarian and Authoritarian Regimes.* Boulder: Lynne Rienner Publishers, 2000.

Lister, Charles R. *The Syrian Jihad: Al-Qaeda, the Islamic State and the Evolution of an Insurgency.* New York: Oxford University Press, 2015.

Litwak, Robert. *Rogue States and U.S. Foreign Policy: Containment after the Cold War.* Baltimore: The Johns Hopkins University Press, 2000.

Long, Jerry M. and Alex S. Wilner. "Delegitimizing Al-Qaida: Defeating an 'Army Whose Men Love Death.'" *International Security* 39 (2014): 126–164.

Lonsdale, David J. *The Nature of War in the Information Age: Clausewitzian Future.* New York: Frank Cass, 2004.

Lubkemeier, Eckhard. "Building Peace under the Nuclear Sword of Damocles." In *Nuclear Weapons in the Changing World: Perspectives from Europe, Asia and North America.* Edited by Patrick J. Garrity and Steven A. Maaranen, 223–238. New York: Plenum Press, 1992.

Lustick, Ian S. *Trapped in the War on Terror.* Philadelphia: University of Pennsylvania Press, 2006.

Luttwak, Edward. "Toward Post-Heroic Warfare." *Foreign Affairs* 74 (1995): 109–122.

Lyons, Martyn. *France under the Directory.* New York: Cambridge University Press, 1975.

MacGinty, Roger. "Irish Republicanism and the Peace Process: From Revolution to Reform." In *A Farewell to Arms? Beyond the Good Friday Agreement.* Edited by Michael Cox, Adrian Guelke, and Fiona Stephen, 124–138. New York: Manchester University Press, 2006.

Machiavelli, Niccolo. *The Prince.* Translated by Harvey Mansfield. Chicago: University of Chicago Press, 1998.

Magaloni, Beatriz. "Credible Power-Sharing and the Longevity of Autocratic Rule." *Comparative Political Studies* 41 (2008): 1–27.

Makarenko, Tamara. "The Crime-Terror Continuum: Tracing the Interplay between Traditional Organized Crime and Terrorism." *Global Crime* 6 (2004): 129–145.

Makiya, Kanan. *Republic of Fear: The Politics of Modern Iraq.* Berkeley: University of California Press, 1998.

Malkasian, Carter. *Illusions of Victory: The Anbar Awakening and the Rise of the Islamic State.* New York: Oxford University Press, 2017.

Mansfield, Harvey. *Machiavelli's Virtue.* Chicago: University of Chicago Press, 1998.

Mansour, Renad and Faleh A. Jabar. *The Popular Mobilization Forces and Iraq's Future.* Washington, D.C.: Carnegie Endowment for International Peace, 2017.

Marx, Anthony W. *Faith in Nation: Exclusionary Origins of Nationalism.* New York: Oxford University Press, 2003.

Marx, Karl and Friedrich Engels. "Manifesto of the Communist Party." In *The Marx-Engels Reader.* Edited by Robert C. Tucker, 331–362. New York: W.W. Norton, 1972.

Mastny, Vojtech. *The Cold War and Soviet Insecurity: The Stalin Years.* New York: Oxford University Press, 2006.

Matthews, Ken. *The Gulf Conflict and International Relations.* New York: Routledge, 1993.

Mayer, Arno J. *The Furies: Violence and Terror in the French and Russian Revolutions.* Princeton: Princeton University Press, 2000.

Mazzetti, Mark. *The Way of the Knife: The CIA, A Secret Army, and a War at the Ends of the Earth.* New York: Penguin, 2013.

McCants, William. *The ISIS Apocalypse: The History, Strategy, and Doomsday Vision of the Islamic State.* New York: St. Martin's Press, 2015.

McCauley, Clark and Sophia Moskalenko. "Mechanisms of Political Radicalization: Pathways Toward Terrorism." *Terrorism and Political Violence* 20 (2008): 415–433.

McIntosh, Christopher. "Counterterrorism as War: Identifying the Dangers, Risks, and Opportunity Costs of U.S. Strategy toward al Qaeda and its Affiliates." *Studies in Conflict & Terrorism* 38 (2015): 23–38.

McNaugher, Thomas L. "Ballistic Missiles and Chemical Weapons: The Legacy of the Iran-Iraq War." *International Security* 15 (1990): 5–34.

McPhee, Peter. *Robespierre: A Revolutionary Life* (New Haven: Yale University Press, 2012.

Mearsheimer, John. *The Tragedy of Great Power Politics.* New York: W.W. Norton, 2001.

Medvedev, Roy. *Let History Judge: The Origins and Consequences of Stalinism.* New York: Columbia University Press, 1989.

Meilinger, Philip. "Busting the Icon: Restoring Balance to the Influence of Clausewitz." *Strategic Studies Quarterly* 1 (2007): 116–145.

Mendelsohn, Barak. *The Al-Qaeda Franchise: The Expansion of Al-Qaeda and Its Consequences.* New York: Oxford University Press, 2015.

——. "Sovereignty under Attack: International Society Meets the Al Qaeda Network." *Review of International Studies* 31 (2005): 45–68.

Merari, Ariel. "Terrorism as a Strategy of Insurgency." *Terrorism and Political Violence* 5 (1993): 213–251.

Meyer, John W., John Boli, George M. Thomas, and Francisco O. Ramirez. "World Society and the Nation-State." *American Journal of Sociology* 103 (1997): 144–181.

Miller, Benjamin. "The State-to-Nation Balance and War." In *Nationalism and War.* Edited by John A. Hall and Siniša Malešević, 73–96. New York: Cambridge University Press, 2013.

Miller, Martin A. *The Foundations of Modern Terrorism: State, Society, and the Dynamics of Political Violence.* New York: Cambridge University Press, 2013.

Miller, Rory. *Desert Kingdoms to Global Powers: The Rise of the Arab Gulf.* New Haven: Yale University Press, 2016.

Milner, Helen V. *Interests, Institutions, and Information: Domestic Politics and International Relations.* Princeton: Princeton University Press, 1997.

Merrit Miner, Steven. *Stalin's Holy War: Religion, Nationalism, and Alliance Politics, 1941–1945.* Chapel Hill: University of North Carolina Press, 2003.

Mishra, Pankaj. *Age of Anger: A History of the Present.* New York: Farrar, Straus, and Giroux, 2017.

Moaz, Zeev and Bruce Russett. "Normative and Structural Causes of Democratic Peace, 1946–1986." *The American Political Science Review* 87 (1993): 624–638.

Mockaitis, Thomas R. *The "New" Terrorism: Myths and Reality.* Stanford: Stanford University Press, 2008.

Moghadam, Assaf. "Failure and Disengagement in the Red Army Faction." *Studies in Conflict & Terrorism* 35 (2012): 156–181.

——. *The Globalization of Martyrdom: Al Qaeda, Salafi Jihad, and the Diffusion of Suicide Attacks.* Baltimore: The Johns Hopkins University Press, 2008.

——. "How Al Qaeda Innovates," *Security Studies* 22 (2013): 466–497.

Moloney, Ed. *A Secret History of the IRA.* New York: W.W. Norton, 2002.

Montefiore, Simon Sebag. *Stalin: The Court of the Red Tsar.* New York: Vintage Books, 2003

Monten, Jonathan. "The Roots of the Bush Doctrine: Power, Nationalism, and Democracy Promotion in U.S. Strategy." *International Security* 29 (2005): 112–156.

Moody, Peter R. "Clausewitz and the Fading Dialectic of War." *World Politics* 31 (1979): 417–433.

Morris, Benny. *1948: A History of the First Arab-Israeli War.* New Haven: Yale University Press, 2008.

Mueller, John E. *Overblown: How Politicians and the Terrorism Industry Inflate National Security Threats, and Why We Believe Them.* New York: Simon & Schuster, 2006.

——. *Policy and Opinion in the Gulf War.* Chicago: University of Chicago Press, 1994.

Mufti, Malik. *Sovereign Creations: Pan-Arabism and Political Order in Syria and Iraq.* Ithaca: Cornell University Press, 1996.

Muller, Edward N. and Karl-Dieter Opp."Rational Choice and Rebellious Collective Action." *American Political Science Review* 80 (1986): 471–488.

Mousseau. Michael. "Market Civilization and Its Clash with Terror." *International Security* 27 (2002): 5–29.

Murray, Williamson, and Kevin M. Woods. *The Iran-Iraq War: A Military and Strategic History.* New York: Cambridge University Press, 2014.

Murphy, David E. *What Stalin Knew: The Enigma of Barbarossa.* New Haven: Yale University Press, 2005.

Naimark, Norman. *The Russians in Germany: A History of the Soviet Zone of Occupation, 1945–1949.* Cambridge: Harvard University Press, 1995.

Nasi, Carlos. "The Peace Process with FARC-EP." In *Truth, Justice, and Reconciliation in Colombia: Transitioning from Violence.* Edited by Fabio Andres Diaz Pabon, 34–49. New York: Routledge, 2018.

Nechaev, Sergey. "The Catechism of the Revolutionist (1869)." In *Voices of Terror: Manifestos, Writings and Manuals of Al Qaeda, Hamas, and Other Terrorists from Around the World and Throughout the Ages.* Edited by Walter Laqueur. New York: Reed Press, 2004.

Neumann, Peter R. *Old and New Terrorism: Late Modernity, Globalization and the Transformation of Political Violence.* Cambridge: Polity Press, 2009.

Neumann, Peter R. and M.L.R. Smith. *The Strategy of Terrorism: How It Works, and Why It Fails.* New York: Routledge, 2008.

Nietzsche, Friedrich. *The Will to Power.* London: Penguin UK Press, 2017.

Nolan, Cathal J. *The Allure of Battle: A History of How Wars Have Been Won and Lost.* New York: Oxford University Press, 2017.

Norton, Augustus Richard. *Hezbollah: A Short History.* Princeton: Princeton University Press, 2014.

Oberschall, Anthony. *Social Movements: Ideologies, Interests, and Identities.* New Brunswick: Transaction Publishers, 1997.

O'Neill, Bard. *Insurgency and Terrorism: From Revolution to Apocalypse.* Dulles: Potomac Books, 2005.

O'Reilly, Kelly P. "Perceiving Rogue States: The Use of the 'Rogue State' Concept by U.S. Foreign Policy Elites." *Foreign Policy Analysis* 3 (2007): 295–315.

O'Rourke, Lindsey. "What's Special about Female Suicide Terrorism?" *Security Studies* 18 (2009): 681–718.

Overy, Richard. *The Dictators: Hitler's Germany, Stalin's Russia.* New York: W.W. Norton, 2004.

——. *Russia's War: A History of the Soviet War Effort, 1941–1945.* New York: Penguin, 1998.

Packer, George. *The Assassin's Gate: America in Iraq.* New York: Farrar, Straus, and Giroux, 2005.

Pape, Robert. *Bombing to Win: Air Power and Coercion in War.* Ithaca: Cornell University Press, 1996.

——. *Dying to Win: The Strategic Logic of Suicide Terror.* New York: Columbia University Press, 2005.

Paret, Peter. "Clausewitz." *Makers of Modern Strategy: From Machiavelli to the Nuclear Age,* edited by Peter Paret. Princeton: Princeton University Press, 1986.

——. *Clausewitz and the State: The Man, His Theories, and His Time.* New York: Oxford University Press, 1976.

——. *Clausewitz in His Time: Essays in the Cultural and Intellectual History of Thinking About War.* New York: Berghahn Books, 2015.

Parker, Tom and Nick Sitter. "The Four Horsemen of Terrorism: It's Not Waves, It's Strains." *Terrorism and Political Violence* 28 (2016): 197–216.

Paul, T.V. "The National Security State and Global Terrorism: Why the State Is Not Prepared for the New Kind of War." In *Globalization, Security, and the Nation State: Paradigms in*

Transition. Edited by Edsel Aydinli and James N. Rosenau, 49–66. Albany: State University of New York Press, 2005.

Pechatnov, Vladimir. "The Soviet Union and the World, 1944–1953." In *The Cambridge History of the Cold War.* Edited by Melvyn P. Leffler and Odd Arne Westad, 90–111. New York: Cambridge University Press, 2012.

Pedahzur, Ami and Arie Perliger. *Jewish Terrorism in Israel.* New York: Columbia University Press, 2011.

Pflanze, Otto. *Bismarck and the Development of Germany: The Period of Unification, 1815–1871.* Princeton: Princeton University Press, 1973.

Pick, Daniel. *War Machine: The Rationalization of Slaughter in the Modern Age.* New Haven: Yale University Press, 1996.

Piekalkiewicz, Jaroslaw and Alfred Wayne Penn. *Politics of Ideocracy.* Albany: State University of New York Press, 1995.

Pollack, Kenneth. *Arabs at War: Military Effectiveness, 1948–1991.* Lincoln: University of Nebraska Press, 2002.

Posen, Barry R. "Nationalism, the Mass Army, and Military Power. *International Security* 18 (1993): 80–124.

Post, Jerrold M. "Terrorist Psycho-Logic: Terrorist Behavior as a Product of Psychological Forces." In *Origins of Terrorism,* edited by Walter Reich, 25–42.

Priest, Dana and William M. Arkin. *Top Secret America: The Rise of the New American Security State.* New York: Little, Brown & Company, 2011.

Ralph, Jason. *America's War on Terror: The State of the 9/11 Exception from Bush to Obama.* New York: Oxford University Press, 2013.

Rangwala, Glen. "The Finances of War: Iraq, Credit and Conflict, September 1980 to August 1990." In *The Iran-Iraq War: New International Perspectives.* Edited by Nigel John Ashton and Bryan R. Gibson, 92–105. New York: Routledge, 2013.

Ranstorp, Magnus. "The Virtual Sanctuary of Al-Qaeda and Terrorism in an Age of Globalization." In *International Relations and Security in the Digital Age.* Edited by Johan Ericsson and Giampiero Giacolmello, 31–56. New York: Routledge, 2007.

Rapoport, David C. "Fear and Trembling: Terrorism in Three Religious Traditions." *The American Political Science Review* 78 (1984): 658–677.

——."The Four Waves of Modern Terrorism." In *Attacking Terrorism,* edited by Cronin and Ludes, 46–73.

Rasler, Karen and William R. Thompson. "Looking for Waves of Terrorism," In *Terrorism, Identity and Legitimacy: The Four Waves Theory and Political Violence.* Edited by Jean E. Rosenfeld, 13–29. New York: Routledge, 2011.

Razoux, Pierre. Translated by Nicholas Elliott. *The Iran-Iraq War.* Cambridge: Harvard University Press, 2015.

Richards, Anthony. *Conceptualizing Terrorism.* New York: Oxford University Press, 2015.

——. *What Terrorists Want: Understanding the Enemy, Containing the Threat.* New York: Random House, 2007.

Rieber, Alfred J. "Stalin as Foreign Policymaker." In *Stalin: A New History.* Edited by Sarah Davies and Joseph Harris. New York: Cambridge University Press, 2005.

Riedel, Bruce. *The Search for al Qaeda: Its Leadership, Ideology, and Future.* Washington, D.C.: Brookings Institution Press, 2008.

Roberts, Geoffrey. *Stalin's Wars: From World War to Cold War, 1939–1953.* New Haven: Yale University Press, 2006.

Roberts, Henry L. "Maxim Litvinov," in *The Diplomats: 1919–1939.* Edited by Gordon Craig and Felix Gilbert, 344–375. Princeton: Princeton University Press, 1981.

Robespierre, Maximilien. "On the Principles of Political Morality That Should Guide the National Convention in the Domestic Administration of the Republic." In *Virtue and Terror.* Edited by Slavoj Zizek, 109–125. London: Verso, 2007.

——. "On the Principles of Revolutionary Government," in *Virtue and Terror,* edited by Zizek, 98–107.

Rose, Gabriel. "Neoclassical Realism and Theories of Foreign Policy." *World Politics* 51 (1998): 144–172.

Rothenberg, Gunther E. *The Art of Warfare in the Age of Napoleon.* Bloomington: Indiana University Press, 1978.

Roxborough, Ian. "Clausewitz and the Sociology of War." *The British Journal of Sociology* 45 (1994): 619–636.

Rubin, Barry. *Revolution Until Victory: The Politics and History of the PLO.* Cambridge: Harvard University Press, 1994.

Rubin, Michael. *Dancing with the Devil: The Perils of Engaging Rogue Regimes.* New York: Encounter Books, 2014.

Ruggenthaler, Peter. *The Concept of Neutrality in Stalin's Foreign Policy, 1945–1953.* Lanham: Lexington Books, 2015.

Russell, James. A. "Into the Great Wadi: the United States and the War in Afghanistan." In *Military Adaptation in Afghanistan,* edited by. Theo Farrell, Frans Osinga, and James A. Russell, 51–82. Stanford: Stanford University Press, 2013.

Ryan, Matthew W.S. *Decoding Al-Qaeda's Strategy: The Deep Battle against America.* New York: Columbia University Press, 2013.

Sagan, Eli. *Citizens & Cannibals: The French Revolution, the Struggle for Modernity, and the Origins of Ideological Terror.* Lanham: Rowman & Littlefield, 2001.

Sageman, Marc. *Turning to Political Violence: The Emergence of Terrorism.* Philadelphia: University of Pennsylvania Press, 2017.

———. *Understanding Terror Networks.* Philadelphia: University of Pennsylvania Press, 2004.

Sassoon, Joseph. *Saddam Hussein's Ba'ath Party: Inside an Authoritarian Regime.* New York: Cambridge University Press, 2012.

Schama, Simon. *Citizens: A Chronicle of the French Revolution.* New York: Alfred A. Knopf, 1989.

Schelling, Thomas C. *Arms and Influence.* New Haven: Yale University Press, 2008.

Scheuer, Michael. *Osama Bin Laden.* New York: Oxford University Press, 2011.

Schroeder, Paul W. *The Transformation of European Politics, 1763–1848.* New York: Oxford University Press, 1994.

Schmid, Alex P. "Frameworks for Conceptualising Terrorism." *Terrorism and Political Violence* 16 (2004): 197–221.

Schmid, Alex P. and Albert J. Jongman. *Political Terrorism: A New Guide to Actors, Authors, Concepts, Data Bases & Literature.* New Brunswick: Transaction Publishers, 1988.

Schmitt, Carl. Translated by George Schwab. *Political Theology: Four Chapters on the Concept of Sovereignty.* Chicago: University of Chicago Press, 2005.

Schuurman, Bart. "Clausewitz and the 'New Wars' Scholars." *Parameters* 40 (2010): 89–100.

Schwarzmantel, John. *The Age of Ideology: Political Ideologies From the American Revolution to Postmodern Times.* New York: New York University Press, 1998.

Sedgwick, Mark. "Inspiration and the Origins of Global Waves of Terrorism." *Studies in Conflict & Terrorism* 30 (2007): 97–112.

Shapiro, Ian. *Containment: Rebuilding a Strategy against Global Terror.* Princeton: Princeton University Press, 2009.

Shapiro, Jacob N. *The Terrorist's Dilemma: Managing Violent Covert Organizations.* Princeton: Princeton University Press, 2013.

Shephard Jr., John E. "*On War*: Is Clausewitz Still Relevant?" *Parameters* 20 (1990): 85–99.

Shy, John. "Jomini." In *Makers of Modern Strategy.* Edited by Peter Paret, 143–185.

Silke, Andrew. "Cheshire-Cat Logic: The Recurring Theme of Terrorist Abnormality in Psychological Research." *Psychology, Crime & Law* 4 (1998): 51–69.

Siracusa, Joseph M. and Aiden Warren. *Presidential Doctrines: U.S. National Security from George Washington to Barack Obama.* Lanham: Rowman & Littlefield, 2016.

Skocpol, Theda and Meyer Kestnbaum, "Mars Unshackled: The French Revolution in World Historical Perspective." In *The French Revolution and the Birth of Modernity.* Edited by Ferenc Fehér, 13–29. Berkeley: University of California Press, 1990.

Sluka, Jeffrey Al. "State Terror and Anthropology." In *Death Squad: The Anthropology of State Terror.* Edited by Jeffrey A. Sluka. Philadelphia: University of Pennsylvania Press, 2000.

Smesler, Neil J. *The Faces of Terrorism: Social and Psychological Dimensions.* Princeton: Princeton University Press, 2007.

Smith, Anthony D. *Nationalism and Modernism.* New York: Routledge, 1998.

Smith, Hugh. *On Clausewitz: A Study of Military and Political Ideas.* New York: Palgrave Macmillan, 2004.

———. "The Womb of War: Clausewitz and International Politics." *Review of International Studies* 16 (1990): 39–58.

Smith, M.L.R. *Fighting for Ireland? The Military Strategy of the Irish Republican Movement.* New York: Routledge, 1995.

———. "Guerrillas in the Mist: Reassessing Strategy and Low-Intensity Warfare." *Review of International Studies* 29 (2003): 19–37.

Smith, Rupert. *The Utility of Force: The Art of War in the Modern World.* New York: Alfred A. Knopf, 2007.

Smith, Steven B. "Hegel and the French Revolution: An Epitaph for Republicanism." In *The French Revolution and the Birth of Modernity.* Edited by Ferenc Fehér, 219–239. Berkeley: University of California Press, 1990.

Snyder, Jack. *Myths of Empire: Domestic Politics and International Ambition.* Ithaca: Cornell University Press, 1991.

Snyder, Timothy. *Bloodlands: Europe between Hitler and Stalin.* New York: Basic Books, 2010.

Soufan, Ali. *Anatomy of Terror: From the Death of Bin Laden to the Rise of the Islamic State.* New York: W.W. Norton, 2017.

Sprinzak, Ehud. "Right-Wing Terrorism in a Comparative Perspective: The Case of Split Delegitimization," *Terrorism and Political Violence* 7 (1995): 17–43.

Steger, Manfred B. *The Rise of the Global Imaginary: Political Ideologies From the French Revolution to the Global War on Terror.* New York: Oxford University Press, 2008.

Stenerson, Anne. *Al-Qaida in Afghanistan.* New York: Cambridge University Press, 2017.

Stern, Jessica. "A Radical Idea," *Hoover Digest,* January 23 2012. https://www.hoover.org/research/radical-idea

———. *Terror in the Name of God: Why Religious Militants Kill.* New York: HarperCollins, 2003.

Stout, Mark, Jessica M. Huckabey, and John R. Schindler. *The Terrorist Perspectives Project: Strategic and Operational Views of Al Qaida and Associated Movements.* Annapolis: United States Naval Institute Press, 2008.

Strachan, Hew. *Clausewitz's On War: A Biography.* New York: Grove Press, 2007.

Sullivan, Brian R. "Intelligence and Counter-Terrorism: A Clausewitzian-Historical Analysis." *Journal of Intelligence History* 3 (2003): 1–18.

Sumida, Jon Tetsuro. *Decoding Clausewitz: A New Approach to* On War. Lawrence: University of Kansas Press, 2008.

Summers, Harry G. *On Strategy: A Critical Analysis of the Vietnam War.* New York: Random House, 2009.

Svolik, Milan W. *The Politics of Authoritarian Rule.* New York: Cambridge University Press, 2012.

Tackett, Timothy. *The Coming of the Terror in the French Revolution.* Cambridge: Harvard University Press, 2015.

Talmadge, Caitlin. *The Dictator's Army: Battlefield Effectiveness in Authoritarian Regimes.* Ithaca: Cornell University Press, 2015.

Tarrow, Sidney. "States and Opportunities: The Political Structuring of Social Movements." In *Comparative Perspectives on Social Movements: Political Opportunities, Mobilizing Structures, and Cultural Framings.* Edited by Doug McAdam, John D. McCarthy and Mayer N. Zald, 41–61. New York: Cambridge University Press, 1996.

Taubman, William. *Stalin's American Policy: From Entente to Detente to Cold War.* New York: W.W. Norton, 1982.

Taylor. A.J.P. *The Origins of the Second World War.* New York: Touchstone, 1996.

Thayer, Bradley A. "The Political Effects of Information Warfare: Why New Military Capabilities Cause Old Political Dangers." *Security Studies* 10 (2000): 43–85.

Thayer, Bradley and Valerie Hudson. "Sex and the Shaheed: Insights from the Life Sciences on Islamic Suicide Terrorism." *International Security* 34 (2010): 37–62.

Thomas, Ward. *The Ethics of Destruction: Norms and Force in International Relations.* Ithaca: Cornell University Press, 2001.

Thurston, Robert W. *Life and Terror in Stalin's Russia, 1934–1941* (New Haven: Yale University Press, 1996.

de Tocqueville, Alexis. *Democracy in America.* Translated by Harvey Mansfield and Delba Winthrop. Chicago: University of Chicago Press, 2000.

———. *The Old Regime and the French Revolution.* Translated by Stuart Gilbert. New York: Anchor Books, 1983.

Tucker, Robert C. *Stalin as Revolutionary, 1878–1929: A Study in Leadership and Personality.* New York: W.W. Norton, 1973.

Tuminez, Astrid S. *Russian Nationalism Since 1856: Ideology and the Making of Foreign Policy.* Lanham: Rowman & Littlefield, 2000.

Ulam, Adam B. *Expansion and Coexistence: Soviet Foreign Policy, 1917–1973.* New York: Praeger, 1974.

———. *In the Name of the People: Prophets and Conspirators in Pre-Revolutionary Russia.* New York: Viking Press, 1977.

U.S. Agency for International Development. "Department of State & USAID Joint Statement on Countering Violent Extremism.". May 2016.

Van Creveld, Martin. *More On War.* New York: Oxford University Press, 2017.

———. *The Transformation of War.* New York: Simon & Schuster, 1991.

Van Hagen, Mark. "The *Levee en Masse* from Russian Empire to Soviet Union, 1874–1938." In *The People in Arms,* edited by Moran and Waldron, 159–188.

Van Linschoten, Alex Strick and Felix Kuehn. *An Enemy We Created: The Myth of the Taliban-Al Qaeda Merger in Afghanistan.* New York: Oxford University Press, 2012.

Varon, Jeremy. *Bringing the War Home: The Weather Underground, the Red Army Faction, and Revolutionary Violence in the Sixties and Seventies.* Berkeley: University of California Press, 2004.

Vasquez, John A. *The War Puzzle Revisited.* New York: Cambridge University Press, 2009.

Vinci, Anthony. *Armed Groups and the Balance of Power: The International Relations of Terrorists, Warlords, and Insurgents.* New York: Routledge, 2008.

Viola, Lynne. *Peasant Rebels under Stalin: Collectivization and the Culture of Peasant Resistance* (New York: Oxford University Press, 1996.

Voegelin, Eric. "The Political Religions." In *The Collected Works of Eric Voegelin, Vol. 5: Modernity Without Restraint,* 19–74. Columbia: University of Missouri Press, 2000.

Wagner, R. Harrison. "Bargaining and War." *American Journal of Political Science* 44 (2000): 469–484.

Waldman, Thomas. *War, Clausewitz, and the Trinity.* New York: Routledge, 2016.

Wall, Irwin M. *France, the United States, and the Algerian War.* Berkeley: University of California Press, 2001.

Walzer, Michael. *The Revolution of the Saints: A Study in the Origins of Radical Politics.* New York: Atheneum, 1976.

Walt, Stephen M. "ISIS as Revolutionary State." *Foreign Affairs* 94 (2015): 42–51.

———. *Revolution and War.* Ithaca: Cornell University Press, 1996.

Waltz, Kenneth N. *Man, the State, and War: A Theoretical Analysis.* New York: Columbia University Press, 2001.

———. *Theory of International Politics.* Boston: McGraw-Hill, 1979.

Wardlaw, Grant. *Political Terrorism: Theory, Tactics, and Countermeasures.* New York: Cambridge University Press, 1989.

Warrick, Joby. *Black Flags: The Rise of ISIS.* New York: Anchor Books, 2016.

Weeks, Jessica L. "Autocratic Audience Costs and Signaling Resolve." *International Organization* 62 (2008): 35–64.

———. *Dictators at War and Peace.* Ithaca: Cornell University Press, 2014.

Weigley, Russell. *The Age of Battles: The Quest for Decisive Warfare from Breitenfeld to Waterloo.* Bloomingon: Indiana University Press, 1991.

Weinberg, Leonard. "Turning to Terror: The Conditions under Which Political Parties Turn to Terrorist Activities." *Comparative Politics* 23 (1991): 423–438.

Weinberg, Leonard and Susanne Martin. *The Role of Terrorism in Twenty-First Century Warfare.* New York: Oxford University Press, 2017.

Weiss, Michael and Hassan Hassan. *ISIS: Inside the Army of Terror.* New York: Simon & Schuster, 2015.

Wendt, Alexander. *Social Theory of International Politics. Social Theory of International Politics.* New York: Cambridge University Press, 1999.

Westad, Odd Arne. *The Global Cold War: Third World Interventions and the Making of Our Times.* New York: Cambridge University Press, 2007.

Whelehan, Niall. *The Dynamiters: Irish Nationalism and Political Violence in the Wider World.* New York: Cambridge University Press, 2012.

Wight, Colin. "Theorising Terrorism: The State, Structure, and History." *International Relations* 23 (2009): 99–106.

Wight, Martin. *International Theory: The Three Traditions.* Leicester: Leicester University Press, 1996.

———. *Power Politics.* New York: Penguin Books, 1986.

Wilkinson, Paul. "Terrorism and the Media: A Reassessment." *Terrorism and Political Violence* 9 (1997): 51–64.

———. *Terrorism Versus Democracy: The Liberal State Response.* New York: Routledge, 2011.

Williams, Brian Glyn. *Counter Jihad: America's Military Experience in Afghanistan, Iraq, and Syria.* Philadelphia: University of Pennsylvania Press, 2017.

Williamson Jr., Samuel R. "July 1914 Revisited and Revised." In *The Outbreak of the First World War: Structure, Politics, and Decision-Making.* Edited by Jack S. Levy and John A. Vasquez, 30–64. New York: Cambridge University Press, 2014.

Wilner, Alex. *Deterring Rational Fanatics.* Philadelphia: University of Pennsylvania Press, 2015.

———. "The Dark Side of Extended Deterrence: Thinking Through the State Sponsorship of Terrorism." *Journal of Strategic Studies* 40 (2017): 1–28.

Wintrobe, Ronald. *The Political Economy of Dictatorship.* New York: Cambridge University Press, 1998.

Woods, Kevin, David D. Palkki and Mark E. Stout. *The Saddam Tapes: The Inner Workings of a Tyrant's Regime, 1978–2001.* New York: Cambridge University Press, 2011.

Woods, Kevin, Michael R. Pease, Mark E. Stout, Williamson Murray, and James G. Lacey. *Iraqi Perspectives Project: A View of Operation Iraqi Freedom from Saddam's Senior Leadership.* Norfolk: Joint Center for Operational Analysis, 2006.

Woods, Kevin, Williamson Murray, Mounir Elkhamri, and Thomas Holaday. *Saddam's War: An Iraqi Military Perspective of the Iran-Iraq War.* Washington, D.C.: Institute for National Strategic Studies, 2009.

Wright, Lawrence: *The Looming Tower: Al-Qaeda and the Road to 9/11.* New York: Vintage Books, 2006.

Wright, Thomas J. *All Measures Short of War: The Contest for the Twenty-First Century and the Future of American Power.* New Haven: Yale University Press, 2017.

Zakharov, Alexei V. "The Loyalty-Competence Tradeoff in Dictatorships and Outside Options For Subordinates." *The Journal of Politics* 78 (2016): 457–466.

Zarakol, Ayse. "What Makes Terrorism Modern?" Terrorism, Legitimacy, and the International System." *Review of International Studies* 37 (2011): 2311–2336.

Ziemke, Earl. "Strategy For Class War: The Soviet Union, 1917–1941." In *The Making of Strategy: Rulers, States, and War.* Edited by Williamson Murray, Macgregor Knox, and Alvin Bernstein, 498–533. New York: Cambridge University Press, 1994.

Zubok, Vladislav. *A Failed Empire: The Soviet Union in the Cold War from Stalin to Gorbachev.* Chapel Hill: University of North Carolina Press, 2009.

Index

About the Author

Eric Fleury is a visiting assistant professor at the College of the Holy Cross in Worcester, Massachusetts.

.

Ingram Content Group UK Ltd.
Milton Keynes UK
UKHW040657210423
420559UK00004B/370